BTS

and the clothes they wear

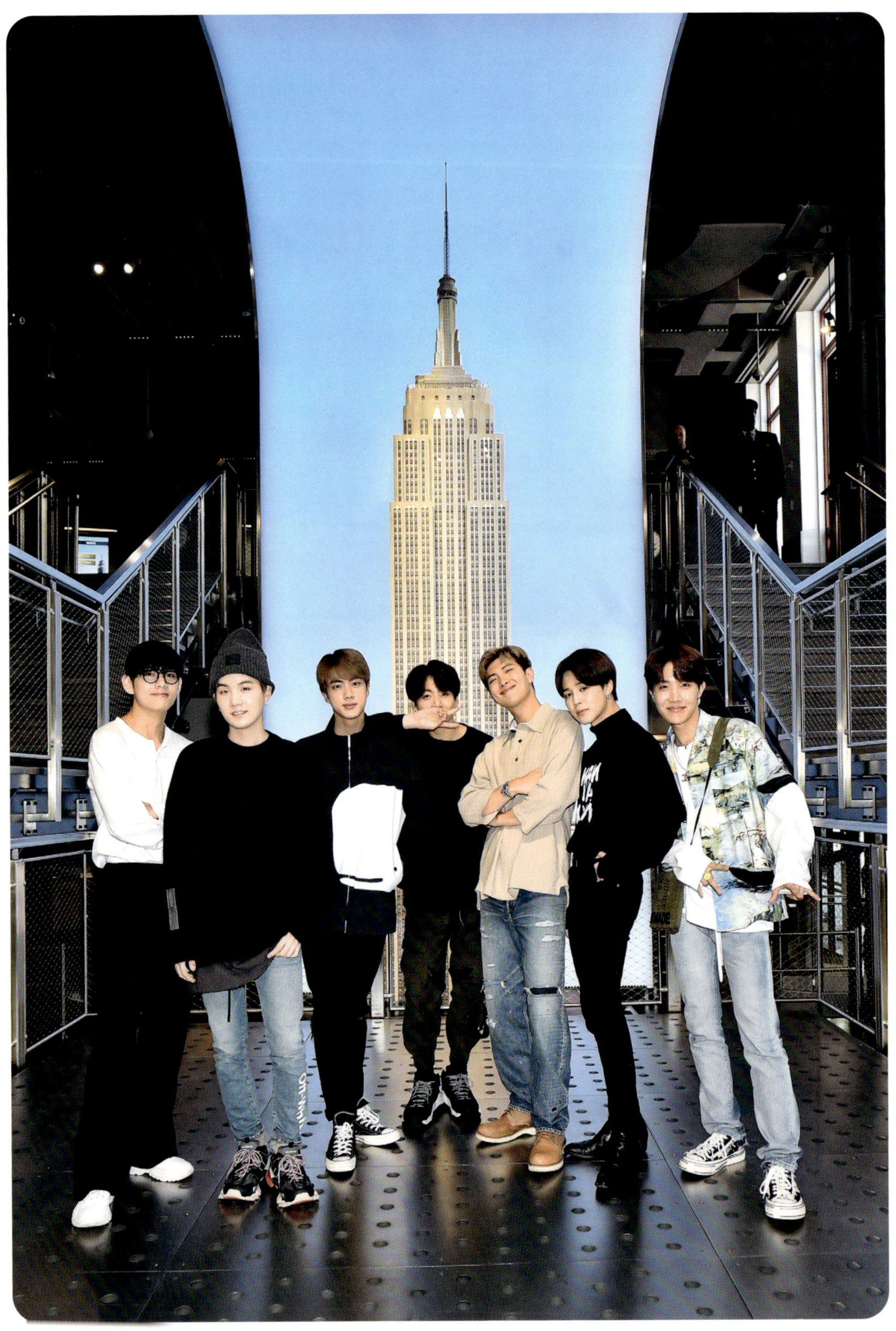

BTS
and the clothes they wear

Terry Newman

ACC ART BOOKS

Introduction

There is something very special about knowing someone when they are young, and ARMY have had the privilege of becoming acquainted with BTS while they were fledgling talents and throughout the process of their growing success. Today, fans know BTS completely and following their journey from obscurity to stardom has created a compelling relationship with potent synergy. ARMY are heartfelt and have, as much as BTS themselves, helped to initiate their achievements. Using social media to hype the band and spread the word, they have sent albums to the top of global charts and made the world sit up and take notice of the boys from South Korea.

Equally, the group feels protective of their supporters. In a 2023 *Dazed* interview feature, Jung Kook reflected: 'Because I get so much love and support from the fans, I want those people to be more confident, to have more self-assurance because of me, and that's the reason why I try to do my best.'

Bulletproof Boy Scouts, as they were initially known, famously debuted in June 2013 by appearing on music channel Mnet's *M Countdown*, the South Korean TV show instrumental in breaking new bands. The boys looked fly and wore the classic hip-hop uniform of black and gold baggy sportswear, snap-back caps, and heavy chains – there were no high-profile labels and their bling was too big to be real. Jin and SUGA were 20, j-hope was 19, RM was 18, Jimin and V were 17 and Jung Kook just 15. On camera, their street posturing and hard rap lyrics belied their baby-faced youth, while offstage their polite charm and persuasive personalities began to weave magic. BTS's music connected with their audience in a powerful way.

Signed to Big Hit (founded in 2005 by Mr Bang Si-hyuk and now called HYBE Corporation), their record company wasn't a major player and certainly not one of South Korea's 'big three' music content makers: SM Entertainment, JYP Entertainment and YG Entertainment who dominated the industry at the time. The boys and their label were outsiders and their debut single album *2 Cool 4 Skool* sold just a few hundred copies. The launch track, 'No More Dream', spoke of the pressures of youthful identity and, over the course of the next few years, the band showed the world how they would rise to the challenge. They sang loud while flashing their abs, break-dancing, and popping, working hard, honing their musical craft and, eventually, morphing into a global powerhouse phenomenon.

For the 600th anniversary episode of *M Countdown*, the boys watched a playback of that first ever performance and reflected on their debut. V admitted that it 'was a chance to show the world I exist', while Jung Kook concedes 'I felt so cool'. They all agreed they would never have believed, back in 2013, that they'd become so 'world-wide'.

Already by 2018 they were conquering the globe. During their Love Yourself world tour, fans just couldn't get enough – all US venues sold out completely – an extra date was added in LA after pre-sale tickets sold out in just *seconds*, and an extra US concert was added in New York. Even that wasn't enough and the whole tour was extended. Eventually by the end of the Love Yourself/Speak Yourself tour in October 2019, they had played a total of 62 dates across 14 countries and drawn crowds of over 2 million. In particular, the huge success in America led to comparisons to The Beatles, the legendary original 'boy band' that revolutionised pop music at home in England and then went on to conquer the States back in the 1960s. But even next to such music industry giants, BTS's careers are largely unparalleled and there are few stars who can compare to their stratospheric achievements. In February 2024, @btschartmaster reported on X that BTS had to date: 'sold over 40 million physical albums on Circle Album Chart', becoming 'the first artist ever to reach the milestone'.

OVERLEAF LEFT: *BTS hanging out with their fans in Times Square, NYC, 31 December 2019.*
OVERLEAF RIGHT: *ARMYs out in force at the BTS 10th Anniversary FESTA in Seoul, 17 June 2023.*

'Do what you like. Don't worry about what other people might think. What's important is what you want.'
— Jin, 'BTS Breaks Down Their Style Heroes' with *GQ*, September 2020.

' Fans watch us as a hobby, you know?
Hobbies are all about enjoying
yourself and being able to laugh,
so I want to look happy for them, not exhausted.
I go out of my way to make funny posts or leave
funny replies on Weverse to make them happier...

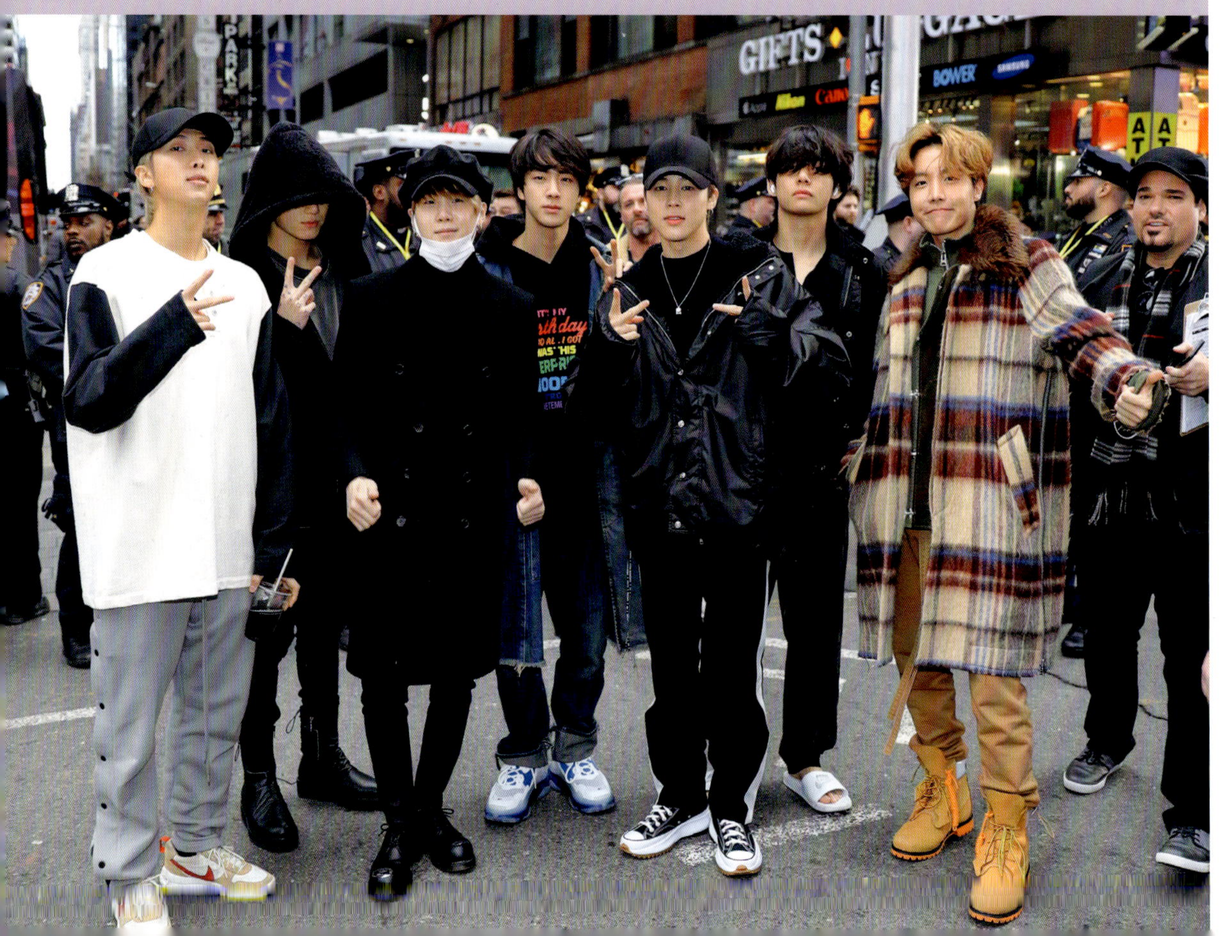

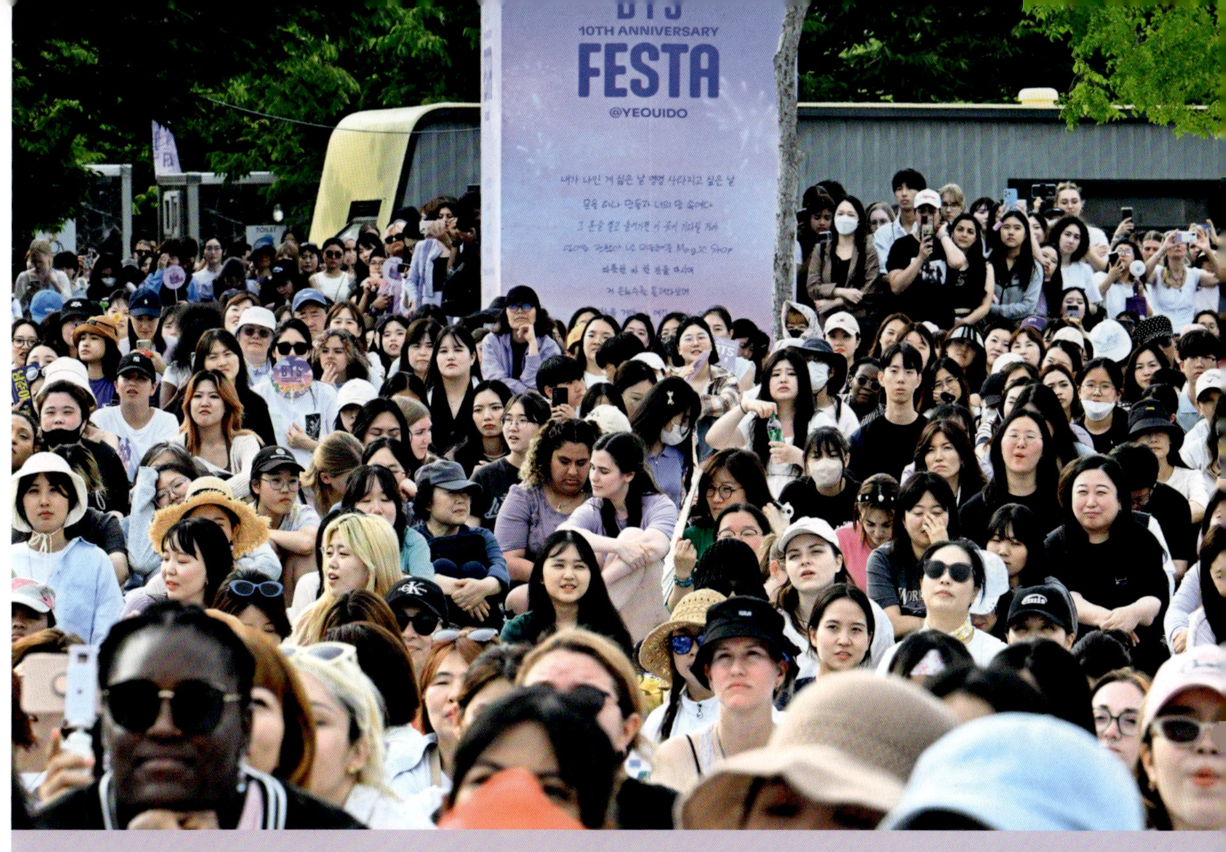

I just hope anyone who likes me is happy.
And I don't want them
to see anything bad.
That's how I feel about my work. ❜

— Jin, *Weverse Magazine*, July 2021.

Although they had to postpone their 2020 Map of the Soul tour, Covid did not halt their runaway success. Bang Bang Con, an online streaming concert, was watched by 50 million fans. In December 2021, they made a return to the stage with four shows at SoFi Stadium in Inglewood, California, selling over 200,000 tickets.

In 2023, the Indonesian Business Post evaluated the 'Bangtan' influence, and noted: 'According to the Hyundai Research Institute in 2019, the overall BTS effect in the economy was 5.56 trillion won per year in South Korea (US$ 4.9 billion). The institute predicted that BTS would create a total of 56 trillion won over 10 years from 2014 to 2023.' Named *Time* magazine 'Entertainer of the Year' in 2020, BTS has broken a ton of records, including in May 2021 when their track, 'Butter', garnered 108 million views and became the most watched YouTube video of all time. In 2022 *Proof* went straight in at #1 and BTS became the first Korean pop group to go to the top of the Billboard 200 with six different albums.

BTS's commercial success is undeniable – they have the Midas touch and even a casual mention of a product can make it sell out. Jung Kook, known as 'The King of Sold Outs', revealed in a fan–chat that Downy's amber blossom scented fabric conditioner was his preferred laundry choice and shortly after there was a state of emergency as it flew off the shelves and caused a shortage. His love of kombucha caused a steep rise of 500% in sales for the Korean tea brand TEAZEN. The boys eat, drink, sleep and play online for their fans to watch and their inclinations become viral moments through a host of livestreams and web shows.

Fans are familiar with the way BTS eat their noodles, brush their teeth and what pyjamas they wear to go to bed and in return buy their records, watch them in concert and organise online campaigns to show their love back. And the love is as big as it gets. *Variety* revealed in 2019 that they generated '$4.65 billion of South Korea's gross domestic product', which puts BTS 'on a par with conglomerates like Samsung and Hyundai'.

As a group they have had the highest achievements, and solo, it's the same story: the sky is the limit. In 2023, Chart Data posted that Jung Kook had topped any K-Pop soloist in Spotify history, with over 3.47 billion streams that year.

Though BTS's path in life has been extraordinary, they began in the familiar environment of the traditional training system for idols in South Korea. It is a gruelling opportunity that young hopefuls aspire to and which, once recruited, demands total dedication. Videos of BTS in their apprentice days reveal the bonding stages of their early career when each member was contracted to Big Hit Entertainment.

After a tape of his rap music impressed the record company, Nam-joon – aka Rap Monster aka RM – was the first of the boys to be signed and moved into their collective dorm in June 2010. Over the next year or two, the whole band came together: Kim Seok-jin 'Jin', Min Yoon-gi 'SUGA'/'Agust D', Jung Ho-seok 'j-hope', Kim

Nam-joon 'RM', Park Ji-min 'Jimin', Kim Tae-hyung 'V', and Jeon Jung-kook 'Jung Kook'. At first all seven slept in bunk beds and shared their dreams working all day and learning to dance, sing and move as a team for up to 15 hours a day. They were young and away from home for the first time, and finding a new family to rely on is important. First impressions count. When the boys first met V, he was wearing a big red North Face puffa jacket, which they laugh about now. V defends his sartorial choices in a live interview, saying: 'My mum didn't want other kids to look down on me in Seoul, so she shipped me that jacket.' Their friendships were necessary to keep going under the pressures, first of training and, later, of extreme fame; and those friendships are clearly real.

In a 2019 time.com interview, BTS's mentor, Bang Si-hyuk – aka Hitman Bang – reflected on the life the band experienced together, which enabled both their focus and also their individuality, saying: 'In our company, we invest a lot of time educating trainees about life as an artist, including social media. After we provide guidance, we choose to let artists be, and leave a window open for them to ask the company anything they need. I think that helped the sincerity get through to the fans.'

One of their early dorms in Seoul has now been converted into a coffee shop, HyuGa Café, and has become a pilgrimage site for fans, displaying art and messages from ARMY around the world.

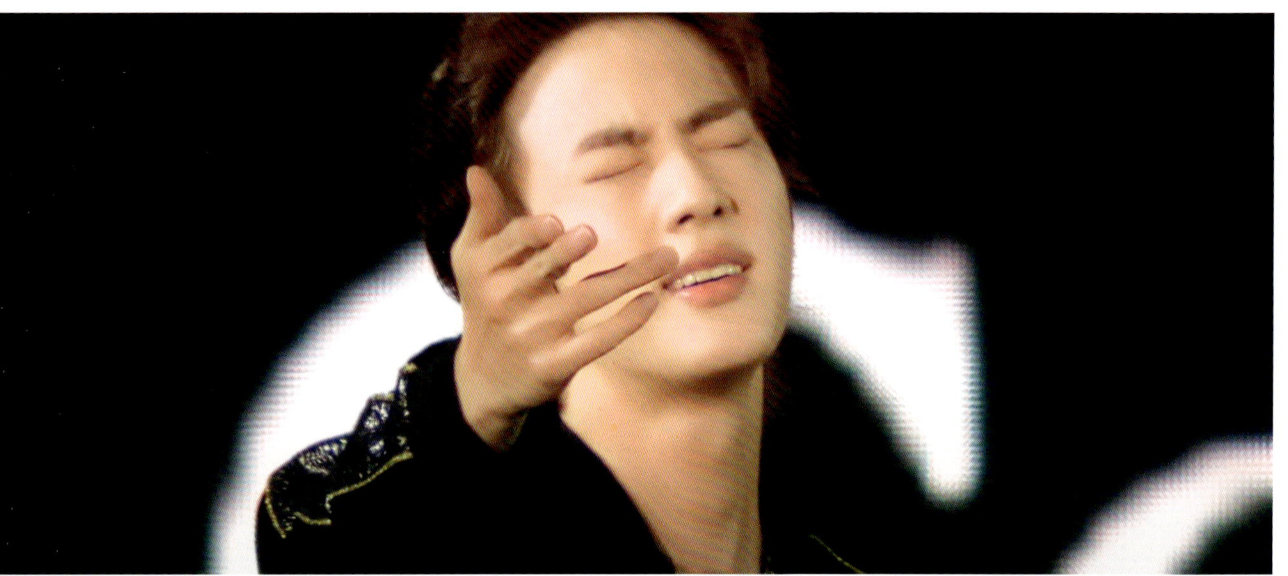

In 2017, the boys moved into an ultra-luxe Seoul residence, Hannam The Hill Apartments, and despite their global success and wealth, it wasn't until 2021 when they all finally moved into their own places. During BTS's 2022 FESTA, the group reflected on the new living conditions, with V saying, 'We became even closer now that we live separately' (koreaboo.com).

Community is at the centre of BTS's achievements and the boys have become global representatives for K–Pop, uniting ARMY around the world, who follow not just their musical energy but their style choices too.

ABOVE AND OPPOSITE: *Stills from* BTS: Yet to Come in Cinemas, *the concert film of the band at the Busan Asiad Main Stadium, 2023*.

As a group of seven, the band has defied the conceivable limitations of the trainee business model and instead created a manifesto for individuality, which is highly valued by the fashion industry.

Together, they worked with creative director Virgil Abloh on collaborations with Louis Vuitton in 2021; separately, they have secured similarly high–profile ambassadorships with the most coveted luxury houses, including Tiffany, Bottega Veneta, Calvin Klein, Valentino and Dior.

Fashion shows, international advertising campaigns and red–carpet moments are all opportunities for the band to showcase these partnerships, but one of the most fun ways to tease a new affiliation is through an extra special travelling outfit. Thanks to BTS, airport

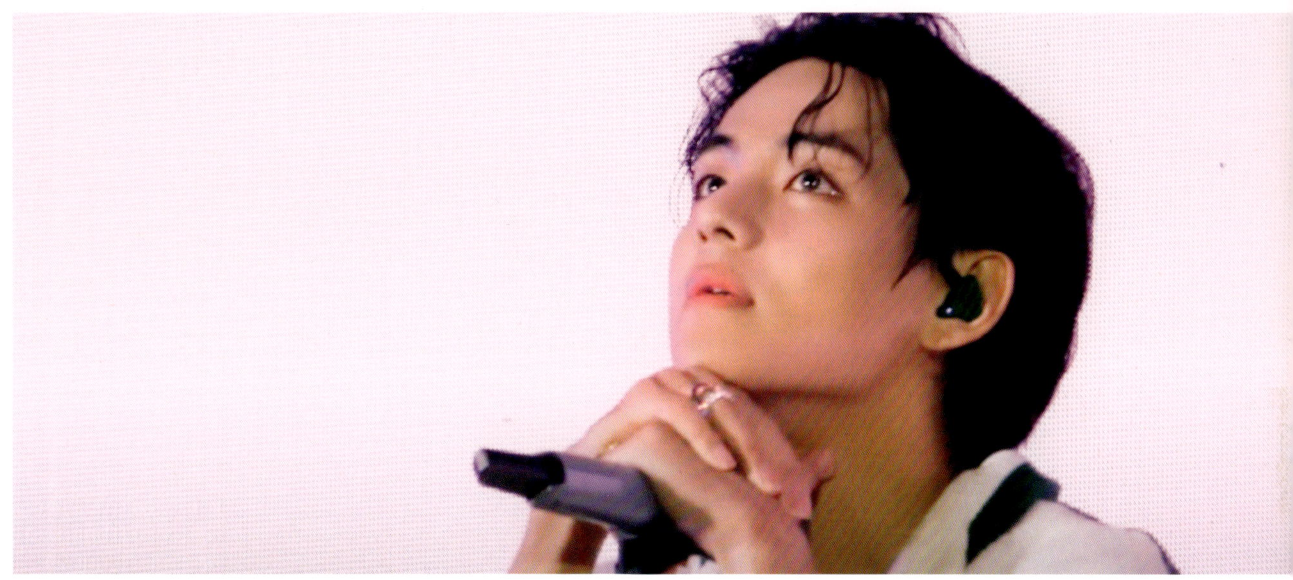

fashion has become a specific wardrobe genre that prompts as many paparazzi pictures as any FROW and leaving South Korea's Incheon Airport has become a literal runway for the boys to parade their favourite pieces. From j-hope's duck-shaped Louis Vuitton shoulder bags and Rick Owens X Converse sneakers, to Jimin's khaki Margiela trench or Jin's favoured Thom Browne mac, a trip away becomes a cavalcade of cool. Each member of BTS's personal flair is forensically tracked and appreciated by fans as a brand in their own right and what they wear is a topic of enthusiastic debate.

In 2018 when j-hope released his mixtape, *Hope World*, it was the beginning of 'Hobicore', his lively retro aesthetic that mashed up smiley-face-pop-art motifs, streetwear, flowers and kidcore nostalgia epitomised by his classic Tonari No Zingaro X Takashi Murakami cartoon hoodie and painted pastel nail varnish. Not afraid to experiment with style, his look has continued to evolve and morph ever since. In 2023, j-hope was appointed Louis Vuitton ambassador and he attended the A/W 2024 show in top-to-toe purple, indigo and black camouflage from the same collection – grown up, yes, but still flourishing a colourful flash of his old-skool hobi-isms.

V confessed to *Vogue Singapore* in September 2022: 'I used to go for the British style before. Nowadays, though, I try to look as comfortable and as "me" as possible by going for something much simpler and more casual'. Celebrated for busting a slightly 1960s beatnik edge and wearing classic-with-a-twist button-up shirts and ties along with tailored trousers, in 2023

Kim Tae-hyung – V – formally joined forces with Celine and Cartier, taking his styling to deluxe fashion rock 'n' roll heights.

Jung Kook's love of streetwear, including Supreme and Nike, means that laid-back fashion choices have always been his thing. He told *Vogue Japan*: 'I mostly gravitate towards things that are comfortable and easy to wear. I like [my clothes] to be a bit oversized and I like shoes that are a bit big. And I like to wear knitted hats!' So it made perfect sense for him to become the first ever K-Pop star to feature on the cover of cult British magazine *Dazed* wearing Georgian designer, Demna Gvasalia's baggy Balenciaga menswear, and to go on to represent Calvin Klein's all-American utility workwear in 2023.

BTS has a staggering command within the fashion and music worlds. However, it is their cultural sway that feels bigger, better and, perhaps, even more important. In a very purposeful way, they have heralded a new and inclusive beautyverse that has helped challenge stereotypes and create new normals for male appearances, not just in South Korea, but globally.

They are idols who have not just embraced soft masculinity, but made it part of their intrinsic DNA and they have done this alongside undertaking compulsory military duties – traditionally the apex of archetypal rugged machismo. They wear make-up and sometimes lots of it. They have produced their own range of ungendered cosmetics and skincare and are celebrated for their all-colours-of-the-rainbow hairstyles.

However, the global popularity of South Korean culture, and especially make-up, is more than just about the permissibility of lip-tints. It's about positively embracing sound mental health and accepting yourself for who you are – whoever and however you might be. Following the release of the first in an album trilogy, *Love Yourself: Her* in September 2017, BTS teamed with Unicef to launch the LOVE MYSELF campaign. It was an extension of their new music's themes and a partnership with Unicef's #ENDviolence programme, created to protect children and young people all over the world from harm.

A year later, BTS were invited to the launch of Generation Unlimited, at the UN General Assembly. RM revealed his own personal struggles, recalling when he was nine or ten years old: 'Looking back, that's when I began to worry about what other people thought of me, and started seeing myself through their eyes. I stopped looking up at the stars at night. I stopped daydreaming. I tried to jam myself into moulds that other people made. Soon, I began to shut out my own voice and started to listen to the voices of others... I have come to love myself for who I was, who I am and who I hope to become.' The group's open vulnerability has helped inspire fans and followers to find help and explore their own dichotomies and

'I don't think success is determined by other people's perspectives. Just experiencing self–satisfaction, being happy, experiencing difficulties, being frustrated – I think in all those moments, "success" is always mixed in with it. For me, instead of chasing success, it's enough to be satisfied. '

Jung Kook, *GQ*, November 2023.

question preconceived notions of gender and identity. BTS clothes, songs and appearances all help support freedom of expression for all. It's a cause that is close to their collective hearts and one that is constantly reiterated. In 2021 they helped to raise $3.6 million towards the Unicef campaign, with the executive director, Henrietta Fore saying: 'The groundbreaking way in which BTS has helped spark a positive message with its ARMY is simply unmatched and incredibly invaluable.' In a five-year anniversary video to celebrate the initiative, SUGA told the world: 'I'm delighted and proud that our Love Myself message comes to many people's minds in their daily lives. But, at the same time, I'm afraid there might be people who still don't know how to love themselves.'

In December 2022, Jin began his military service in Korea, followed by j-hope in April the next year – each member subsequently committing, with Jung Kook and Jimin the last to go in December 2023. Enlisting in the army is compulsory and an important duty for all South Korean men, but an amendment to law meant that BTS were allowed to defer until they were 30, which gave relief to fans and enabled Big Hit to roll out consecutive content from the band to bridge the gap until they return to civilian life in 2025.

During their 2022 FESTA dinner, RM was philosophical about the group's way forward, not just because of the military stint but also in the context of the members as solo artists, saying:

'I think we should spend some time apart to learn how to be one again.' j-hope added: 'I hope you don't see this as a negative thing, and see it as a healthy plan. I think BTS will become stronger that way.' In a Weverse live, RM encouraged fans, saying: 'We'll go and come back healthy and smiling. Jin will return quickly and fill the empty space.' And for their supportive fans, the hiatus has not been cheerless: BTS worked hard before going away, preparing exciting content like j-hope's documentary *Hope on the Street*, as well as SUGA's concert film *SUGA/Agust D: Tour D-Day*, which were both released in early 2024 while they were away. But it was perhaps, BTS's free concert, 'BTS, Yet to Come' hosted way back in 2022 to support South Korea's bid to host the 2030 World Expo that fills fans with most hope. At the time, Jimin reassured the audience saying: 'Although it's so sad that the concert is ending already, it's not like we only have today. We will continue for 30 years ... and even perform when we are 70 years old.'

We can't wait to see their outfits!

A café in Seoul declares ARMY's love and willingness to wait for the boys to be reunited after military service.

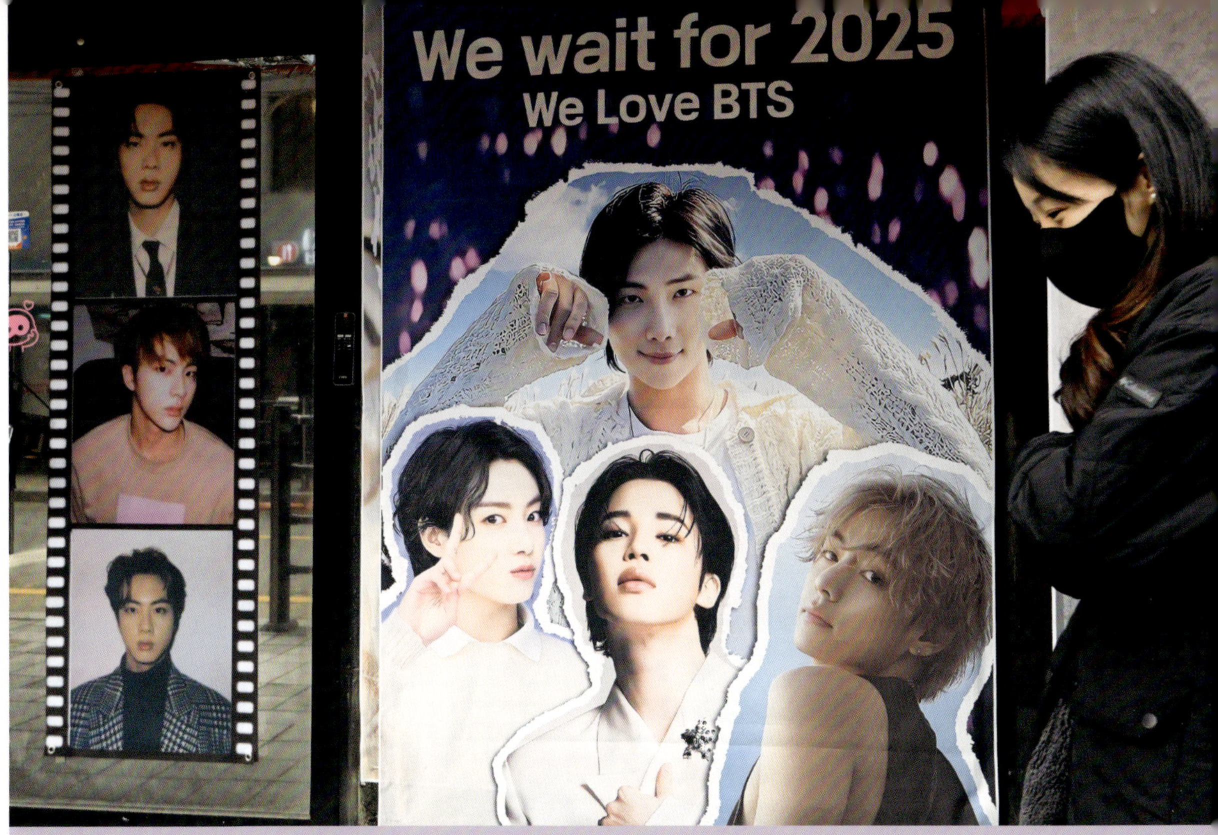

'We were born at the right time.
Without social media we wouldn't have been
so successful. '
— BTS, K–Pop: Korea's Secret Weapon.

Top Boys

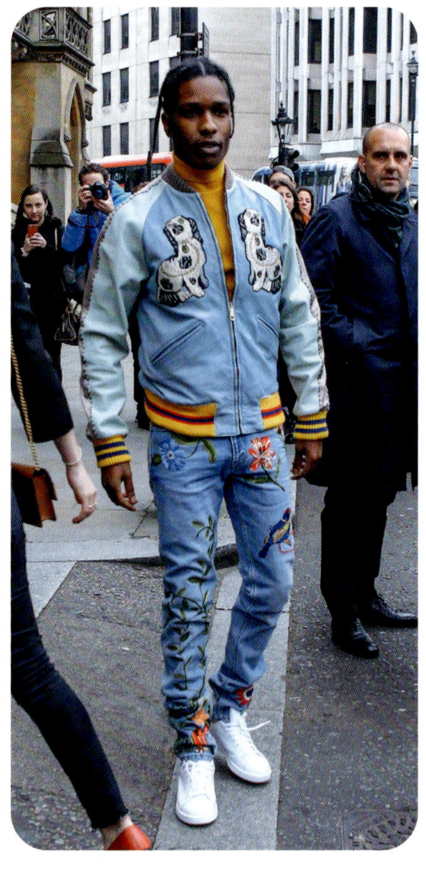

In October 2017, BTS registered on US Billboard's Hot 100, entering at 85 and climbing to 67 with their track, 'DNA' from the album *Love Yourself: Her*. It was only the second time a Korean language single charted and ARMY around the world rejoiced. The following month, the band appeared for the first time on the American Music Awards to sing it. They were introduced by The Chainsmokers' Andrew Taggart and Alex Pall who, conscious of the historic moment, said: 'To be honest I'm a little bit nervous to be announcing this next performance'. Although they didn't take home any awards that night, BTS stole the show and revealed to the world not just the magic of their music, but their sartorial swag too. They arrived wearing Saint Laurent by Anthony Vaccarello but hit the stage wearing Gucci by Alessandro Michele, establishing their confident fashion prowess. RM sported the memorable puppy bomber jacket embroidered with spaniels, a version of which A$AP Rocky had worn at the 2017 Gucci Cruise show in London. j-hope donned a Coco Capitán X Gucci old-skool logoed T-shirt scrawled with 'tomorrow is now

THIS PAGE: *A$AP Rocky styling the Gucci puppy jacket.*
OPPOSITE: *Ripping it up at the AMAs in Gucci, Microsoft Theater, LA, 19 November 2017.*

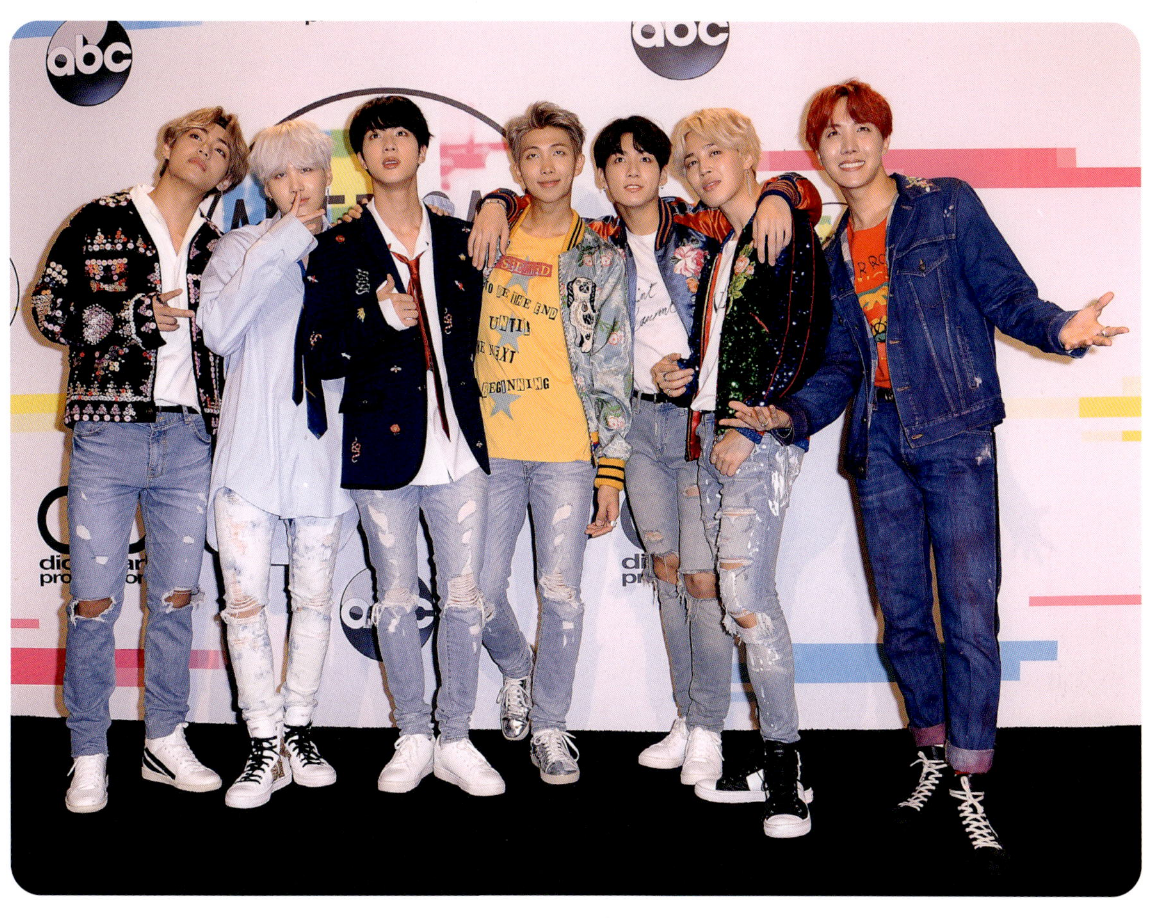

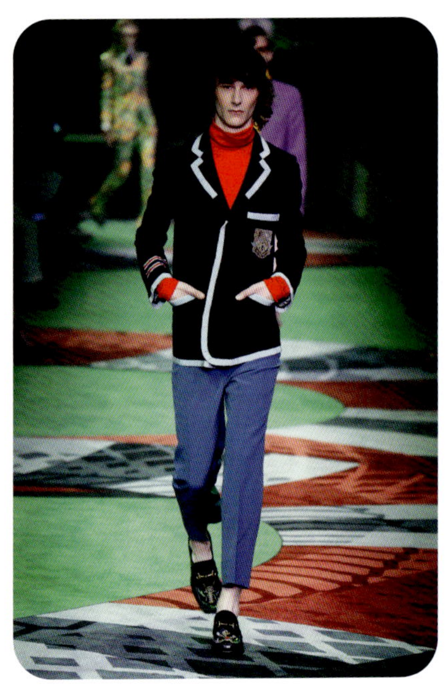

yesterday' under a 'modern future' studded denim jacket. Jimin chose a sequined jacket embellished with a rose, and Jung Kook selected the same silhouette but in satin with a floral motif. Jin meanwhile selected a formal blazer with cute all-over motifs.

The following year at the 2018 Billboard Music Awards, BTS chose to wear Gucci again and didn't disappoint. SUGA's baby-blue pierced heart shirt won love, and V's formal navy-blue sports jacket over a white polo, teamed with striped cropped tracksuit trousers and Gucci sneakers was a distinctive look. The BBMAs were the first American awards ceremony to recognise BTS. In 2017, when they won the prize for Top Social Artist, RM told refinery29.com: 'We feel that music is the international language, and we feel the love from all over the world through that.' And the BBMA love kept flowing the following year: not only did they scoop Top Social Artist again, but the video of them performing their new single, 'Fake Love', was viewed 35.9 million times in the first 24 hours of release! According to forbes.com, it was the highest 24-hour YouTube debut in 2018! Now no-one could deny BTS's success.

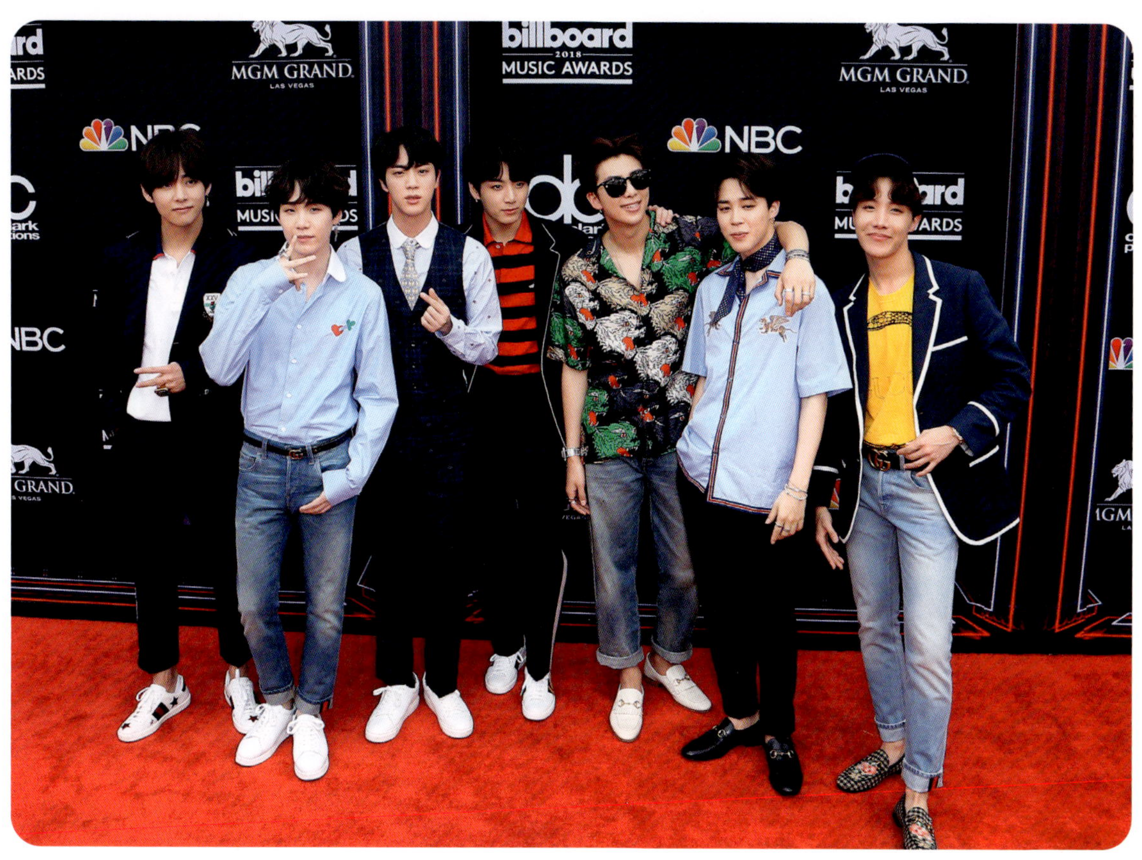

OPPOSITE: *Gucci by Alessandro Michele, S/S 2017, Milan Men's Fashion Week, June 2016.*

THIS PAGE: *Giving it some Gucci red-carpet swag at the 2018 BBMAs. L–R: V, Jin, Jung Kook, Jimin, RM, SUGA and j-hope – MGM Grand Garden Arena in Las Vegas.*

In 2021 *Billboard* magazine featured the group on the cover but ran an interview that questioned them about charting tactics, irking ARMY enough to campaign to boycott *Billboard*. RM responded calmly saying: 'If there is a conversation inside *Billboard* about what being No. 1 should represent, then it's up to them to change the rules and make streaming weigh more on the ranking. Slamming us or our fans for getting to No. 1 with physical sales and downloads, I don't know if that's right … It just feels like we're easy targets because we're a boy band, a K–Pop act, and we have this high fan loyalty.' Winning globally has always meant fans first for BTS and their careers have been based on this rather than waiting for the traditional music industry gatekeepers to approve them. Their success is forever on their own blazing–a–trail terms and, ultimately, the best reward is ARMY love.

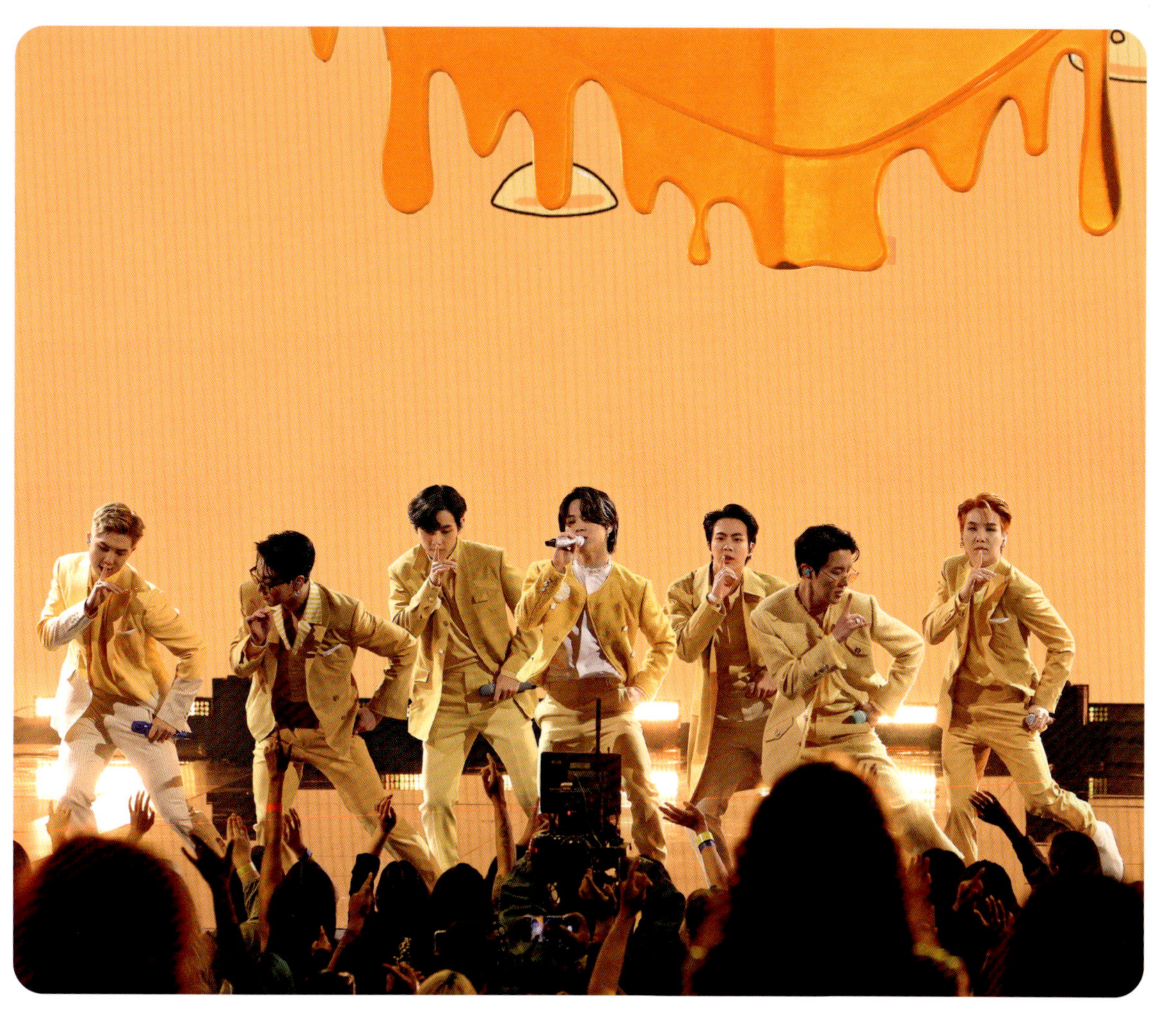

Mellow yellow. L–R: RM, Jung Kook, V, Jimin, Jin, j–hope and SUGA onstage during the 2021 American Music Awards at the Microsoft Theater, LA, 21 November 2021.

Californian Dreaming

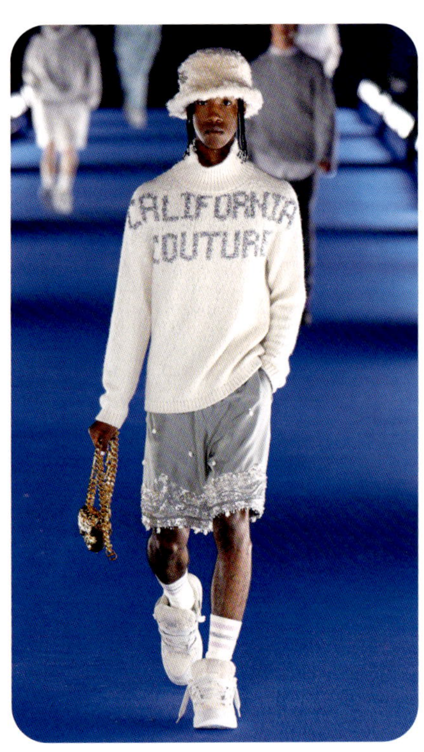

When you're invited on the biggest live TV party in America, *Dick Clark's New Year's Rockin' Eve* shown on ABC, you must be a very special VIP. Clark, who passed away in 2012, began the tradition when he launched the show back in 1972, and was famously known as 'the world's oldest teenager'. Throughout his career, he championed many talented music stars, so it was fitting that one of the world's most loved modern idols was asked to perform on the 50th anniversary show. j-hope ticked all the boxes on 31 December 2022, and the bash, filmed live in New York's iconic Times Square was one of the most highly anticipated ever. It wasn't the first time j-hope had rocked Times Square; he'd played there with the whole band in 2017 via a pre-recorded segment and then live in 2019. This time he flew solo, and a solo show by one of BTS called for a spectacular outfit. j-hope rose to the challenge picking out something superior especially to sing three tracks: 'Butter', 'Chicken Noodle Soup' and '= (Equal Sign)'. He told koreaboo.com afterwards: 'I looked up Lookbooks and there was the perfect outfit. That's why I picked this outfit.'

THIS PAGE: *Dior Men's S/S 2023 collection in LA, 19 May 2022.*
OPPOSITE: *Hope for the future – j-hope performs during the Times Square New Year's Eve Celebration, 2022.*

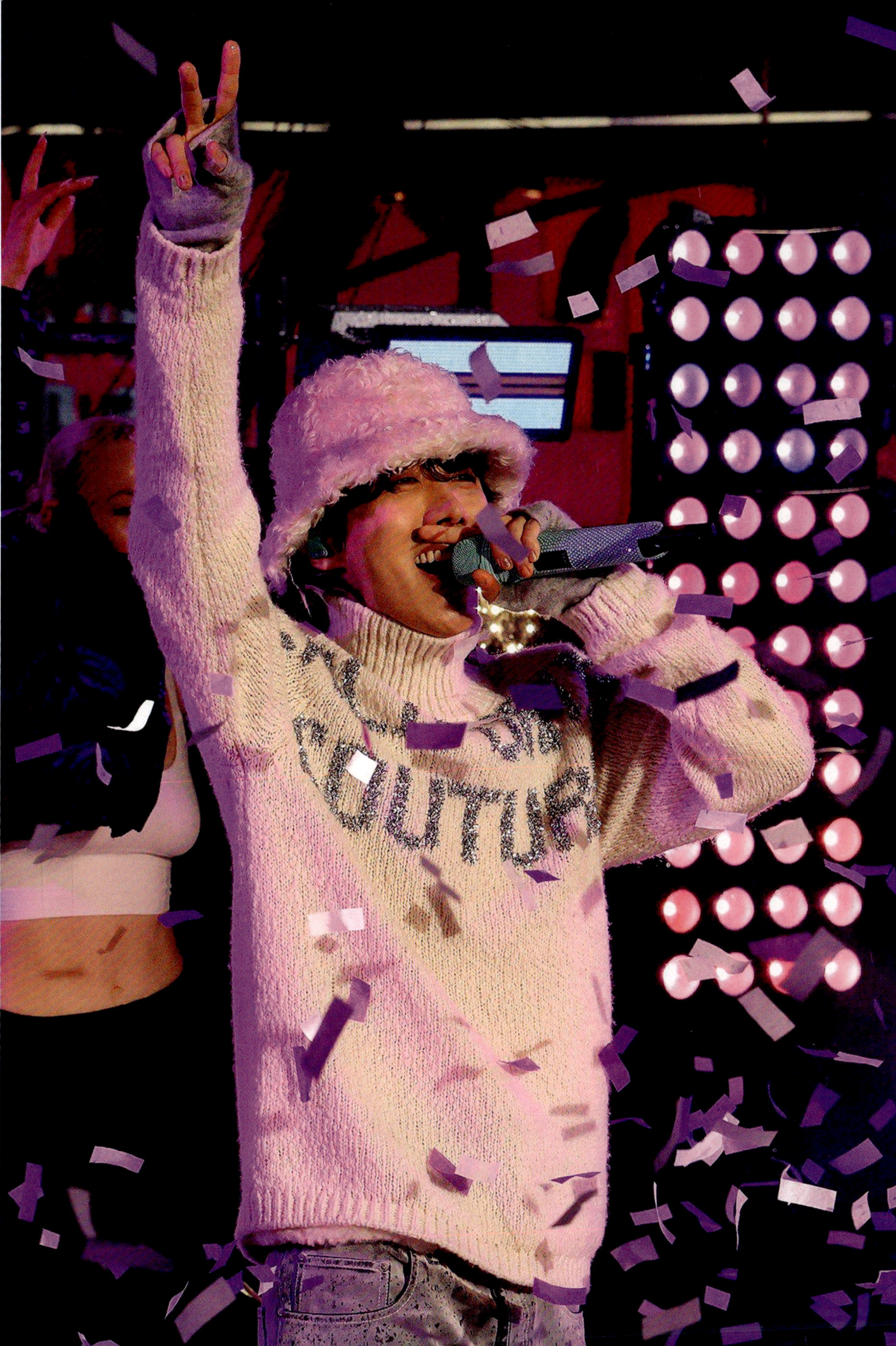

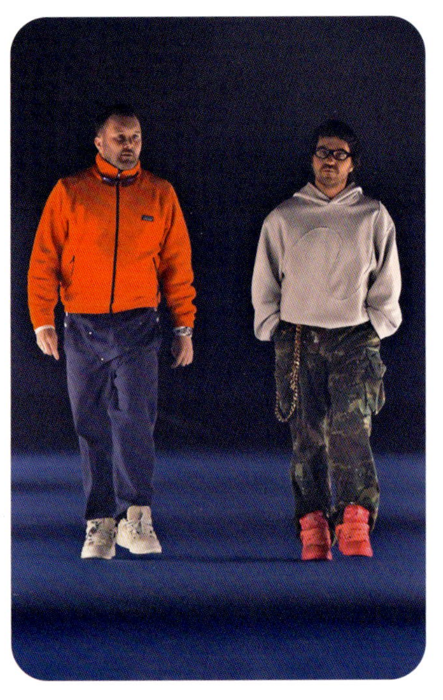

j–hope had homed in on one of the most well–received menswear collections of 2022, Kim Jones's Dior collaboration with ERL's Eli Russell Linnetz. Venice Beach based, ERL started out making T–shirts and quickly evolved into a fully fledged label, going on to be shortlisted for the LVMH Prize for Young Fashion Designers in 2022, winning the Karl Lagerfeld prize. Dior X ERL for Spring 2023 was all about streetwise skater silhouettes, the powder–blue skies of Venice Beach and the cool of Parisian finery. In a May 2022 interview, Kim Jones explained his inspiration to Hypebeast: 'I love Los Angeles. It's the American way, the American way of looking at sportswear.' j–hope chose one of the fine white sweaters emblazoned with 'Californian Couture' and a matching fluffy white bucket hat. j–hope loves attention to detail and remarked: 'Wearing different accessories is nice. But I thought it would be nice to wear gloves and give off a winter vibe for the first time in a while.' The fingerless gloves were another clever pick, showing off his 'least excessive' sparkly silver manicure, which helped add shine to an already super–shiny evening.

THIS PAGE: *Designers Kim Jones and Eli Russell Linnetz walk the runway for the Dior Men's S/S 2023 collection in LA, 19 May 2022.*
OPPOSITE: *j–hope, Times Square NYC, New Year's Eve 2022.*

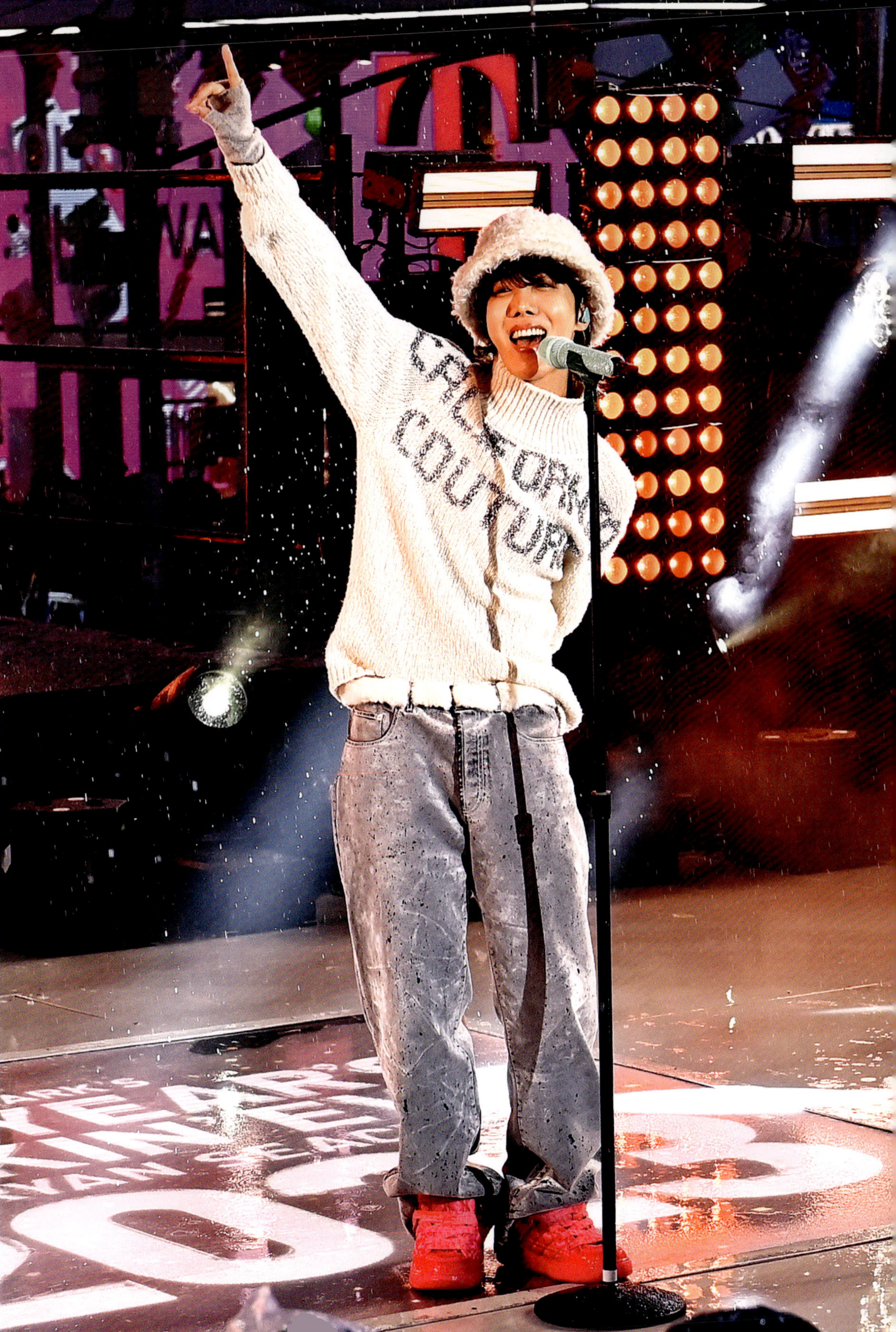

Fashion Graduate

— Jimin, *Weverse* magazine, June 2022.

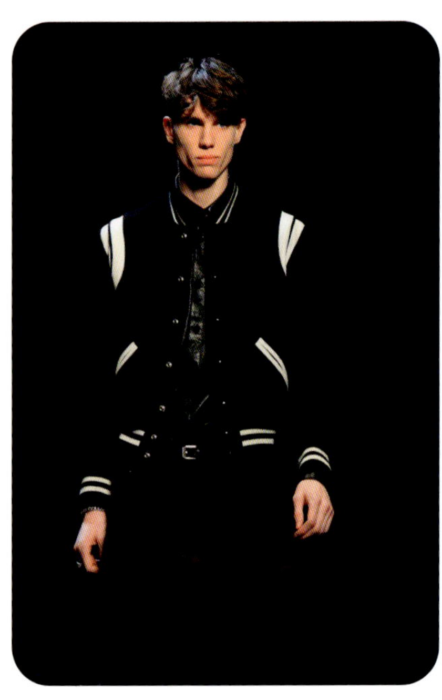

Jimin is a thoroughbred clothes horse. His styling changes as often as his hair colour, making him an inspiration for daredevil fashion followers the world over. Back in 2020, BTS appeared on the *Today* show to announce their new album, *Map of the Soul: 7* and, as with any new release from the boys, it was a moment to savour, not just for the music itself but also for the clothes they wore to promote it.

Jimin went kitted out in Celine's signature varsity jacket, mixing up the classic college look with a deep–brown shade. Hedi Slimane took the helm at Celine and launched its first menswear line in 2018, having left Saint Laurent a couple of years earlier – it was at YSL that he'd launched a version of the varsity jacket in his grungy A/W 2013 collection. Music drives the edge of Slimane's work, which is infused with an androgynous appeal, fitting right in with Jimin's aesthetic. Slimane's rockstar designs have long been worn by all genders and, in his hands, the historic jock jacket has become a stylish gender–fluid wardrobe option.

THIS PAGE: *The original St Laurent version of Hedi's baseball jacket. Hedi Slimane for Yves Saint-Laurent Men's A/W 2013–14 collection, Paris Fashion Week, 20 January 2013.*
OPPOSITE: *Jimin, better and cooler in Manhattan, 21 February 2020.*

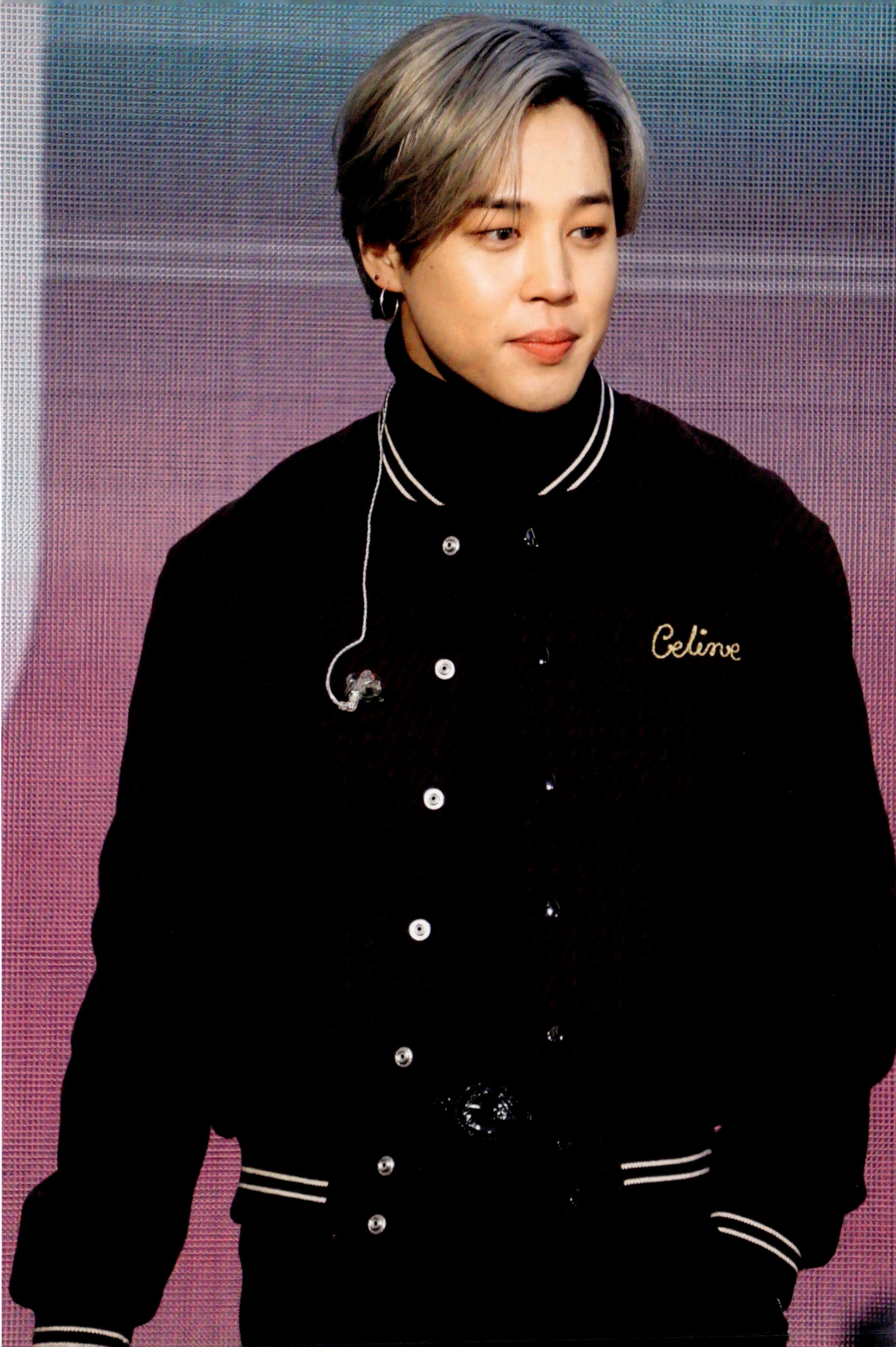

Adore You More

> ' ... he's got a very pure soul. Jin is also very talkative. **He's the most talkative one in his group.** He really loves to talk, like... I can never say everything I want when I'm with him, because he **pretty much doesn't let me talk. '**
> — **Kim Nam-gil,** *You Quiz on the Block* **tvN TV show, September 2023.**

In July 2022, just five days after the Gucci Lovelight range was released online, Jin was spotted wearing the collection's flying comet-heart cream patch cardigan while walking the red carpet at the Seoul premiere of the disaster action thriller movie, *Emergency Declaration*, starring Jin's self-confessed hero, the Korean actor Kim Nam-gil.

The cardigan was one of the last Gucci pieces designed during Alessandro Michele's reign as creative director. Teamed with button-up striped blue shirt, slip-on loafers, and Pee-wee Herman-length black trousers, Jin and his bowl-cut hair looked every inch a preppy dream, described in December 2023 by Elle.in as belonging to the 'Light Romantic Academia' style aesthetic. The Lovelight series, intended by Michele as 'an expression of adoration, both to oneself and to others', featured a light and summery selection of flowers and clouds adorning its Americana-inspired bowling shirts, hoodies, and trackpants. Debuting its key knitwear piece, Jin met with his ARMY fans, bowing to show his gratitude for their support.

Jin looking adorable in his Gucci comet cardigan.

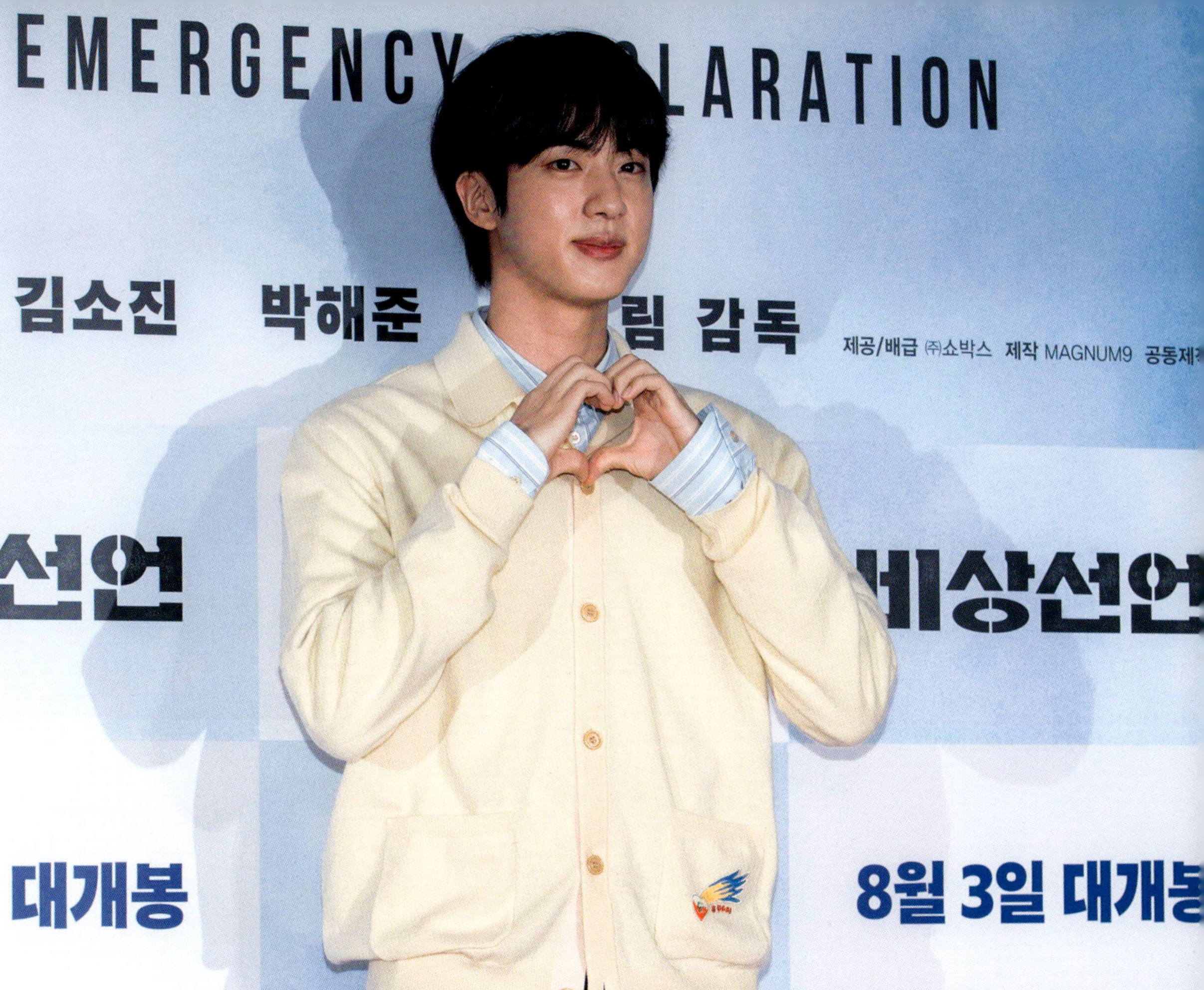

' He was proven to be our
forever 'manner idol'
here again. '
— All About BTS Jin, *YouTube* channel, July 2022.

Are We Family?

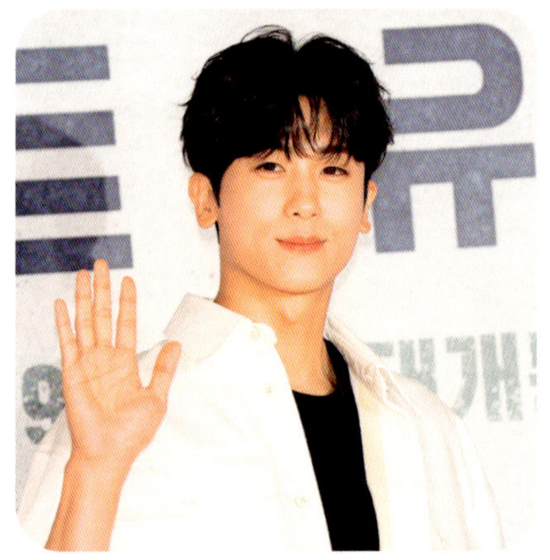

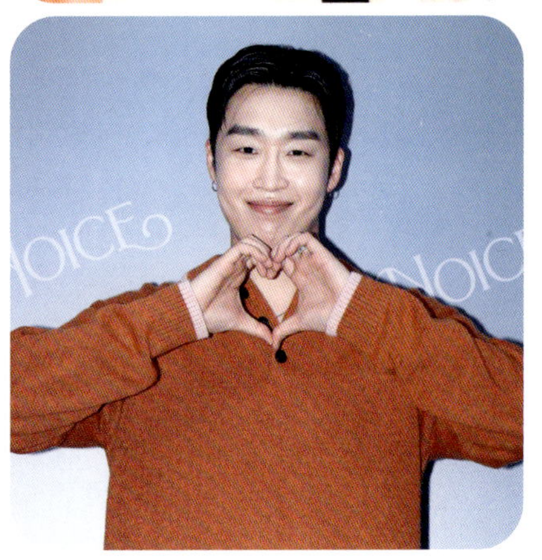

V will be forever known as BTS's vocalist and lead dancer, but the Daegu-born Capricorn has a solid crew in the form of his WOOGA Squad too. He first met actors Park Seo-joon and Park Hyung-sik (who was also in the boy band, ZE:A and its spin-off, ZE:A Five), when he won a part in KBS2's period drama, *Hwarang: The Poet Warrior Youth*, in 2016. The three became fast friends and later when Park Seo-joon introduced his *Hwarang* crew to fellow actor, Choi Woo-shik and rapper Peakboy, the fivesome became close and famous as the WOOGA Squad (short for *Woori-ga Gajok-inka* = Are We Family?).

So, it was no surprise to V's global fan base that he would make a special effort to attend the VIP premiere of Park Seo-joon's 2023 film *Concrete Utopia* at the Lotte Cinema World Tower in Songpa-gu, Seoul. It was a star-studded event and V dressed accordingly: along with Celine Chelsea boots he wore a cherry-red tweed jacket and ripped jeans trimmed in fake leopard fabric by 4SDesigns – a label created in 2020

THIS PAGE TOP: *Actor/singer Park Hyung-sik, 2023.*
THIS PAGE BOTTOM: *Rapper Peakboy (aka Kwon Sung-hwan), Seoul, September 2023.*
OPPOSITE: *V supports his Squad in style at a photo call before the VIP preview of* Concrete Utopia, *Seoul, August 2023.*

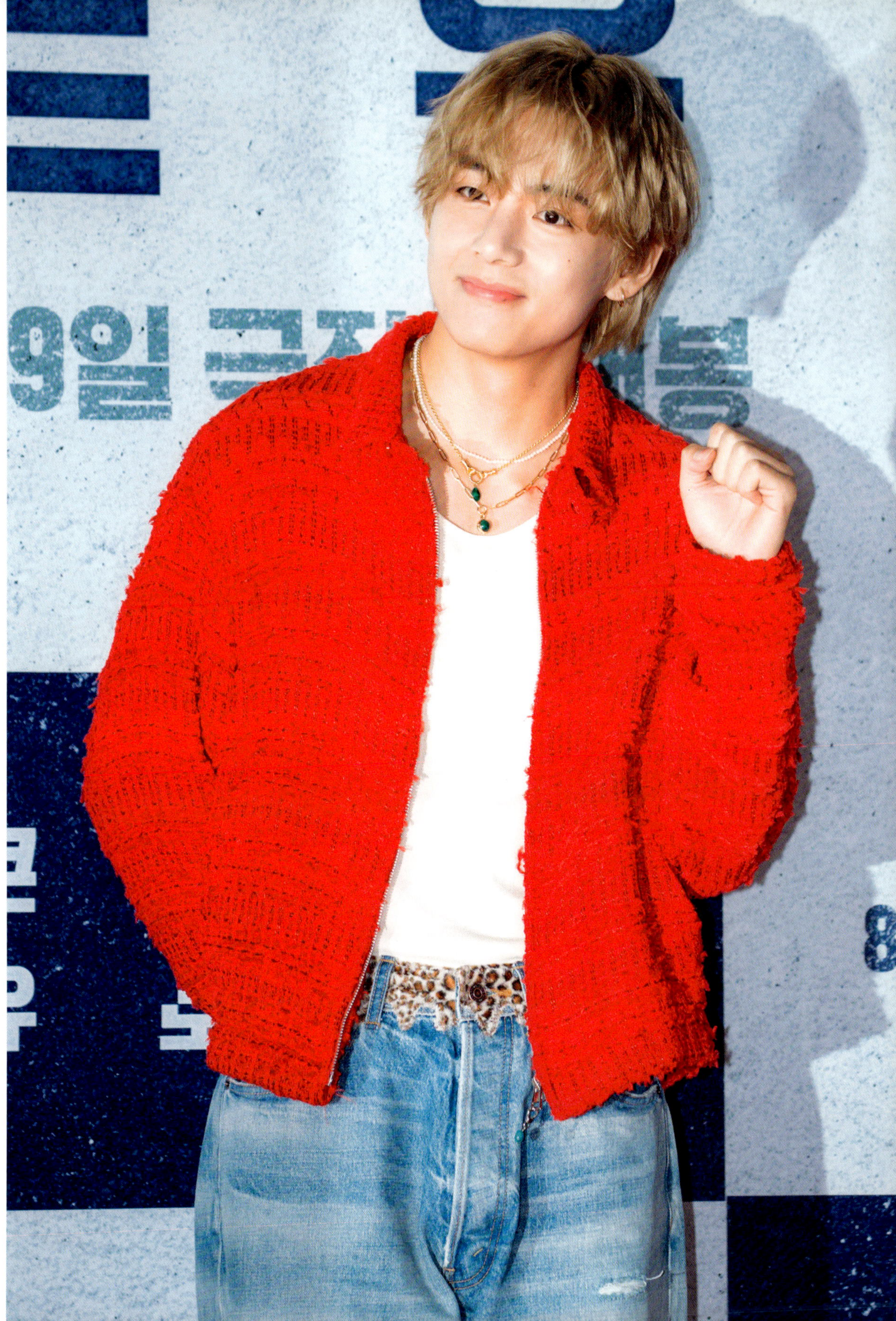

9월

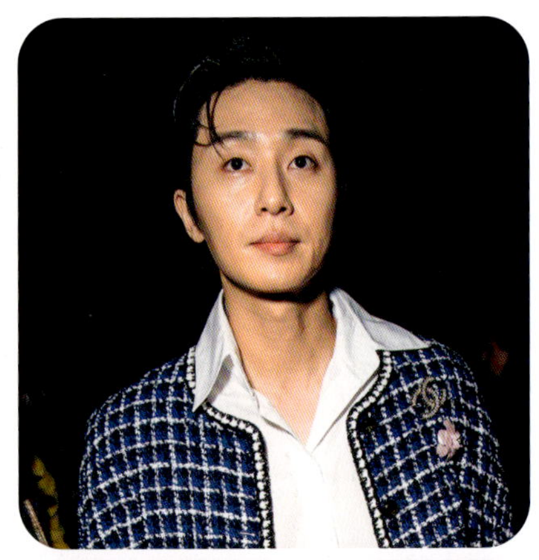

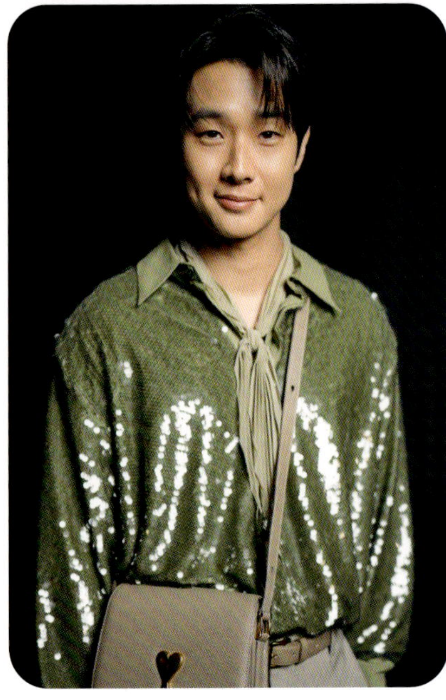

by Angelo Urrutia, the New York menswear fashion maestro born in San Miguel, El Salvador. Urrutia is vocal about his love of Chanel and the jacket V sported evidenced the sartorial codes laid down by Coco when she invented the boxy Chanel suit back in 1925. The androgynous look V wore was further emphasised with an 'In Good Hands' Harris Reed X Missoma pendant necklace, which became an international sell-out piece, not least because V adopted it for his own. The accessory was made with loving vibes, and the Central St Martin's graduate, Reed, told grazia.com in November 2023: 'I just love that people love this idea of two hands coming together, being there for someone, taking their hand and leading them to somewhere new', making it particularly apt for V to wear for his WOOGA pal's special event, also championed by fellow WOOGA affiliate, Park Hyung-sik and reportedly his BTS brother, Jung Kook – making it a real family affair.

THIS PAGE TOP: Hwarang *co-star Park Seo-joon, 2023.*
THIS PAGE BOTTOM: *Choi Woo-shik at AMI Alexandre Mattiussi Men's Autumn 2024 show.*

'I need to know who
I am as Kim Tae-hyung,
as a regular person. It's hard for me
to think ahead about what to
wear and how to present myself
tomorrow. So, I try to wear what
best expresses who I am
as a person every day,
or how I feel each day. '

V, *Vogue Korea*, September 2022.

Blazing a Trail

Jung Kook's solo album *Golden* dropped in November 2023. To celebrate, he travelled to the States and appeared on NBC's *Today* show Concert Series, playing at the Rockefeller Plaza on 8 November. The set featured three tracks: 'Standing Next to You', 'Seven' and '3D' – all songs that have gilded his international success as a solo star, true to his 'Golden Maknae' nickname. Forbes called 'Standing Next to You' 'the biggest song in the world', and it's hard to argue with that considering its immediate #1 chart position on the Billboard Global 200 along with an impressive 81.6 million streams and 121,000 copies sold instantly after its 3 November release.

The youngest member of BTS hit the Plaza stage early in the morning looking pitch-perfect for the thousands of ARMY who had turned out to see him. Jung Kook wore a slightly oversized double-breasted blazer, embellished with hundreds of crystal beads, teamed with dark trousers and contrasting white socks.

Jung Kook performs on NBC's Today *show Concert Series at the Rockefeller Plaza, 8 November 2023.*

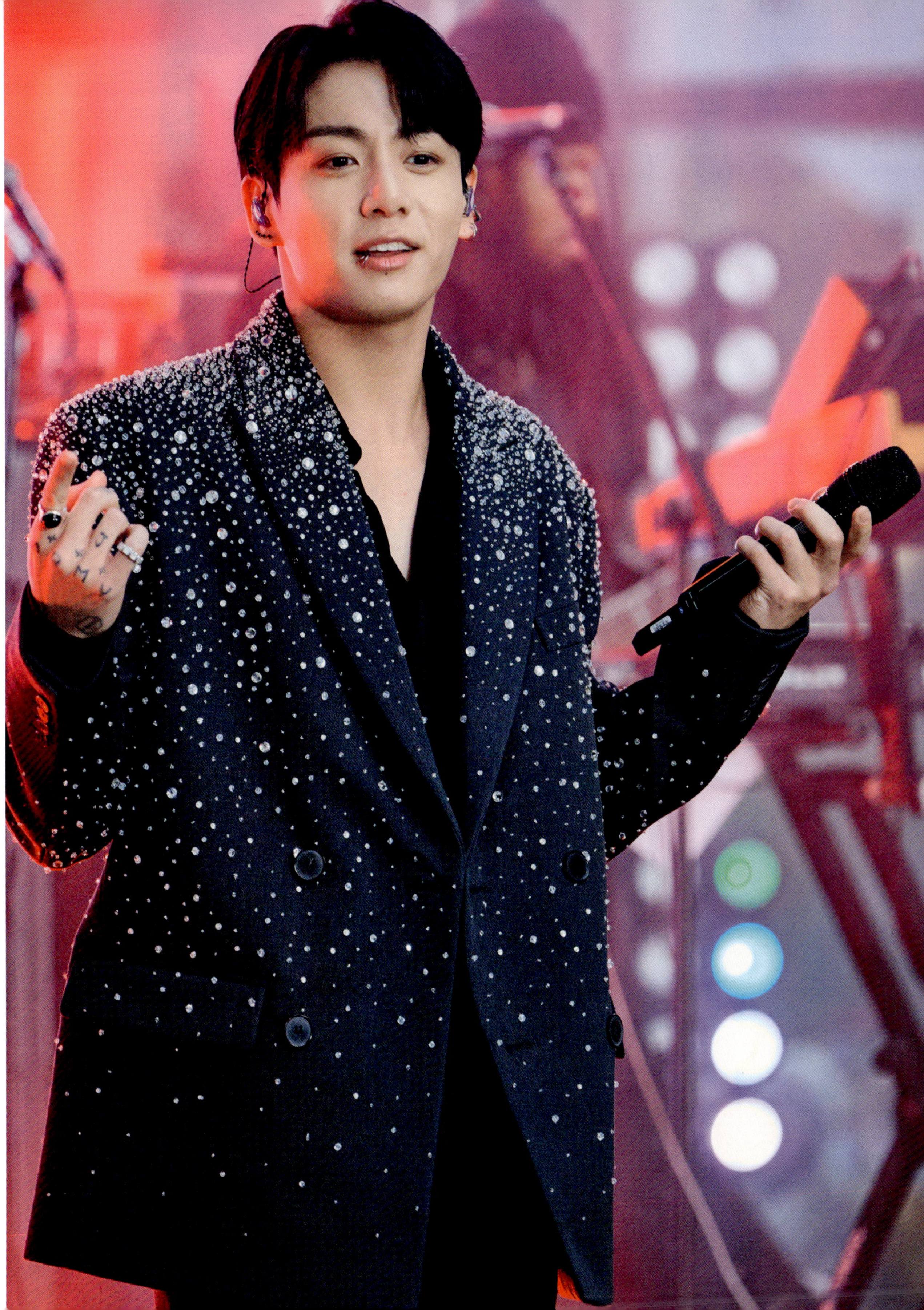

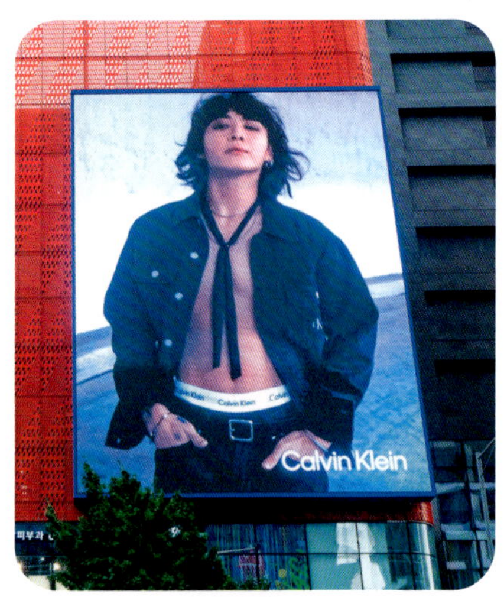

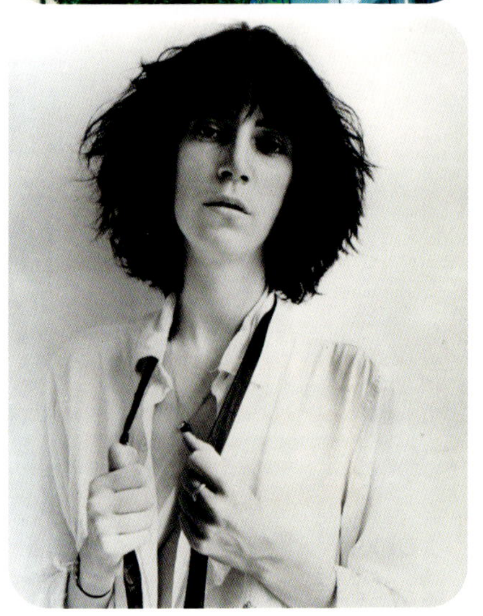

The next day his busy schedule saw him playing Times Square. The show, also streamed by Twitch, ensured fans caught a glimpse of him in full Calvin Klein Ambassador mode, wearing the American brand's signature inky jeans and a co-ordinating denim shirt. Earlier that year he had starred in the brand's Autumn campaign. The film was shot by fashion photographer couple Inez & Vinoodh (Inez van Lamsweerde and Vinoodh Matadin) in LA and styled by the ex-Editor-in-chief of French *Vogue*, Emmanuelle Alt. Looking flawlessly beautiful, Jung Kook danced to Gary Numan's new wave classic late-70s track 'Cars', his chest bare and accessorised with a skinny tie in a nod to androgynous songstress Patti Smith. The music and fashion moment was as exciting for Jung Kook as it was for the rest of the world, as he told kpoplife.com: 'My music is how I communicate with my fans around the world, and I see this partnership as an opportunity to connect with them in a new way. I'm incredibly excited for people to see a new side of me in this first campaign for the brand.'

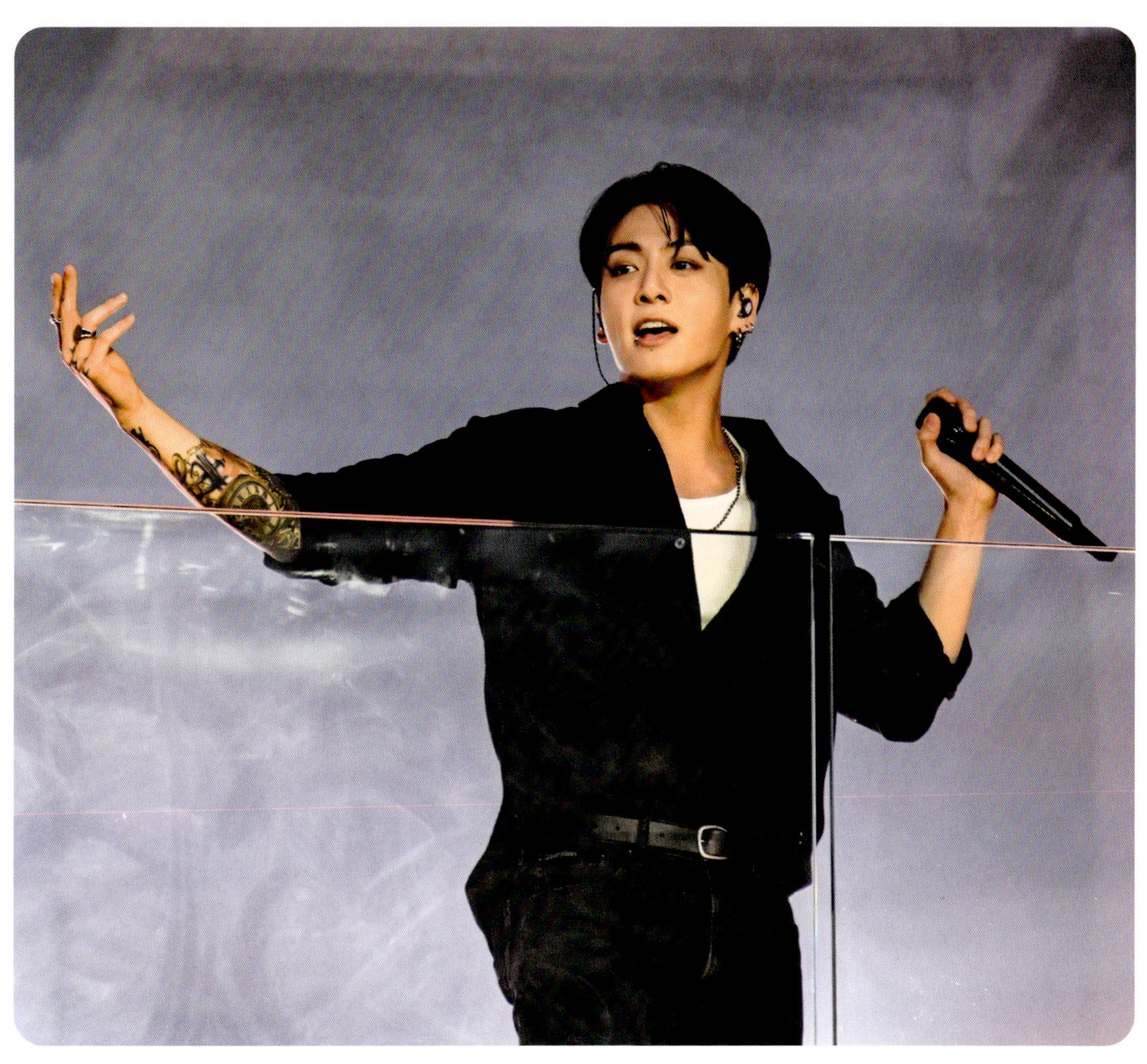

OPPOSITE TOP: *A video for the Calvin Klein Autumn 2023 campaign starring Jung Kook shown on an LED board in Seoul.*
OPPOSITE BOTTOM: *Rock chic, Patti Smith, 1975.*
THIS PAGE: *Jung Kook performs during a surprise concert in Times Square, NYC, 9 November 2023.*

Grey Slay

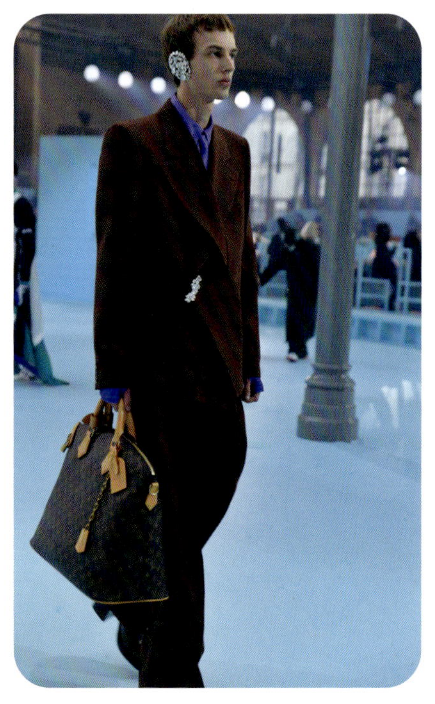

BTS were nominated for the Best Pop Duo/Group Performance 2022 Grammy and, to ARMY's approval, also performed their hit 'Butter' live at the ceremony. It was a massive night for the band. RM hit the red carpet with his hair shaded ashen. His Louis Vuitton brown double-breasted jacket, trousers with a slight kick-flare, co-ordinating purple shirt and tie teamed with a diamanté brooch gave off fun '70s disco vibes. But the 'fit – an exclusive custom look from the Autumn 2022 runway shown in January earlier that year – was a serious fashion statement; it had been Virgil Abloh's final collection. The fly suiting sported by RM and the rest of the band showcased Abloh's legacy perfectly. The band looked and sounded super-strong. For many fans expectation was high – BTS had lost out the year before for their song 'Dynamite'. Much to the fans' exasperation, the Grammy eluded them again in 2022, but the band lit up social media with their electrifying routine and their super-stylish outfits slayed anyway. As highsnobiety.com reported at the time: 'Objectively the world's biggest boy band, BTS won the Grammys without even taking home a single trophy.'

THIS PAGE: *Louis Vuitton RTW Men's Autumn 2022 show in Paris, 20 January 2022.*
OPPOSITE: *RM looking slick at the 64th Annual GRAMMY Awards, MGM Grand Garden Arena in Las Vegas, 3 April 2022.*

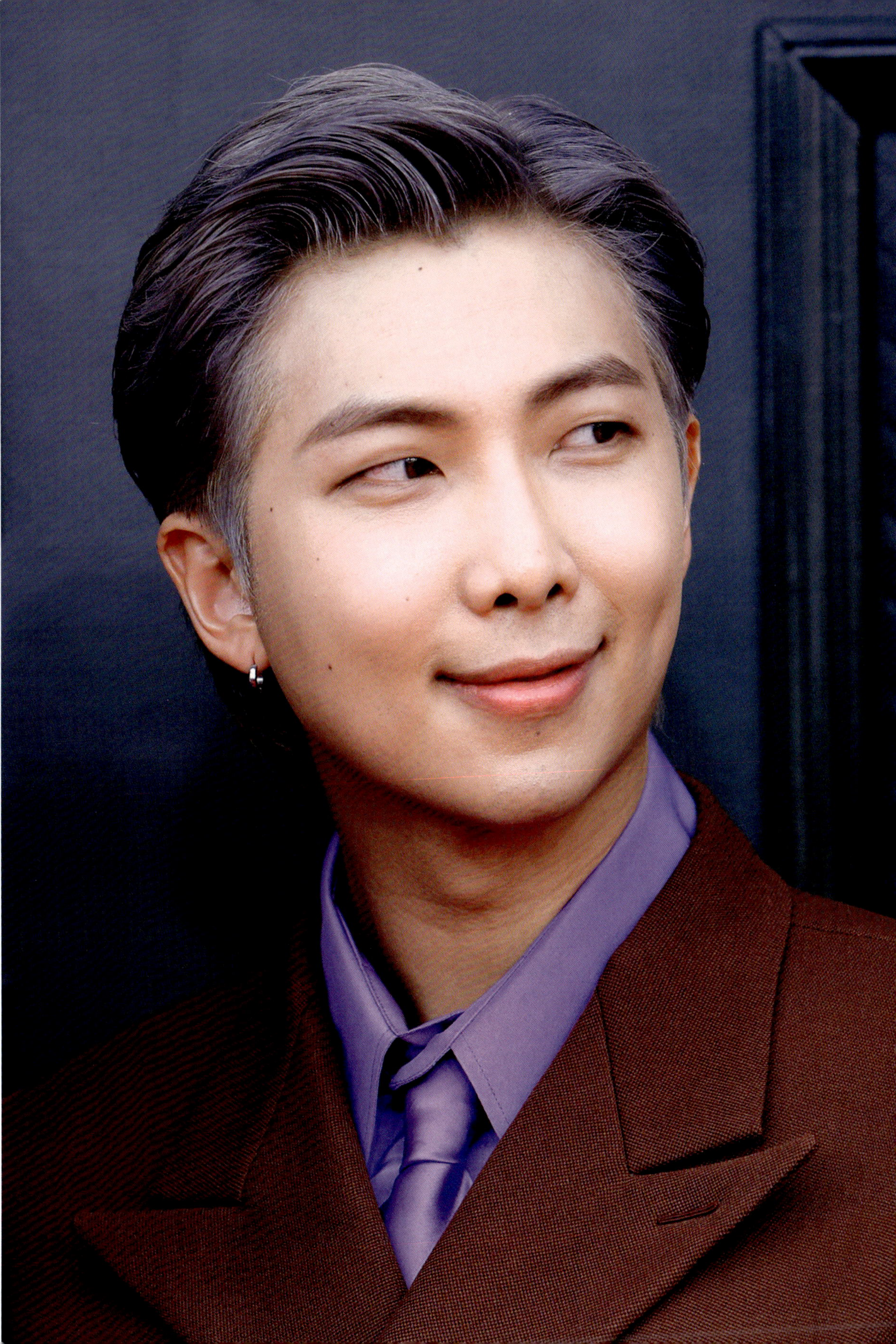

DI.VA for Ever

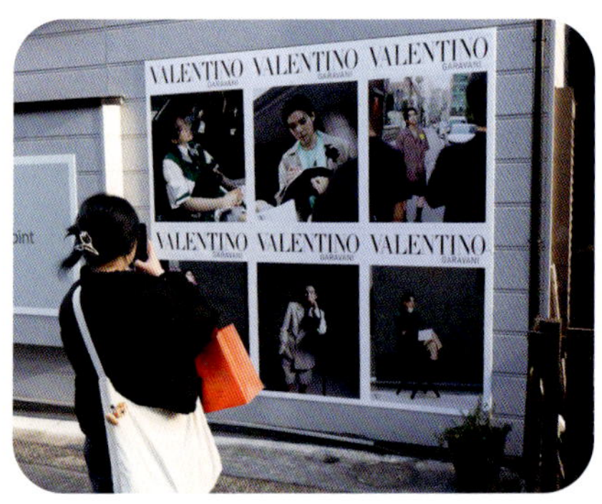

In January 2023 Italian fashion house Valentino signed SUGA as their new DI.VA (= Different Values) ambassador, joining Zendaya and Lewis Hamilton. An Instagram post pronounced: 'SUGA reflects the values of the Maison, speaking to a generation through his contemporary ideals'.

SUGA was selected by then creative director, Pierpaolo Piccioli to star in the Maison's menswear Essentials campaign, because 'his unique style and music world is a way to convey values that lead to a change, and embodies identity values that chime with the DI.VA ideals to inspire diversity and equality.'

The rapper returned the love, telling *Marie Claire Korea*: 'Flexibility is an important value for me when making music, and as I communicate and work with Valentino, I get the impression that it's a very flexible brand. That's why I enjoy collaborating with them. People around me also commented that its style suits my own, which is another aspect I'm happy about.'

THIS PAGE: *A fan snaps a pic of brand ambassador SUGA's Valentino campaign posters in Tokyo's fashion district Harajuku, 2024.* **OPPOSITE:** *SUGA striding it out at* The Devil's Deal *VIP premiere at Megabox COEX in Seoul, 28 February 2023.*

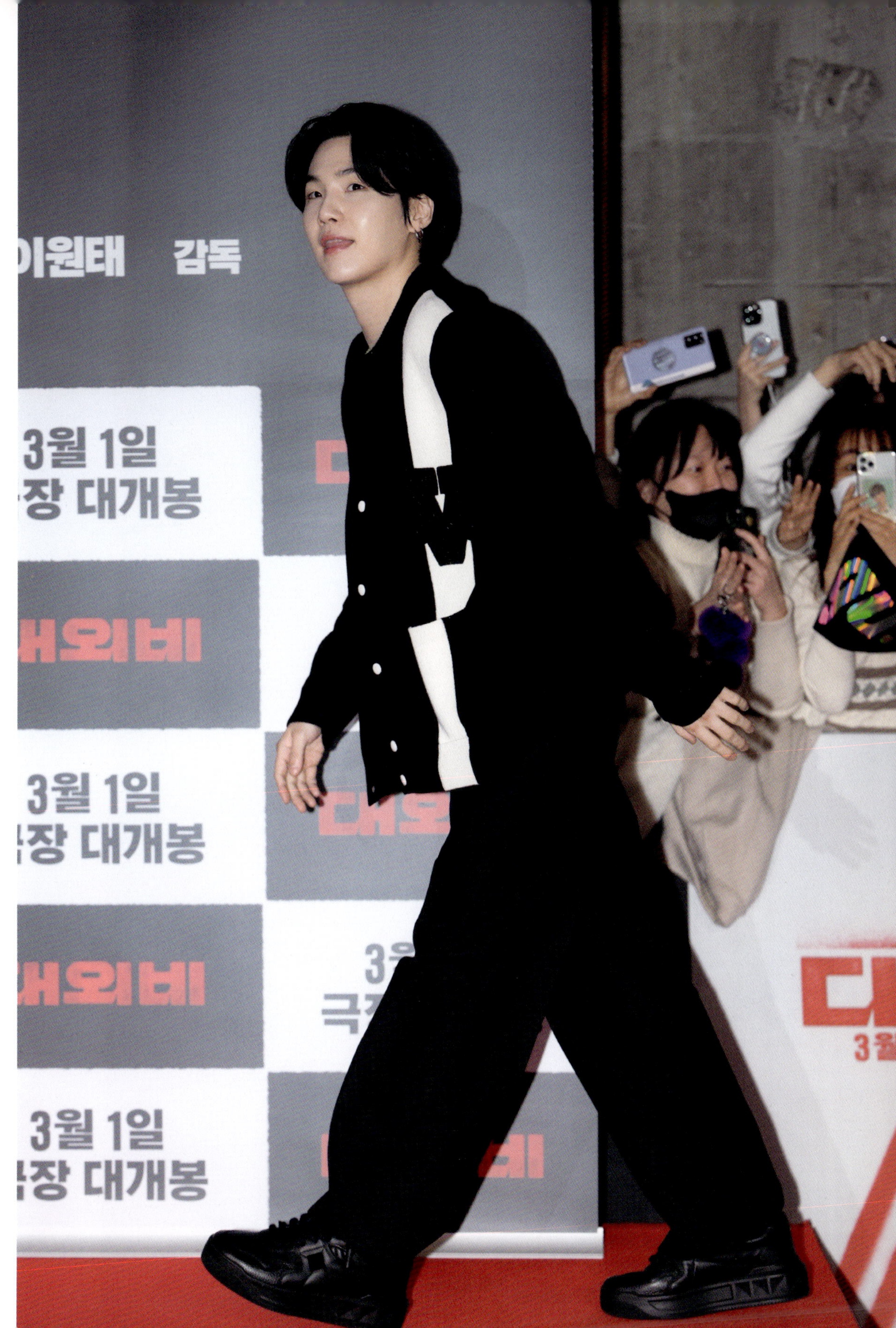
이원태   감독
3월 1일
장 대개봉
대외비
3월 1일
장 대개봉
대외비
3월
극
3월 1

The Essentials collection is a range of relaxed suiting – sportily suave silhouettes with a contemporary edge. Classic pieces include pink anoraks, crisp shirting and fun Bermuda shorts that fit SUGA's modern-flex perfectly. So, when he made an impromptu appearance at the Seoul movie premiere of Lee Won-tae's stylish thriller, *The Devil's Deal*, it was only natural that SUGA should appear in top-to-toe Valentino: he sported a Valentino V-3D embellished cardigan, wide co-ordinating pants, and Valentino Garavani one-stud XL low-top sneakers.

The icing on the cake was SUGA's brand new hair-trim, seen here for the first time. When ARMYs screamed their approval, Daegu-born Min Yoon-gi – aka SUGA, aka Agust D – rewarded them by running to the crowd and high-fiving some of the lucky ones. It was the beginning of a year that put him firmly in the spotlight. His debut official solo album *D-Day* was released in April and broke records selling a million copies in its first day.

'All individuals have different dreams and values. Maison Valentino and Creative Director Pierpaolo Piccioli have been supportive of diversity which is something that I also believe in. I am happy to be joining as DI.VAs and to collaborate on this amazing campaign with Maison Valentino Essentials.'

SUGA, Valentino press office statement, January 2023.

Tux Deluxe

There are many firsts when it comes to the phenomenon that is BTS. In 2019, the boys became the first Korean band to present an award at the Grammys (Best R&B Album to H.E.R.). They were also probably the only K–Pop group who had ever been caught on camera grooving to country and western singer Dolly Parton, who was at the ceremony that evening singing her classic, 'Jolene', much to their approval.

The boys had the best time, even though earlier on the red carpet they confessed they were super nervous and could only do it 'together'. And for their important evening, instead of working their own looks, they went unified, and all wore classic black tuxedos. BTS's group fashion statement that night honoured their favourite Korean designers. Their tailoring was crafted by two of South Korea's most famous designers: Kim Seo Ryong and JayBaek Couture. Outfitting j–hope for the Grammys, Kim Seo Ryong is the designer to go to when elegant menswear is required. The brand JayBaek Couture, which dressed the rest of the band, is no

BTS jump for Jolene at the 61st annual Grammy Awards held at Staples Center in Los Angeles, 10 February 2019.

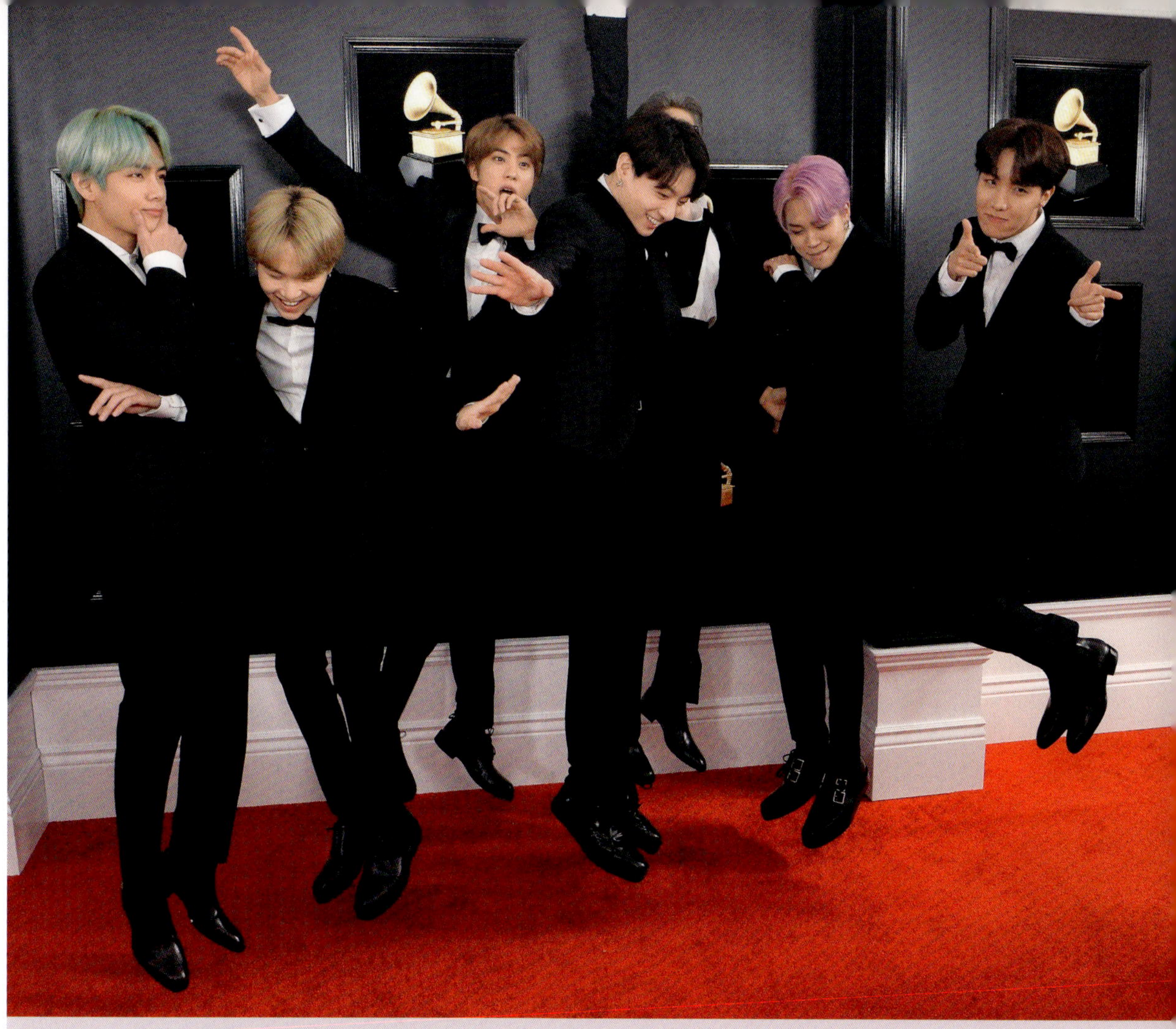

'We're living the dream.
So, we just want to say thanks to all the ARMYs. They made us.
They gave us force. '
— RM, Grammys red-carpet interview, *Billboard News*, 2019.

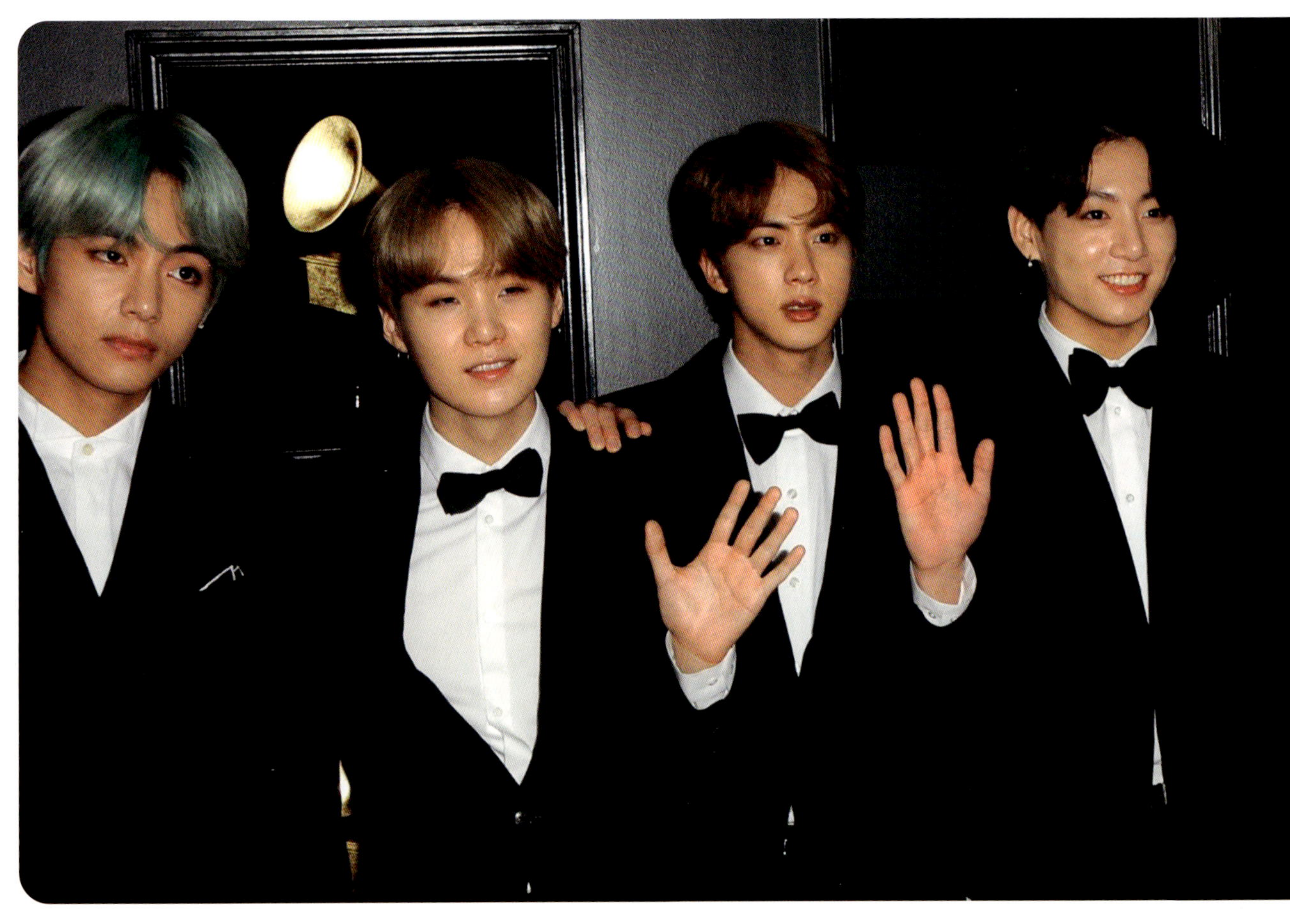

stranger to working with the super famous either – household names such as the star actors Yoo Ah-in and Hyun Bin are customers. CEO Jay Baek explained to kpopherald.com: 'I want the person who is wearing my outfit to take the lead role in their life... I like people who love themselves and who want to discover their beauty. Because when you love yourself, you can love others and discover the beauty of life.' That night the world loved BTS just a tiny bit more and it was clear for all to see they were indeed living their best lives and shining a light on their fellow Korean creatives.

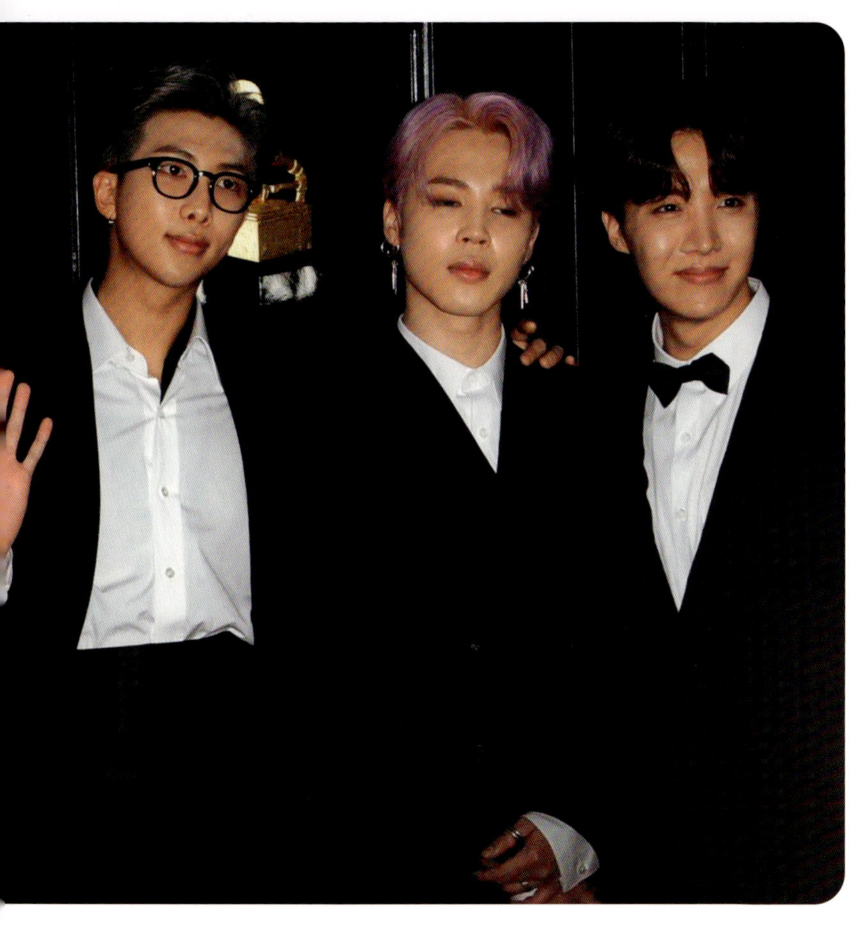

A suave line-up showcasing South Korean designers at the Grammys, Staples Center, Los Angeles, 10 February 2019.

All the President's Men

Looking cool, bold, and brave, BTS met up with American president, Joe Biden in 2022. They had been invited to talk about Asian representation. It was a landmark for both the band and the American government, as korea.net reported, the group was 'the first Korean artist to visit the White House for talks with the U.S. president'.

Following the previous year's COVID-19 Hate Crimes Act there was plenty to review in the 35 minutes they spent together. Jimin reflected how sad they were at the then rise of anti-Asian hate crimes, and that they were there 'to put a stop on this and support the cause', taking 'this opportunity to voice ourselves once again'. On the @potus Instagram, RM modestly said 'we just want to be a little help'. The meeting went viral; there couldn't be a better envoy to champion such a crucial issue.

BTS proudly underlined their heritage to the world with their choice of smart, sharp black suits by Tailorable. They had worn the Korean brand before, when they appeared on the cover of *Time* magazine in April that year.

The White House walk with Joe Biden, 31 May 2022.

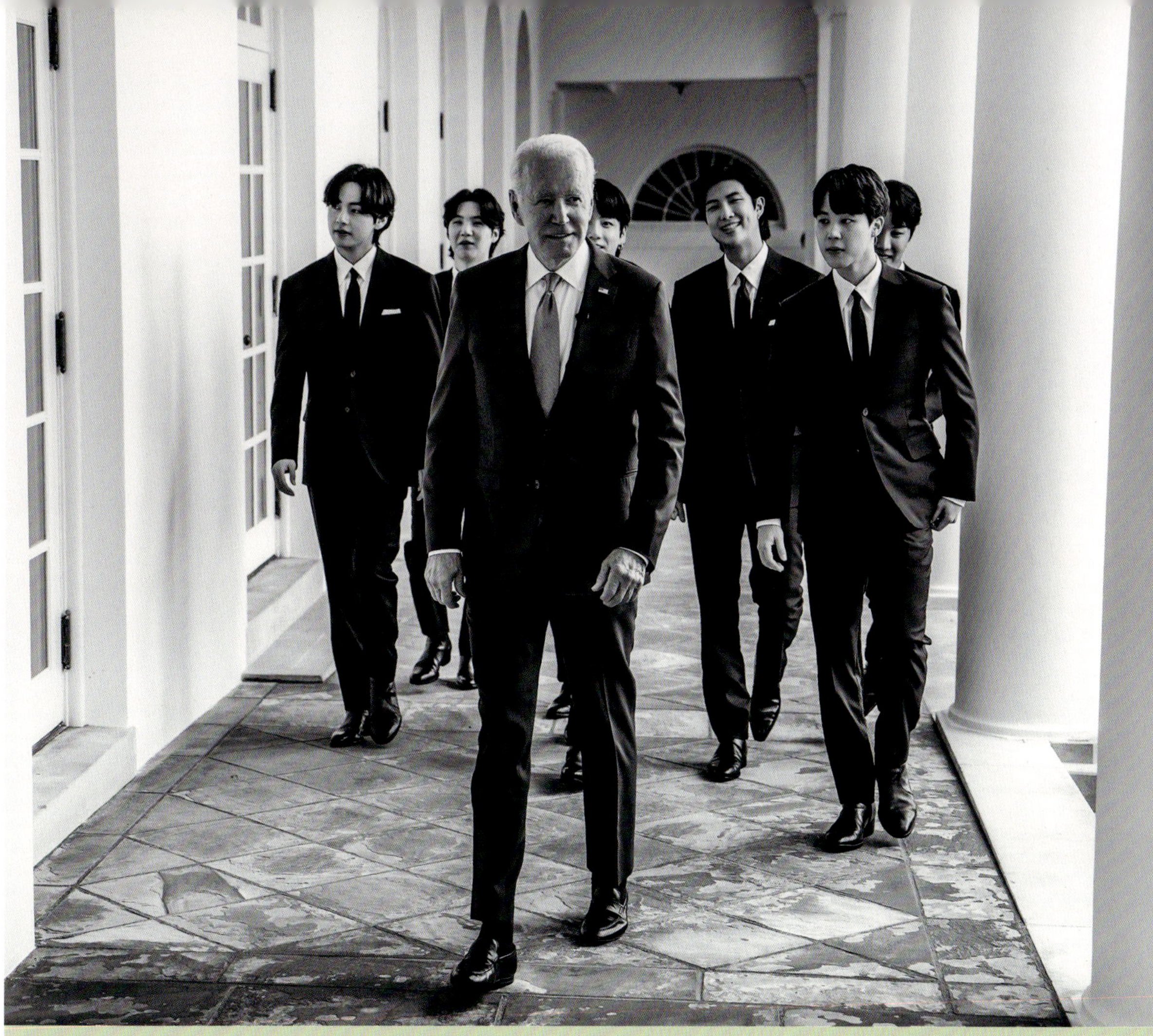

'People care a lot about what you say, and what you're doing is good for all people. It's not just your great talent, it's the message you're communicating. It matters. '

— President Biden, White House news briefing, 31 May 2022.

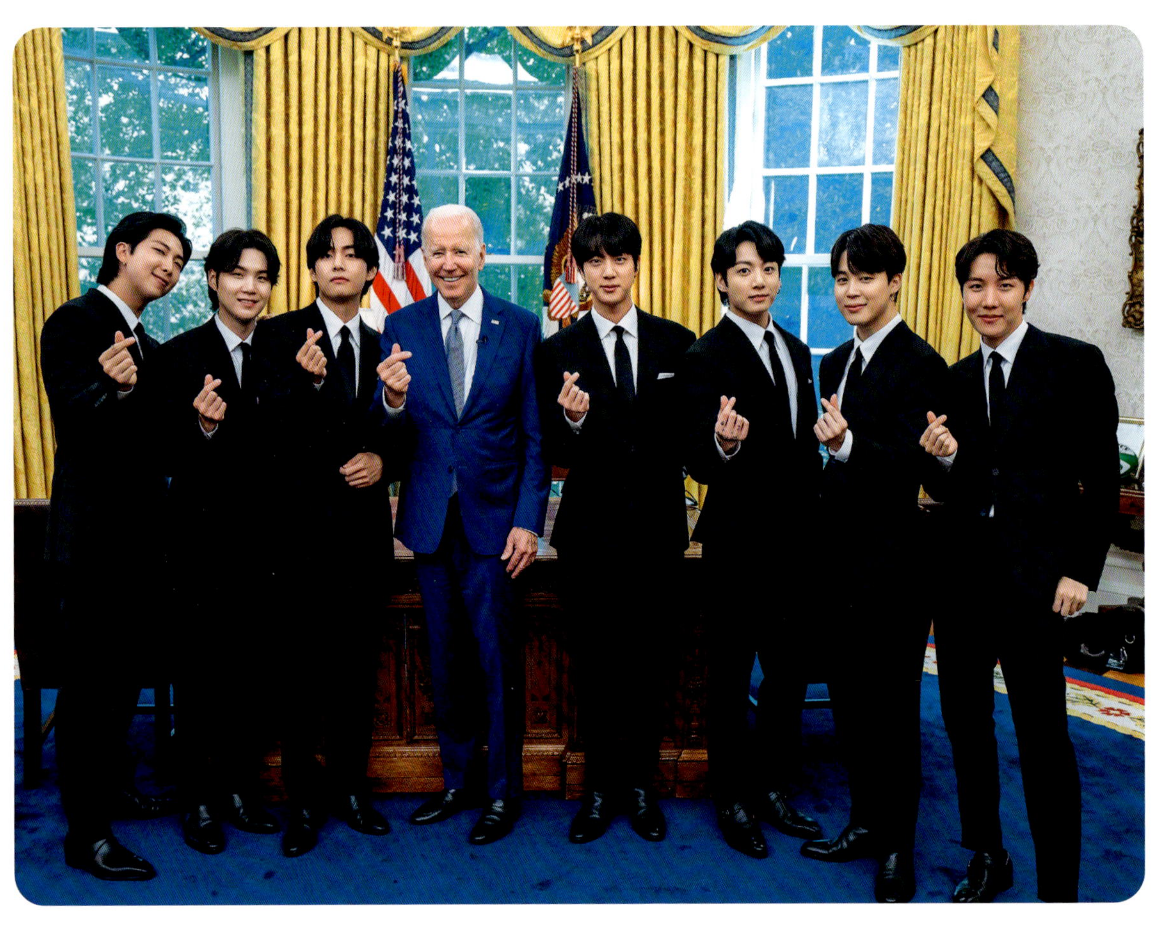

U.S. President Joe Biden and BTS unite to show their love, making the finger heart gesture during a video message on hate crimes against Asian Americans in the Oval Office of the White House, 31 May 2022.

Musical Youth

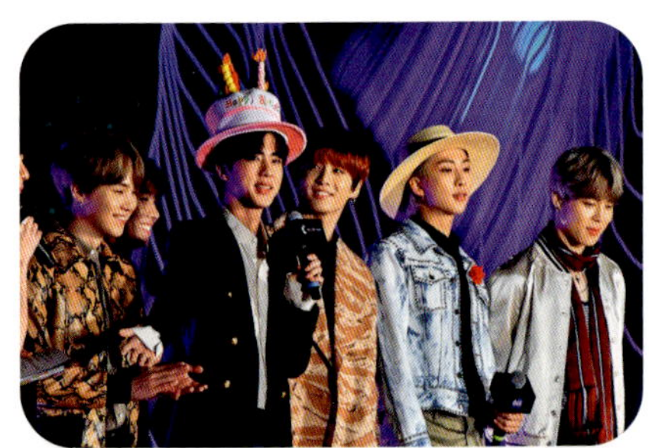

At the 2019 MAMAs, BTS won BIG, taking home all four Daesangs (Grand Prizes): Album of the Year for *Map of the Soul: Persona*, Worldwide Icon of the Year, Artist of the Year and Song of the Year for 'Boy with Luv'. RM gave a shout out to fans, saying: 'This year we released an album called *Persona* and you guys gave us our persona. We love you ARMYs.'

Their personas that evening were dressed by Celine: They arrived sporting snakeskin, satin and gold leather bombers, camo-coats and stone-washed denim jackets from Hedi Slimane's Celine S/S 2020 menswear collection, which melded Lou Reed–era downtown New York glam with the heady psychedelic Rolling Stones '70s styling. The collection, in collaboration with Brooklyn artist David Kramer, emblazoned the slogan of the season, 'I have nostalgia for things I probably have never known' across T-shirts and bags, reaffirming Slimane's reveries for subcultural halcyon days never actually experienced. The BTS boys are similar in their post-modern appreciation of fashion and during their

THIS PAGE TOP: *Jin wearing his birthday hat.*
THIS PAGE BOTTOM: *Celine S/S 2020 snakeskin bomber.*
OPPOSITE: *All kitted out in Celine at the Mnet Asian Music Awards in Nagoya, Japan, 4 December 2019.*

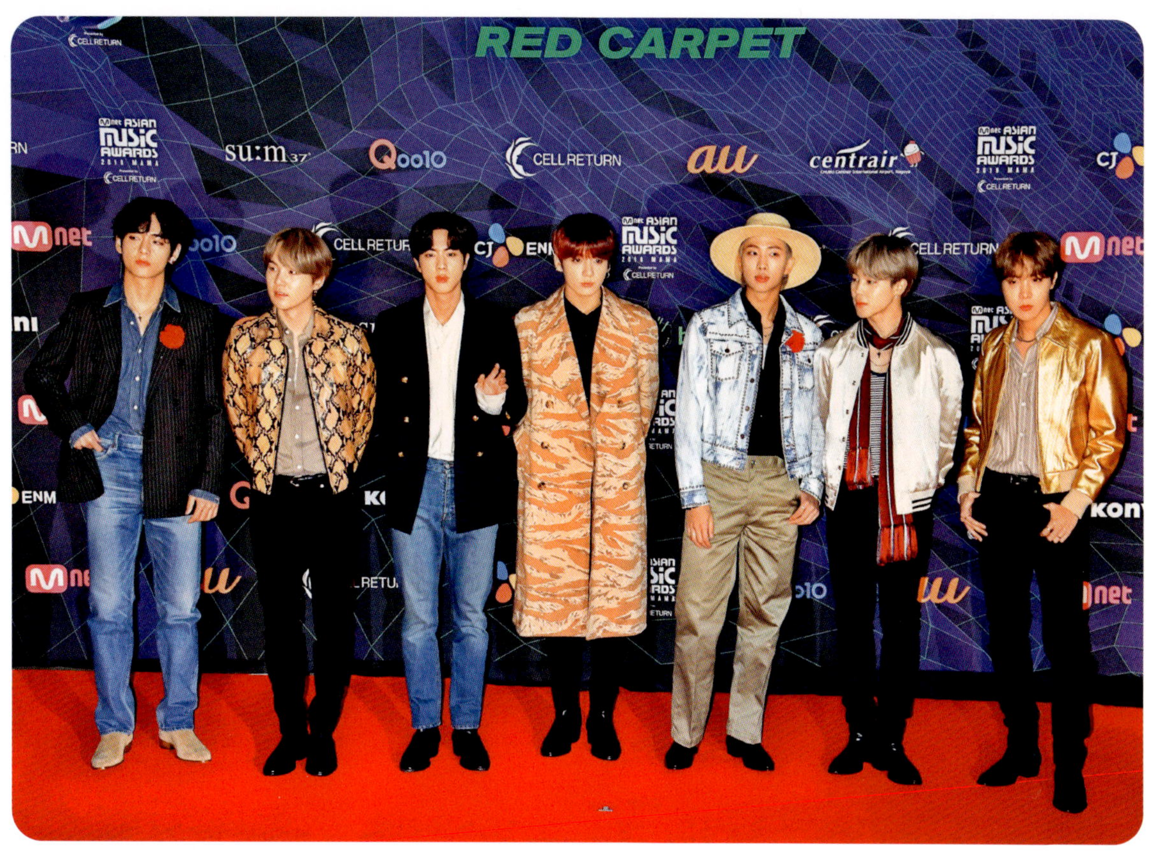

career have intuitively cut and pasted retro vibes making them new and fresh for a forward-looking audience. It's no surprise then that Slimane and BTS have become fast friends; especially V, who was named an official ambassador for Celine in March 2023. Apart from the wild silhouettes, the evening was made even more entertaining as it was 'World-Wide Handsome' Jin's 27th birthday and he donned a very swish foam party hat to celebrate.

LV Luv

— BTS, Louis Vuitton press release, April 2021.

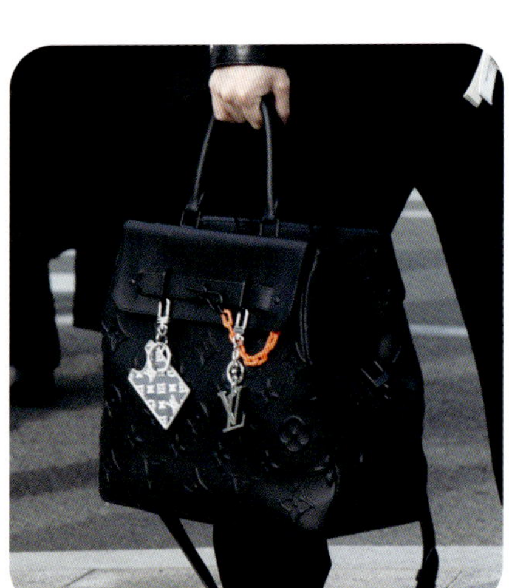

In 2021, BTW collaborated officially for the very first time with a big luxury fashion house, partnering with Louis Vuitton back when American–Ghanaian designer Virgil Abloh was still Creative Director. It was an exciting time and Abloh reflected: 'I am looking forward to this wonderful partnership which adds a modern chapter to the House, merging luxury and contemporary culture.' LV sent the news out online via Twitter (now X) which, as voguehk.com reported at the time: 'went on to become the brand's most popular tweet [to date] with shy of a million likes'.

Louis Vuitton's 'spin-off' 34-piece Fall 2021 menswear collection was presented alongside seven pieces from the original Winter collection in a mesmeric film directed by Jeon Go-woon. The movie, shown at the Bucheon Art Bunker B39, in Gyeonggi-do in South Korea, starred the band wearing a choice outfit each and was, according to an LV

THIS PAGE: *Swag bag, SUGA with LV in hand, Incheon International Airport, 17 November 2021.*
OPPOSITE: *Showing the L(u)V. L-R: V, SUGA, Jin, Jung Kook, RM, Jimin, and j-hope at iHeartRadio 102.7 KIIS FM's Jingle Ball 2021 presented by Capital One at The Forum, LA, 3 December 2021.*

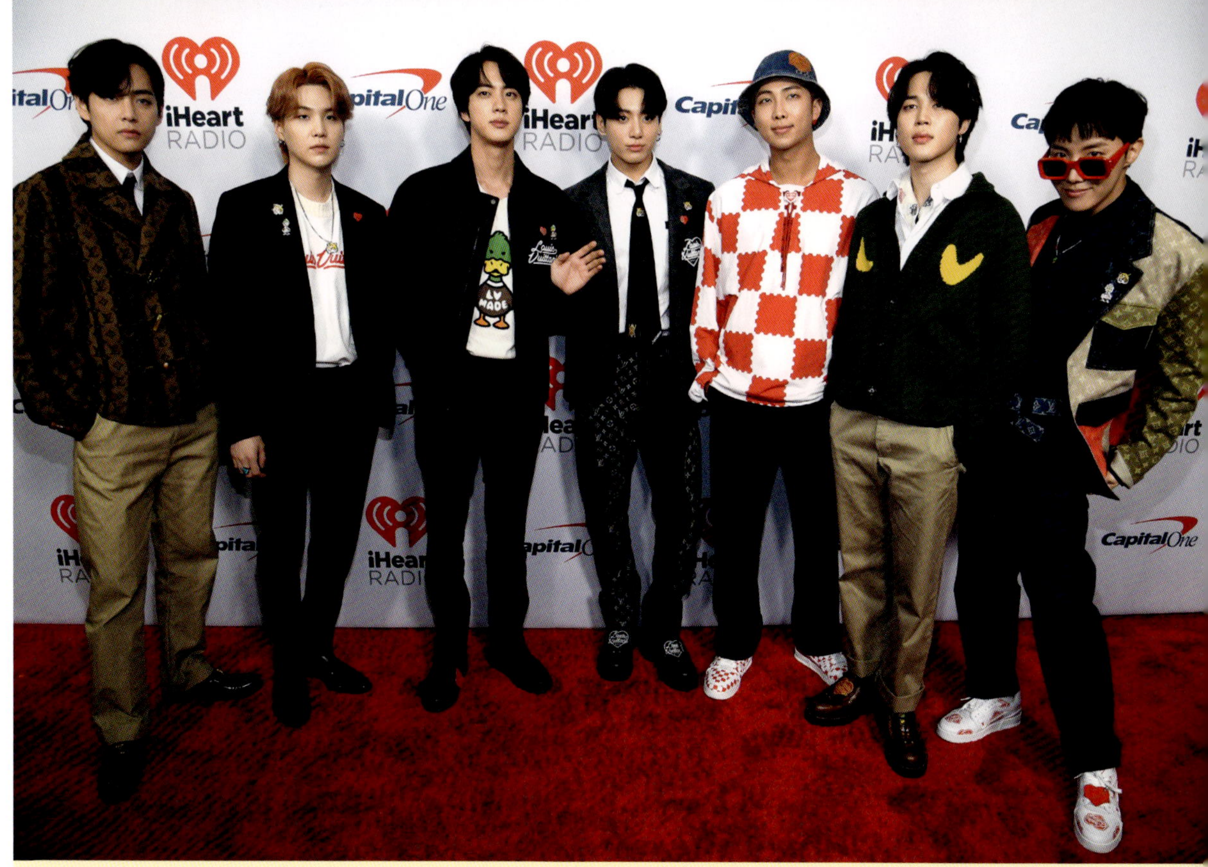

' Seoul has such unique energy and
BTS embody this vibe completely.
They add their spin to the collection,
make it their own and
take it to new heights. '
— Virgil Abloh, *koreaboo.com*, July 2021.

press announcement, intended to: 'stage a conversation between space, movement and global connectivity central to our moment in time.' Abloh and BTS's understanding of their fashion fans as a global community resonated, and the partnership sealed a very modern moment for how the very biggest creatives collaborate.

Abloh's unique fusion of style and luxe streetwear suited BTS to perfection and the boys' high-profile events that year became a brilliant catwalk for his work. In December 2021, the boys opened the legendary KIIS FM Jingle Ball with a performance of their hit tracks 'Dynamite' and 'Butter' sporting logo-embellished Louis V from top to toe. It was just a month after Abloh's heart-breakingly premature death, and their colourful 'fits were a celebration of the creative's pioneering handiwork and accomplishments while at the storied Parisian house.

SUGA looking like dynamite in Louis Vuitton, iHeartRadio 102.7 KIIS FM's Jingle Ball 2021, LA, 3 December 2021.

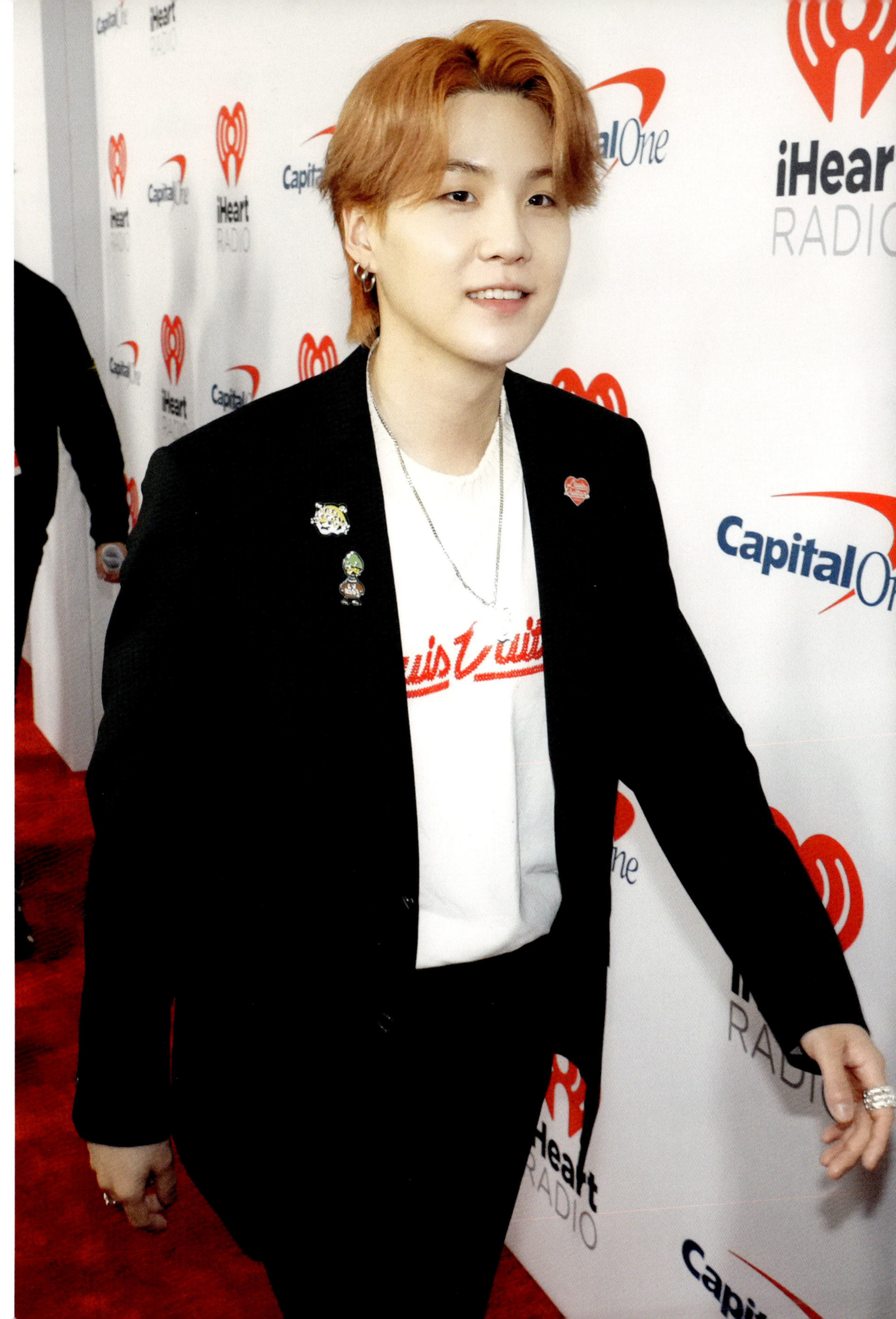

Soul Love

BTS love designer trainers. From SUGA's oblique-printed high-top Diors, to V's Balenciaga black speed knit sock, to Jung Kook's Visvim Skagway Lo G Patten low-top sneaker created with a special handmade Japanese canvas fabric… the band has always shown a choice understanding of not just what looks good, but also performs well. As trainees, they were coached for up to 12 hours every day until they became dope dancers; today, when they hit the stage and slide into action, it shows. They move as well as they sing *and* as well as they dress. In 2018, they partnered with Puma and designed a floral-logoed black, white and gold basket shoe featuring a hand holding a flower on the sole.

A year later, their footwear expertise was put once more to the test and BTS signed to become the face of sportswear brand Fila, originally founded in Italy in 1911, starring in subsequent campaigns. Later in 2022, the band collaborated on a range of Fila X BTS athleisure-wear including, of course, sneakers, as well as some cute socks embroidered with a special dance move from each member.

Keeping his feet on the ground. SUGA in Dior oblique-printed high-tops during BTS's performance on ABC's Good Morning America, *NYC, 15 May 2019.*

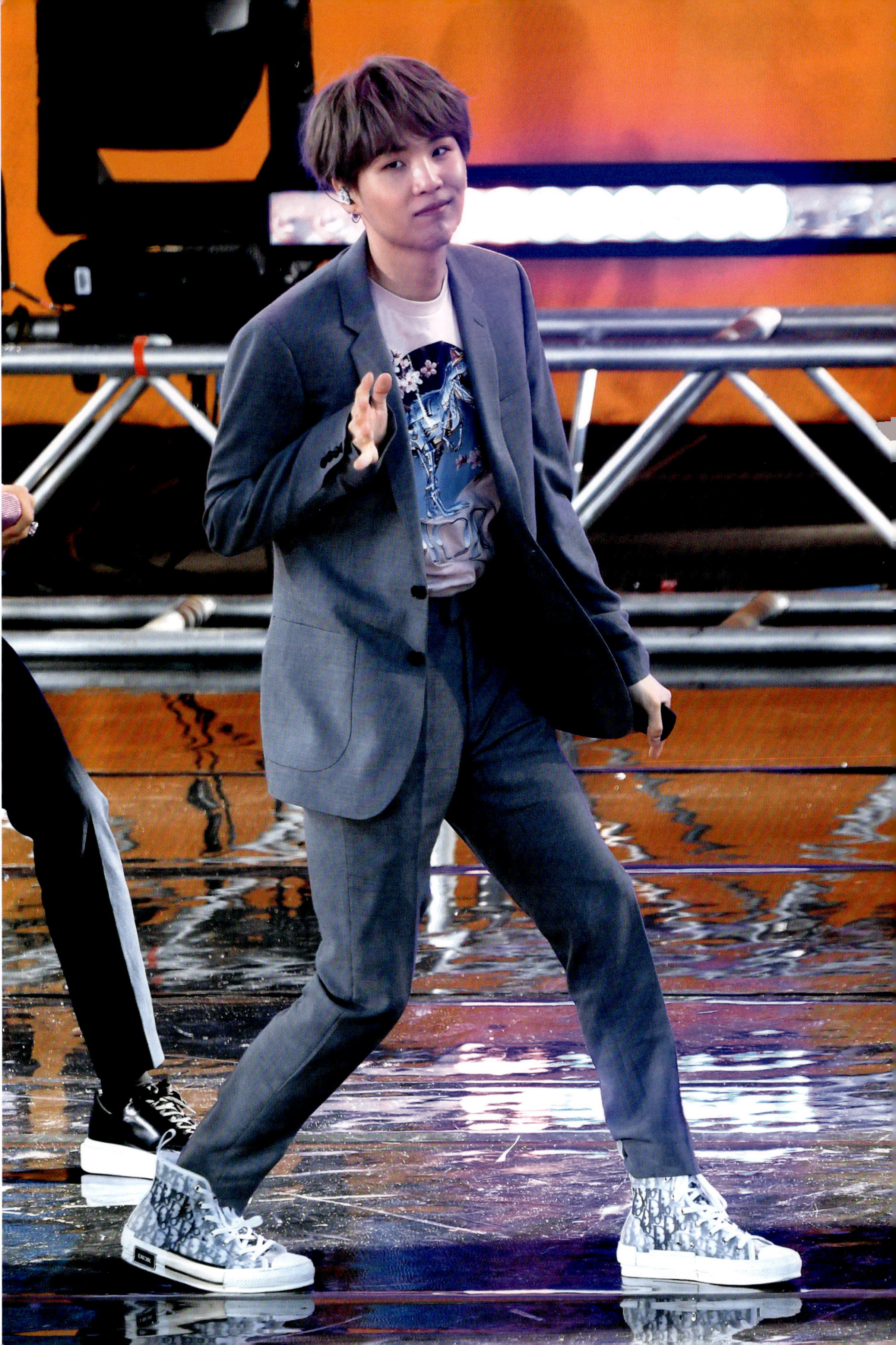

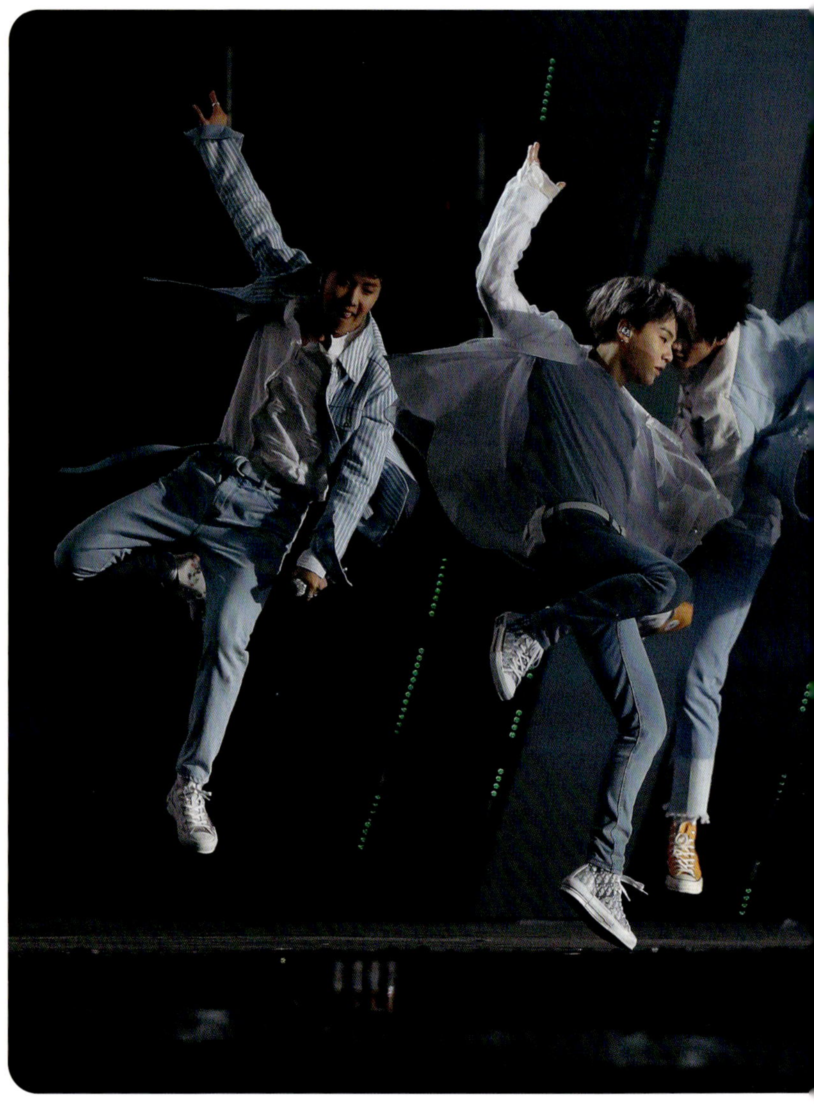

The most entertaining sneaker partnership, however, was unofficial. After BTS endorsed McDonald's with a 2021 Meal alliance that hit record sales, the Singapore-born artist Josiah Chua, re-assembled the packaging to create a pair of lilac and buttercup-yellow cardboard sneakers. They blew up online and had fans taking inspiration and upcycling their own McNuggets boxes into a variety of home-made, Maccy-D

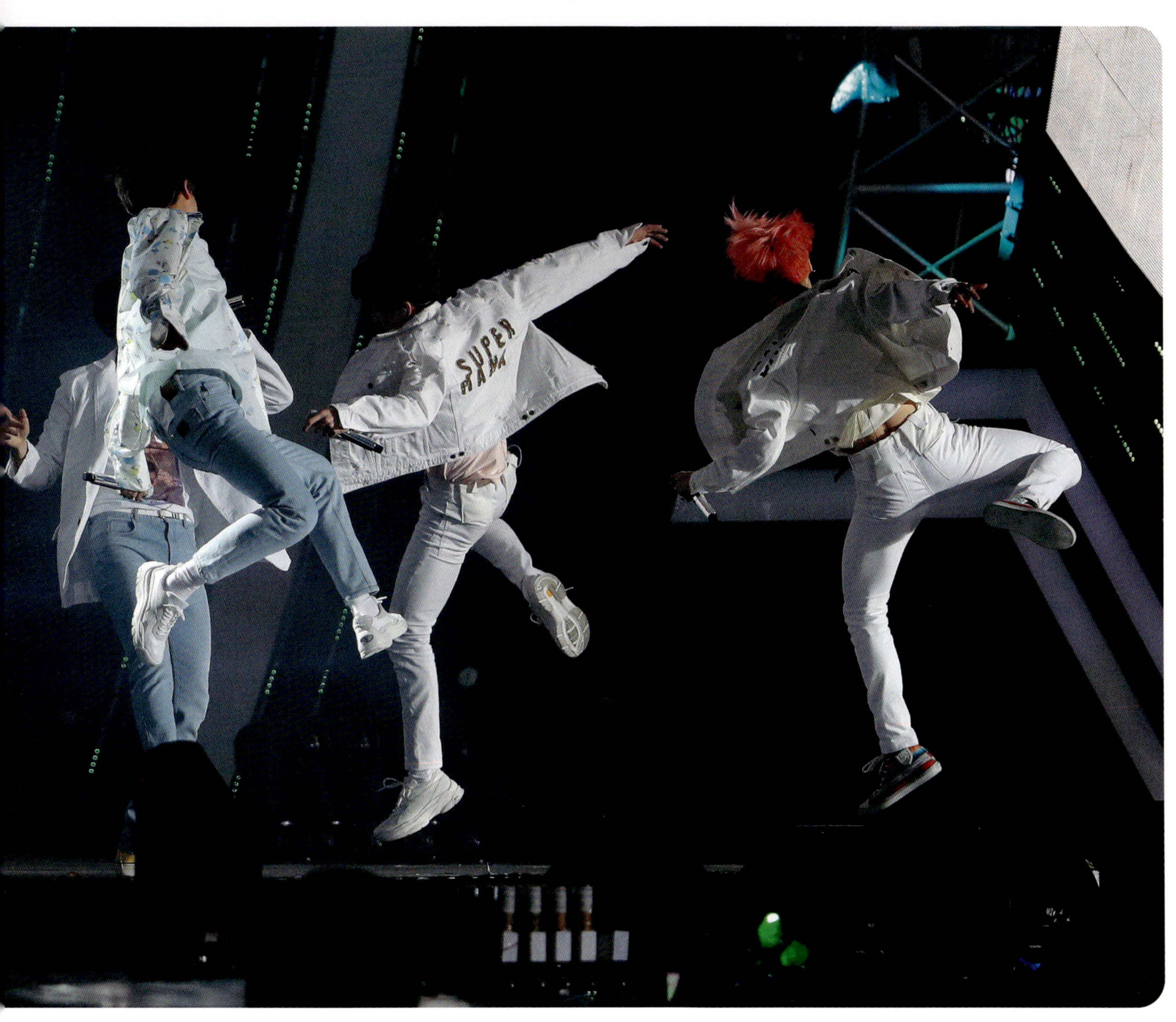

memorabilia. Chua told nylon.com: 'The point is really to have fun and not be serious about everything. Something like packaging can be made fun and interesting with a dose of creativity!' *Sole* food indeed!

Air time. BTS show off their moves at a concert to promote the 18th FINA World Championships, Gwangju, 28 April 2019.

Fly Style

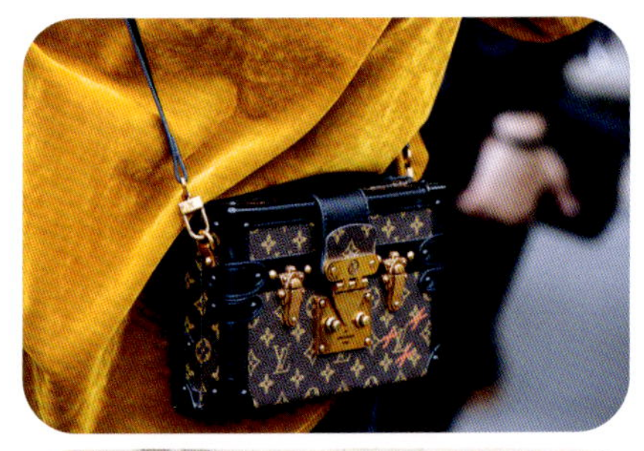

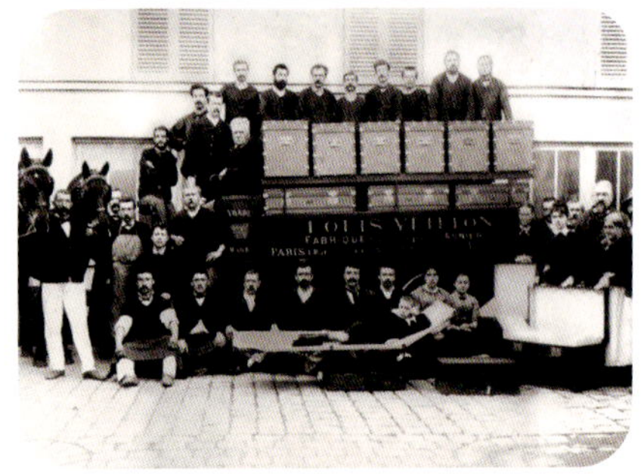

There are many ways to love BTS and their fashion choices and one of the most valuable for style-watchers is checking out their airport looks. Originally it was a moment for fans to see their idols wearing informal and cosy travel attire picked to relax in during a long journey. However, airport fashion has evolved into a voguish statement and now what stars wear to travel is as important as what they wear on stage. The K–Pop influence is so great that it has become a trend genre all of its own and a riveting way to catch a peek of our favourite celebrities busting new garms and showing allegiance to their preferred labels.

On 17 November 2021, BTS left Incheon, South Korea to fly to their 'Permission to Dance on Stage' LA concert in casually classic designer wear with stand-out accessories. Jimin carried a black Louis Vuitton Petite Malle handbag crossbody, Jin a Damier duffle bag and SUGA a large steamer tote embossed with the LV house insignia. j–hope, meanwhile, wore a gold Vuitton X Yayoi Kusama infinity scarf. In a major

THIS PAGE TOP: *LV Petite Malle bag, Paris Fashion Week, 2016.*
THIS PAGE BOTTOM: *Old school Louis Vuitton luggage luxury. With the man himself in the driver's seat, c.1890.*
OPPOSITE: *Jin, V, Jung Kook, Jimin, SUGA, RM and j–hope crossing the tarmac in style, Incheon International Airport, 17 November 2021.*

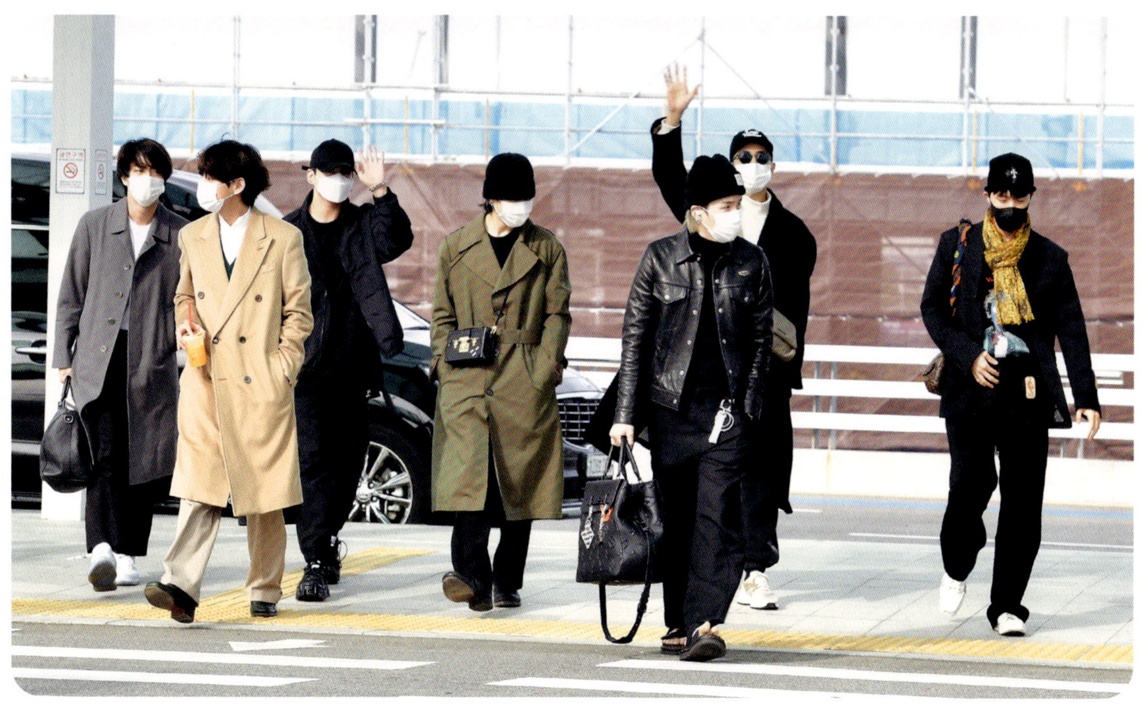

coup, LV had signed the entire band in April that year as
global brand ambassadors, and with Virgil Abloh at the helm,
they were regularly seen sporting the fashion House's most
covetable pieces. Louis Vuitton Malletier founded his Parisian
luggage company in 1854 and became known for his elegant
travelling trunks. Originally made with a grey Trianon canvas,
it wasn't until 1896 that Vuitton's son, George, introduced
the now legendary LV logo to the world. Today, it's worn and
carried by fashion forward style-lovers, making it once again
a touring essential, and super-suitable airport attire for BTS.

Hobi-Core

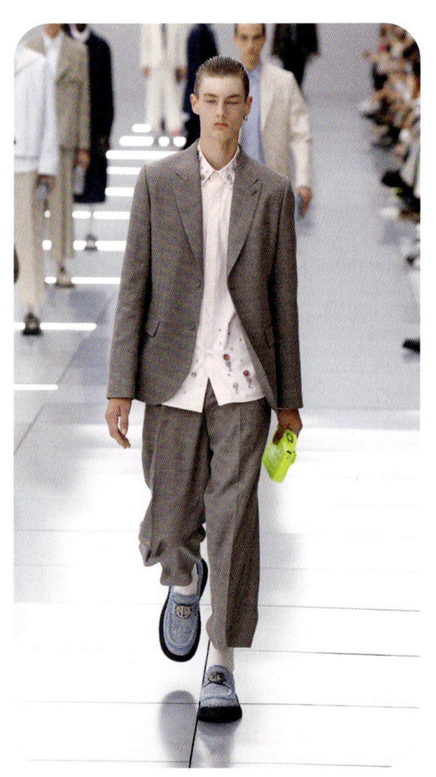

Even before j-hope's official announcement as ambassador for Dior, fans scrutinising BTS airport fashion detected that he was happy to work an en-pointe full 'fit for the French fashion house. In late November 2022, he travelled out of Incheon Airport to go to the MAMAs, where he sang three tracks from his album, *Jack in the Box*, becoming the first member of BTS to appear solo at the awards ceremony. As ever, it was the star's airport style that heralded this huge deal and his outfit that day was fully noted. 'Hobi' totally embraced the Dior X Cactus Jack S/S 2024 collab collection, which included stand-out accessories: a vital element of any airport styling. He elegantly rocked a Dior slogan beanie emblazoned with: 'If you can read this, I must love you to let you this close', signed, as the label described, 'with the Dior logo reinvented by Travis Scott', along with Jordan X Travis Scott trainers and a Cactus Jack brooch designed by Kim Jones. j-hope completed his look with a mini saddle bag.

THIS PAGE: *Dior Homme Menswear S/S 2024 show, Paris Fashion Week, 23 June 2023.*
OPPOSITE: *j-hope looking fly leaving Incheon International Airport, 28 November 2022.*

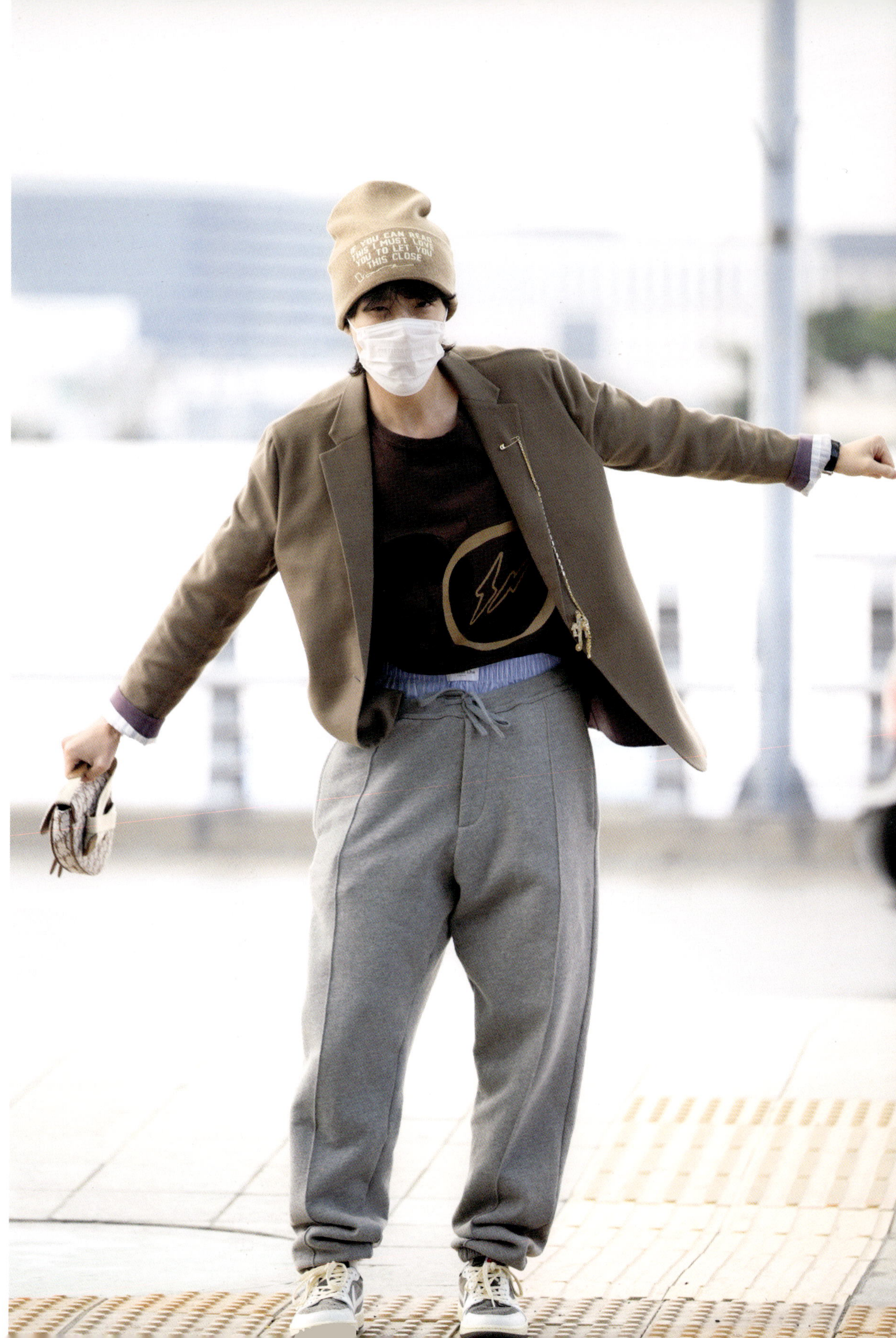
IF YOU CAN READ
THIS I MUST LOVE
YOU TO LET YOU
THIS CLOSE

The design was first introduced for the S/S 2000 collection by John Galliano when he was creative director of the brand, and has subsequently become legendary and a favourite of style icons, including Beyoncé and Rihanna. It's a shape that gets reinvented season after season, and today is seen equally on both men's and women's Dior runways. j-hope teamed the smart bag, which could also be worn on a belt, with a formal mushroom-coloured blazer and contrasting low-rise jogging pants and stripy blue boxer shorts that could be glimpsed peeping out, causing a stir online. The outfit typified Kim Jones's high-meets-street-fashion methodology to luxury design, which is echoed in many respects by j-hope's own particular sartorial approach, making them a model combination.

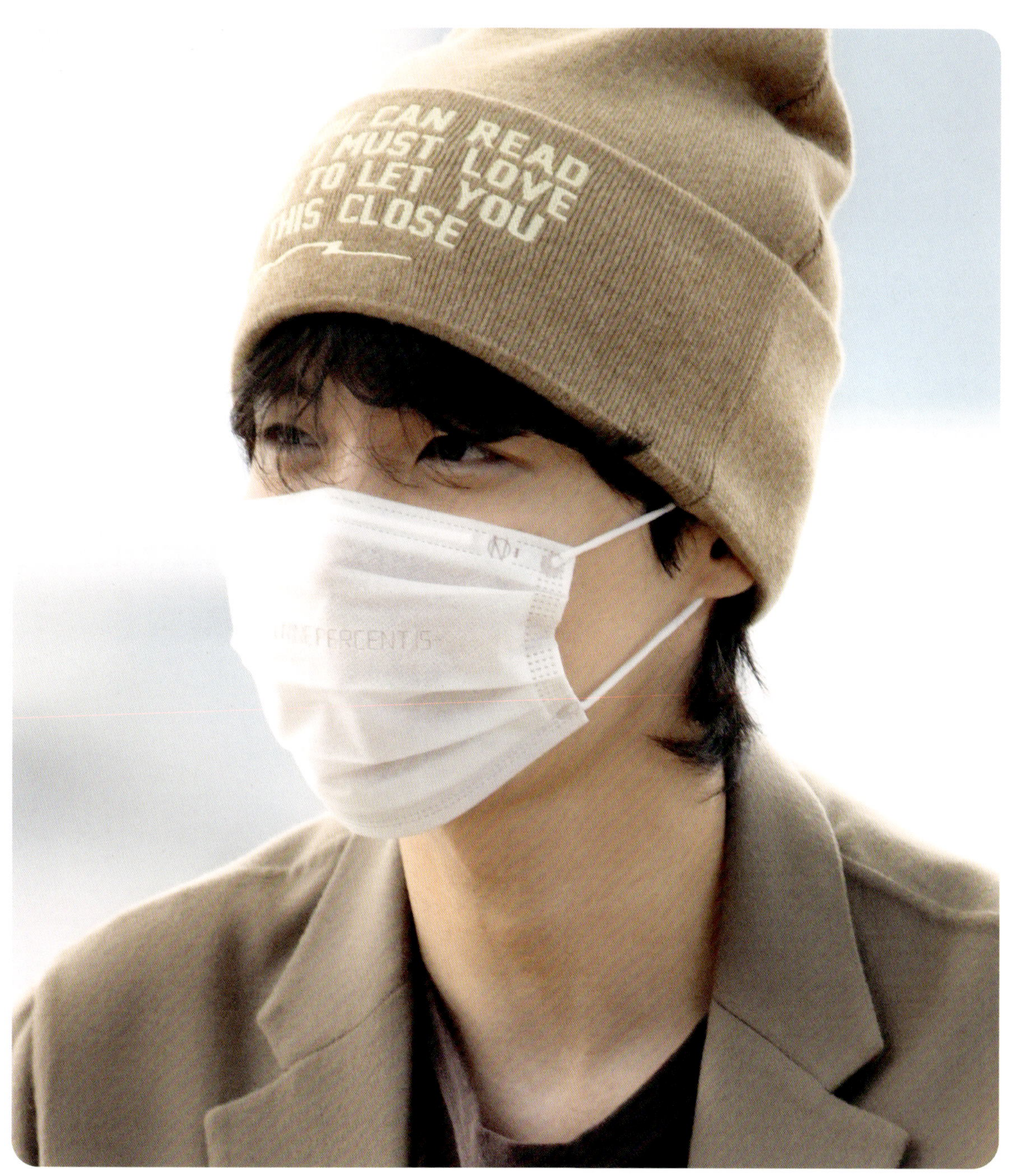
I CAN READ
I MUST LOVE
TO LET YOU
THIS CLOSE

It's a Tradition

**Fashionista Jin,
hanbok this time?'**
**— Jung Kook, episode 34, *Run BTS!* series,
aired via Naver's V app (now Weverse), 2 January 2018.**

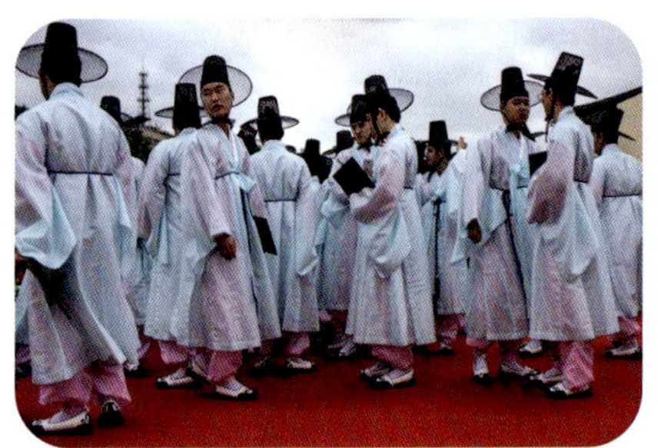

One of the key reasons BTS have garnered so many loyal fans is because although they are super famous, and shut it down with their looks and music, they are always in the room with you and relatable. Not least because of their Weverse hit series, *Run BTS!* that shows the band messing around, being real and having fun. In episode 34, the band played their usual variety of games finishing with, as kopherald.com reported: 'a spot-the-difference puzzle and game of bingo'. ARMYs know that the loser of these competitions is often tasked with wearing a 'forfeit' outfit and look forward to spotting it. Previously, BTS members have been seen wearing sunflower heads and bunny ears because of these escapades, and this time it was Jin's turn, as he was challenged to wear traditional hanbok to the airport en route to the November 2017 Mnet Asian Music Awards.

THIS PAGE: *South Korean students at a traditional coming-of-age ceremony at Namsangol Hanok Village in Seoul on 15 May 2017. The ceremony marks the age of 19, at which a person is legally able to make life choices like voting and drinking alcohol.*
OPPOSITE: *BTS's 'moon' pays his forfeit. Wearing traditional Korean costume, Jin waves to fans as he arrives at the Hong Kong International Airport for the 2017 Mnet Asian Music Awards.*

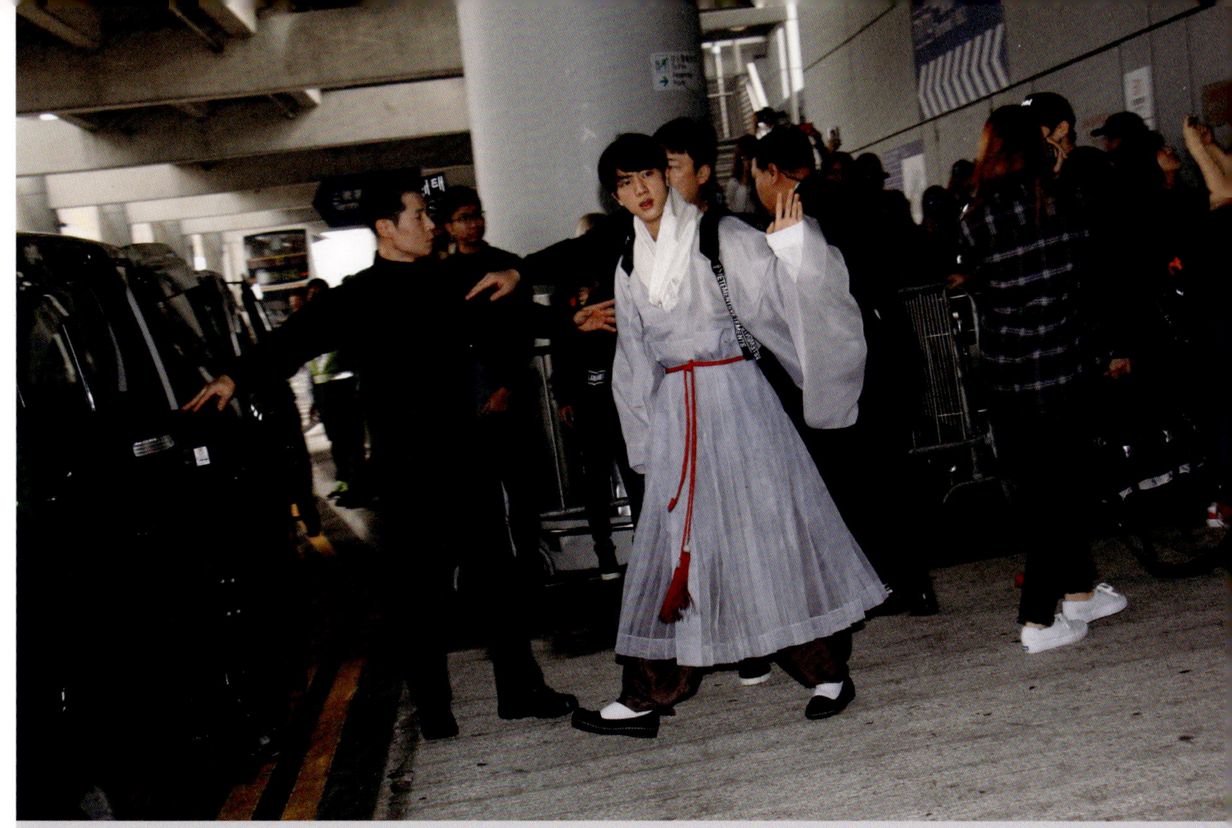

— Jin, *Twitter (now X)*, 29 November 2017.

Anytime the group sets off on a trip via Incheon International Airport they hit the headlines. Their outfits are always big news when travelling and when the group touched down in Hong Kong for the ceremony taking place at the AsiaWorld–Expo, photographers were waiting and astonished to see Jin sporting the traditional garb of a young Joseon dynasty pupil. The costume is still worn today in South Korea for special occasions including holidays and birthdays, but rarely for world–wide music events, especially by global pop stars just about to win the Daesang prize, Artist of the Year, for the second time in a row. Fittingly enough, BTS has gone on to secure the honour a massive lucky seven times in total to date, confirming they have substance and style as well as a fantastic sense of humour.

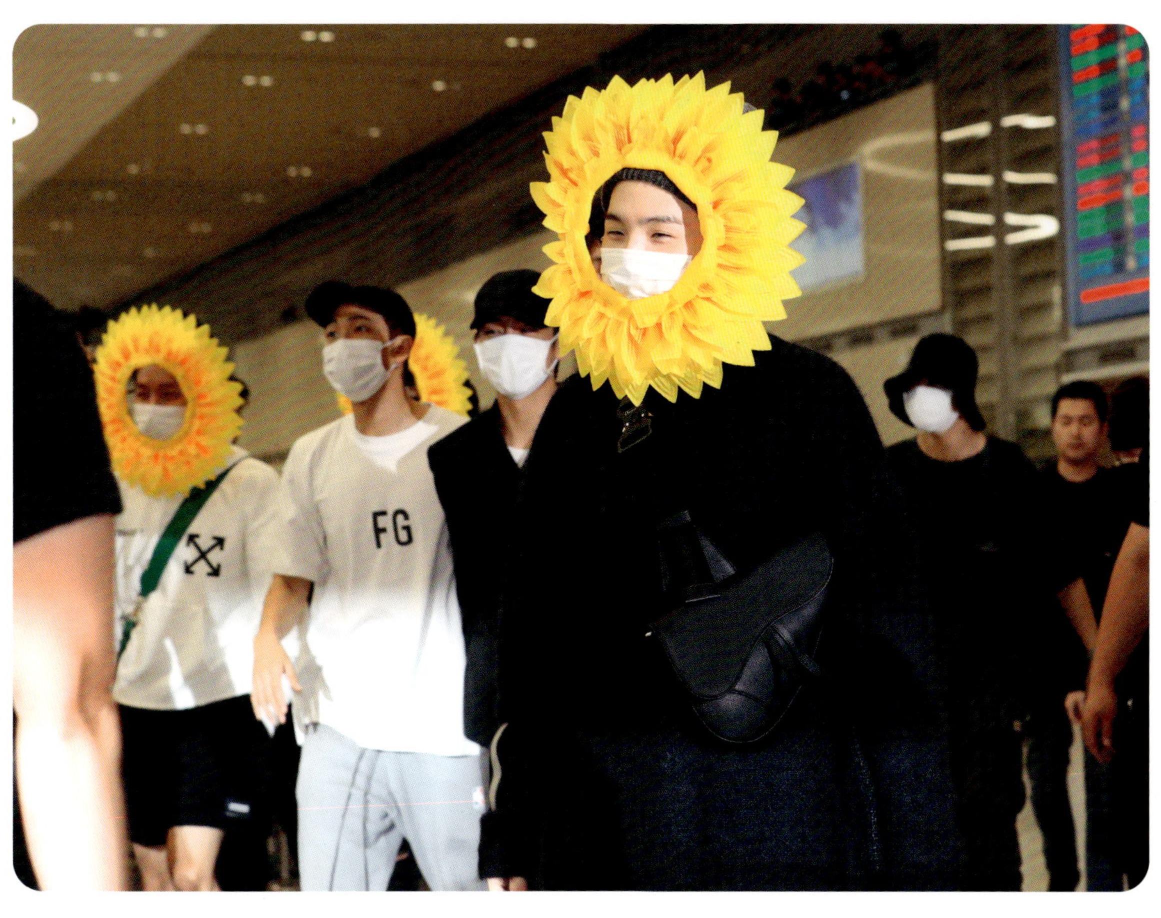

Flower power. BTS back from their European tour arrive at Incheon International Airport, 10 June 2019.

I Purple U

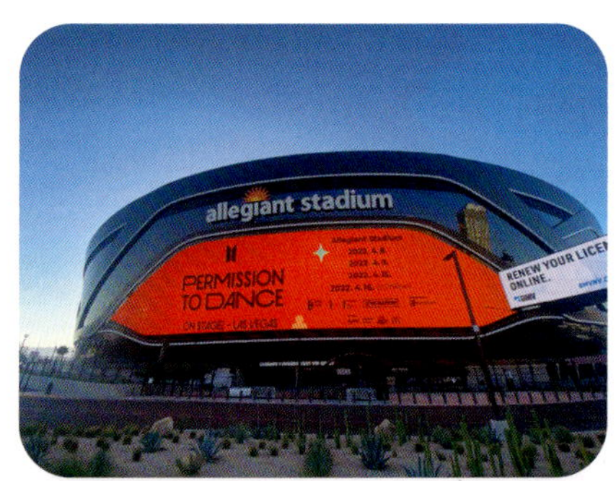

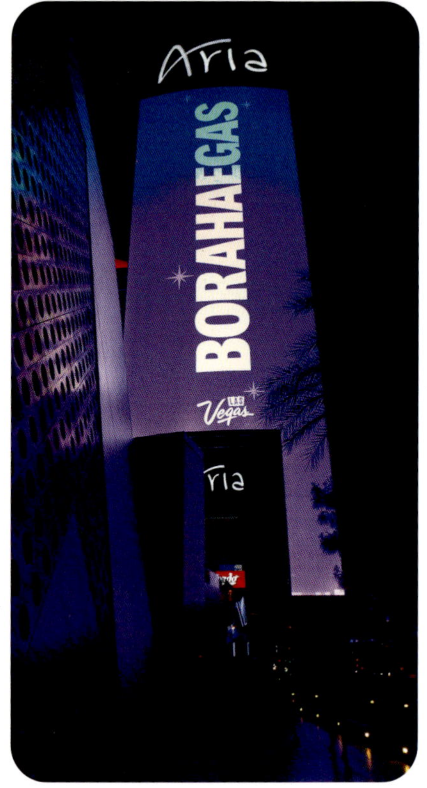

It seems a lifetime ago, but in April 2022 when BTS flew back to Incheon airport, from playing their four blockbuster 'Permission to Dance on Stage' Las Vegas concerts, life was still getting back to normal post-Covid. The American leg of the tour had virtual attendees as well as, much to ARMY's delight, a live crowd. Billboard reported that 'the in-person portion...was attended by around 200,000 people, while the number of online viewers who dialled in to the livestream reached around 402,000 in 182 countries/regions on the concluding day on Saturday'. Just in case anyone didn't know what was going on, while they were in residence, the band spotlit a message of love to their fans, shining 'BORAHAEGAS' – 'I Purple U' – onto buildings all over town. The concerts were a festival of fun and the boys enjoyed flirting with the crowd. Afterwards, exhausted but happy, they headed home to Seoul and, in classic BTS form, busted a stand-out selection of legendary airport styling. SUGA showed off a cult, rave-tastic Smiley T-shirt by Belgian designer Raf Simons and loose-fitting Wooyoungmi pants, topped with

THIS PAGE TOP: *Permission to Dance. The Allegiant Stadium, Las Vegas, 6 April 2022.*

THIS PAGE BOTTOM: *The Aria Resort & Casino declares its purple love to ARMY, 7 April 2022.*

OPPOSITE: *SUGA wearing a Raf Simons T-shirt.*

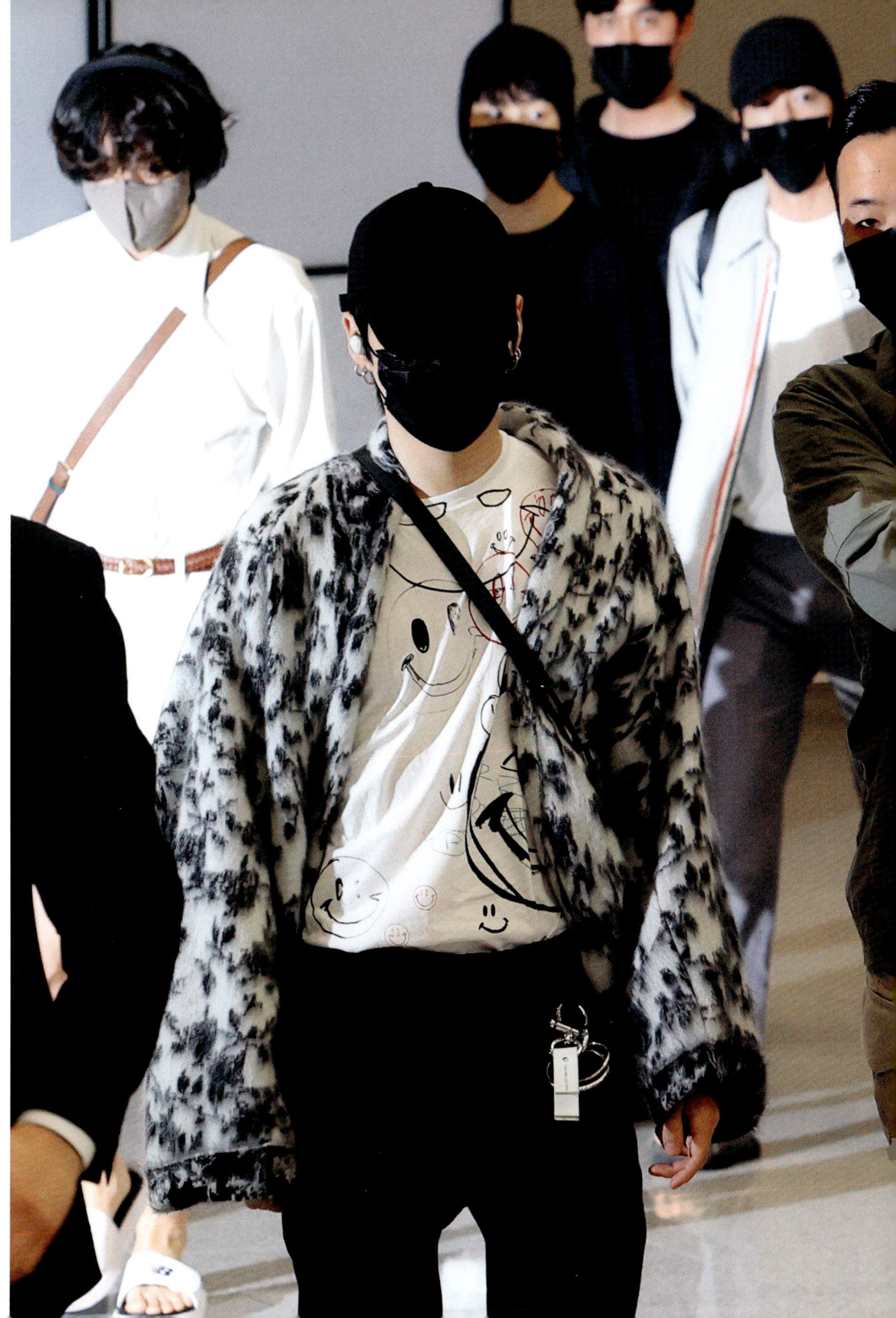

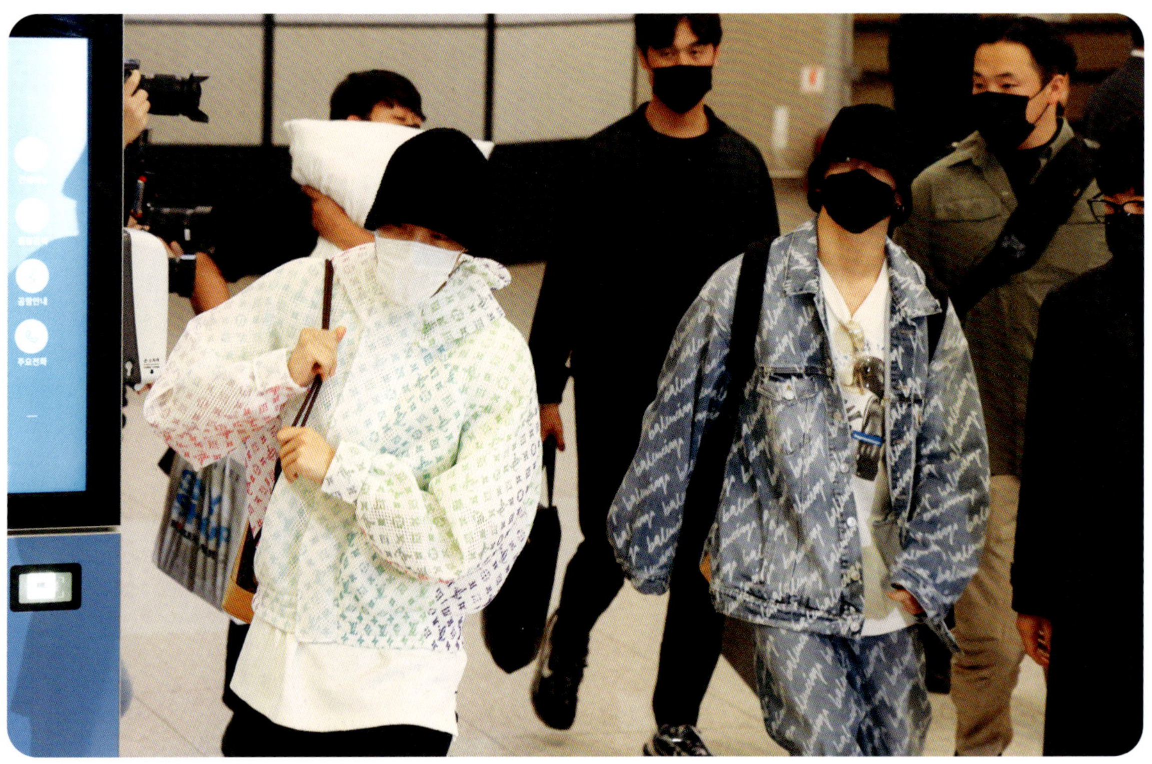

a deluxe Saint Laurent cardigan. Designer labels were out in full force, with j-hope's Louis V monogram blouson and shorts co-ordinating fiercely alongside an LV X Nigo brown Reverso Stripe Monogram Randonnee Messenger over his shoulder. Meanwhile Jung Kook sported double faded denim, a scribble-print jacket and high-rise baggy jeans from Balenciaga and a streetwear savvy T-shirt by Travis Scott X Fragment X Jordan. V sported preppy white shirting and tailored shorts by Polo Ralph Lauren, and Jin looked easily smart in Thom Browne slacks and oversized jacket. Despite not picking up a Grammy earlier that year, BTS had still managed to win big. Viva Las Vegas!

j-hope and Jung Kook on their way home after their Las Vegas gigs, Incheon International Airport, Seoul, 19 April 2022.

'We didn't come to Vegas
for the Grammys.
We came to focus
for the ARMYs!
The records, the titles,
accomplishments, the trophies,
they're really important, but that
wasn't the first thing, the first reason
why we started all these things.
These two hours of community,
energy, eye to eye, singing along,
dancing together,
this communication,
this is everything,
this is why we're doing this, right?
I hope you know it. I love you!
Let the haters hate, let the lovers love. '

**RM, 'Permission to Dance on Stage' concert,
Las Vegas, April 2022.**

Prada Group

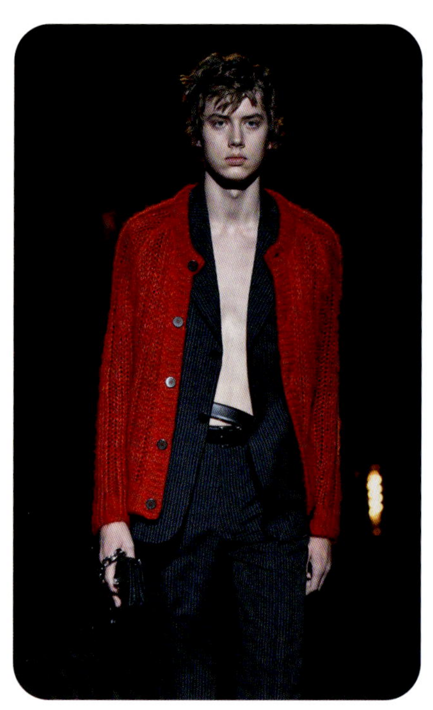

In August 2019, when BTS told the world they were taking a break, it was the start of a new calibration of the band, giving them space to develop their independent projects; they reunited after a month with fresh ideas. The boys attended the Melon Music Awards later that year in November at the Gocheok Sky Dome and presented an extended show featuring eleven songs, including 'Intro: Persona', and 'Dionysus' paired with individual choreographed elements, during which each band member shone equally bright. Jung Kook's water-dance accompanied 'Save Me' and wowed the crowd, while j-hope popped and breaked along to 'Fake Love' in co-ordination with a dazzling light spectacle. Alone they were impressive, and together they were invincible – winning four Daesangs that night, including Album of the Year with *Map of the Soul: Persona*, and Song of the Year for their track 'Boy With Luv'.

THIS PAGE: *Prada Menswear A/W 2019–20, Milan Fashion Week, 13 January 2019.*
OPPOSITE: *BTS parade the Prada at the Melon Music Awards at Gocheok Sky Dome in Seoul, 30 November 2019.*

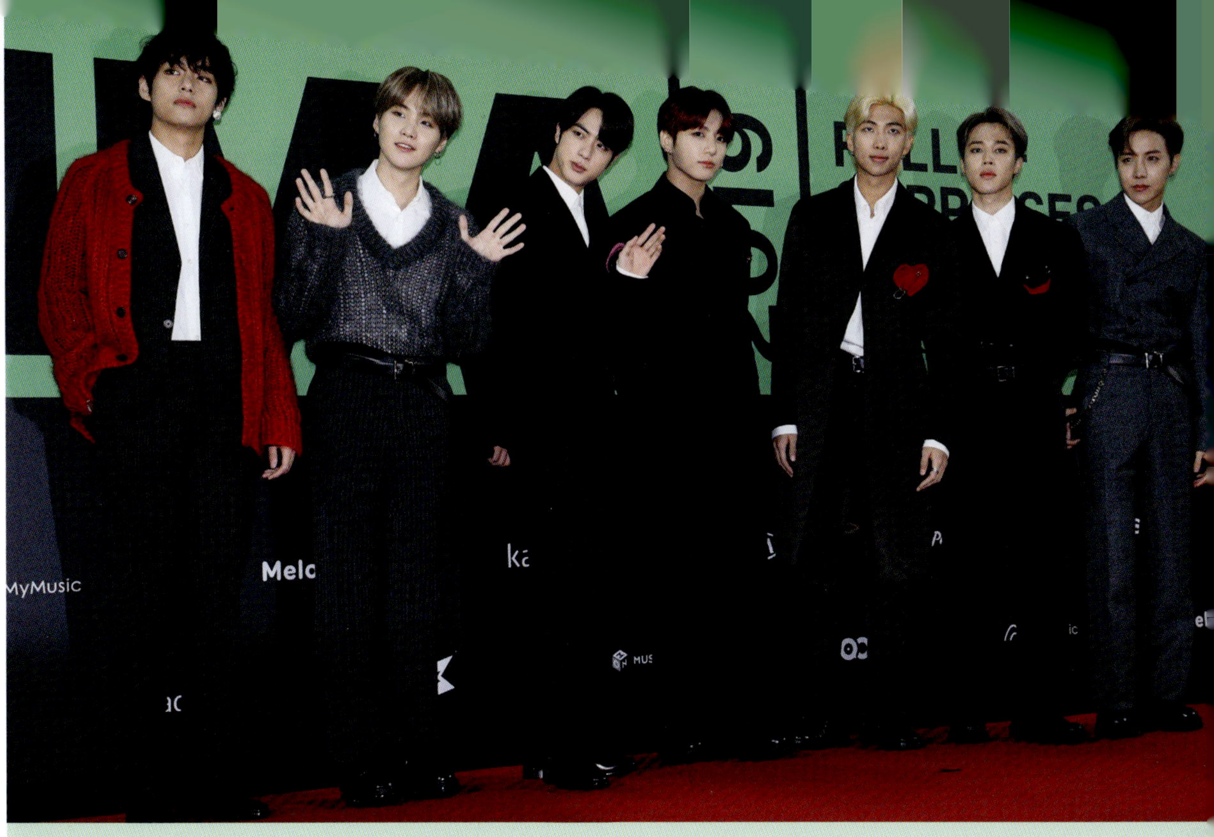

' We do make sure that one person doesn't
stand out. But then we are really unique.
We all have our style,
so I think we all stand out.
We each have our own roles and
positions in the band and then we
work together to make sure
we all try hard for the ARMY. '
— Jung Kook, *Ms Vogue*, 2018.

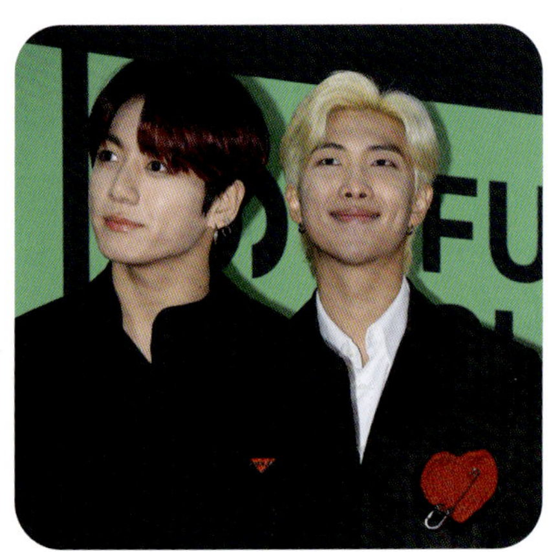

Fashion watchers acknowledged the band triumphed in the fashion stakes too. They arrived on the red carpet wearing pieces chosen from Miuccia Prada's A/W 2019/20 menswear runway. Jimin and RM strode out sporting suiting embellished with a hand-knitted heart, safety-pinned to their lapels, while V's pinstripe outfit's semiotics were deconstructed by styling it up with a red woollen cardigan. Prada's clothes are clever, sometimes funny, and always interesting. That season's collection was inspired by cult films, including *The Rocky Horror Picture Show* and the 1931 classic *Frankenstein* – both movies about alienation, which helped fuel Prada's reflective response to making clothes that fit in with an overwhelming world; existential themes and ideas that BTS have not been nervous to address in their music either. A year later, in November 2020, the world had changed again, and their seminal 'letter of hope' album, *BE*, was released – a reaction to the Covid pandemic; in pop-speak it told of the band's own solitude and sentiments about isolation, but proving, as the eponymous title of the first track says: 'Life Goes On'.

THIS PAGE: *Lapel luv. Jung Kook and RM.*
OPPOSITE LEFT: *V's comfy cardy.*
OPPOSITE RIGHT: *Jimin, Prada suited and booted.*

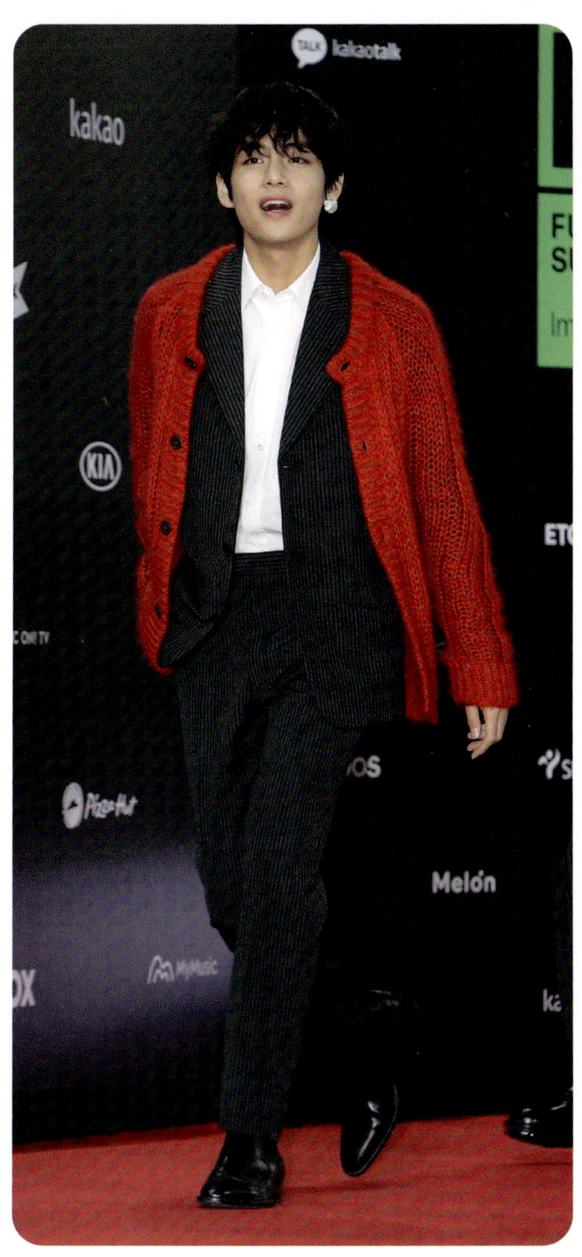

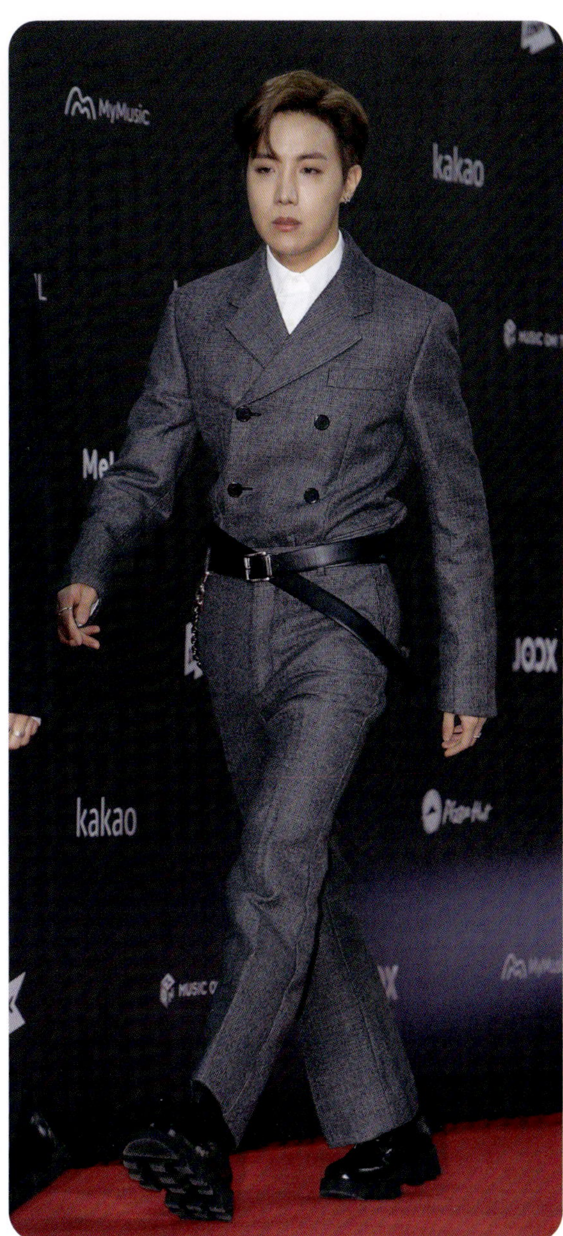

Dreaming Big

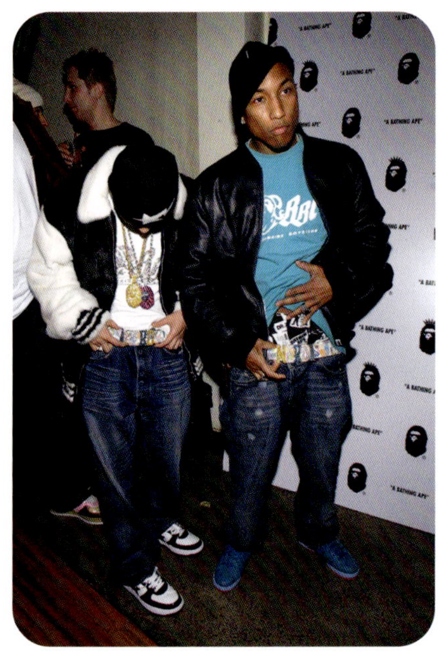

Wearing swag knee-high socks, Nike Air Jordans and Y-3 high-top trainers, BTS strode onto the stage to sing their debut single, 'No More Dream', taken from the *2 Cool 4 Skool* album. This was the Mnet 'M Count Down' at CJ ENM Studio Center in Seoul on 4 July 2013, and it seemed like the beginning of everything for the septet singers. At the very start of their careers, their streetwear hip-hop look was strong: beanies and snapbacks, and bling sportswear co-ordinated in classically fly black and gold colourways. Chains were big as per the trail blazed by fashion and music icons such as Pharrell Williams. BTS would go on to win the 2013 Melon Music Award 'Rookie of the Year' prize, although their track, released on Bang Si-hyuk's K-Pop label, Big Hit Entertainment, registered only a modest success on the then Gaon (now Circle) Digital Chart. In 2020, ARMYs revived the retro favourite and took it to #2 in Billboard's World Digital Song Sales charts, and in 2024 to #1 during the band's hiatus for military service. Fans adore looking back on baby BTS. They were fresh out of training and had lived together

THIS PAGE: *Fashion designer/DJ Nigo and Pharrell at the opening of Nigo's A Bathing Ape store, New York, 11 January 2005.*
OPPOSITE: *In chains. Early days BTS at the Incheon Korean Music Wave photocall, September 2013.*

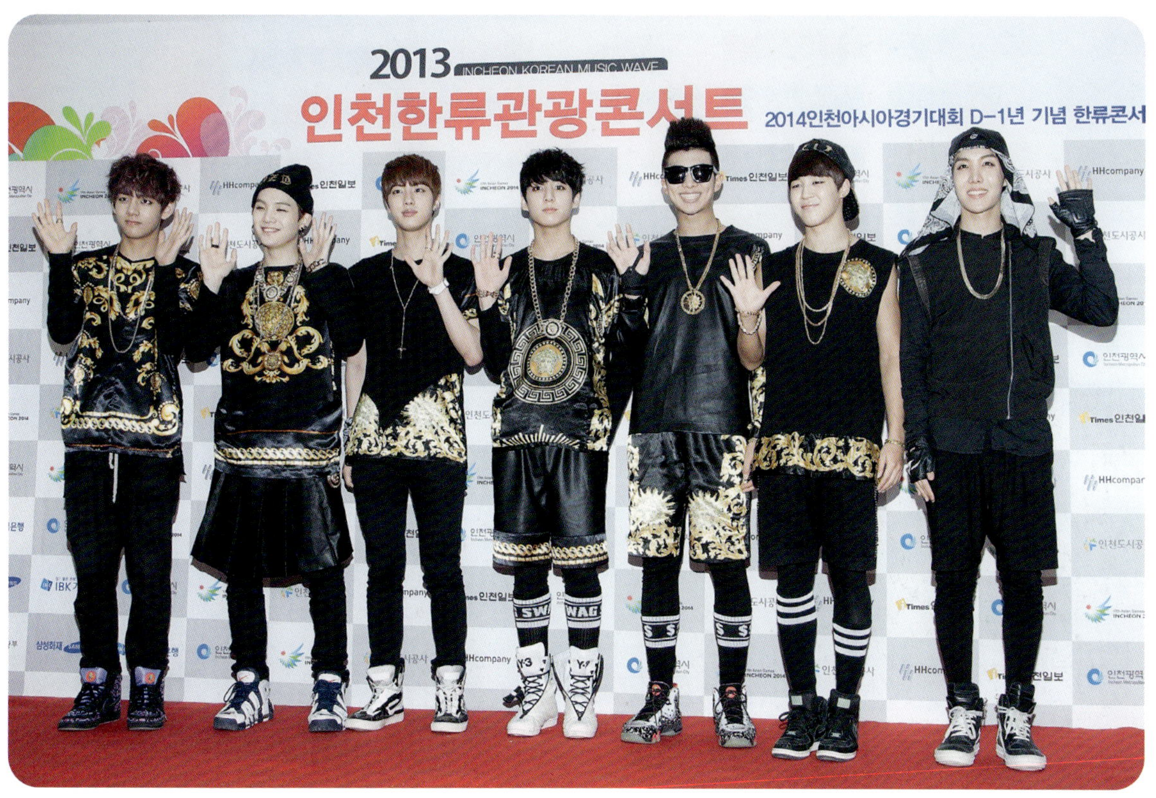

in a tiny dorm, working hard since the auditions in 2010/11 in search of a brand-new boyband. Their followers have always been the backbone of their success. In a 2019 time. com interview, Bang Si-hyuk admitted: 'BTS's success in the U.S. market was achieved by a formula different from the American mainstream formula. Loyalty built through direct contact with fans had a lot to do with that.' Their supporters are the most dedicated in the world and continue to champion BTS's career as their sound and vision evolve. They've since experimented with pop, R&B and EDM and collaborated with the highest profile designers, confirming that the magic that came together while preparing for stardom and hanging out at Hakdong Park and eating at Yujeong Restaurant was real.

School's Out

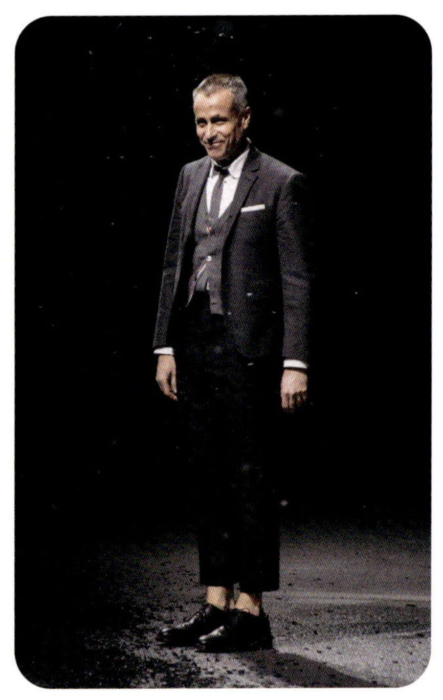

In February 2014, to showcase their second mini album, the 9-track *Skool Luv Affair*, BTS visited the Lotte Card Art Center in Seoul. They used the event as a platform not just to present their new music but also to play around with some fresh looks. Arriving in rock 'n' roll biker jackets, ripped jeans and denim, their appearance fine-tuned the previous year's hip hop 'fits. Still nodding to the streets, this time their wardrobe was more grunge and less showy.

That was until they took to the stage in their concept image of teenage college-kids wearing a school uniform of suiting. It was the kind of silhouette U.S. designer Thom Browne has made his own since he debuted a small collection of five suits way back in 2001 in Manhattan. It was also perfectly reflective of the much-anticipated BTS album material all about the trials of adolescent love, curiosity and yearning.

THIS PAGE: *Thom Browne's school days. The designer shows how to wear his schoolboy designer suiting at his Menswear A/W 2015–16 show, Paris Fashion Week, 25 January 2015.*
OPPOSITE: *Skool of Rock. BTS showcase at Lotte Card Art Center, Seoul, 11 February 2014.*
OVERLEAF: *Biker grunge. Arriving at the Lotte Card Art Center before they smartened up for their performance.*

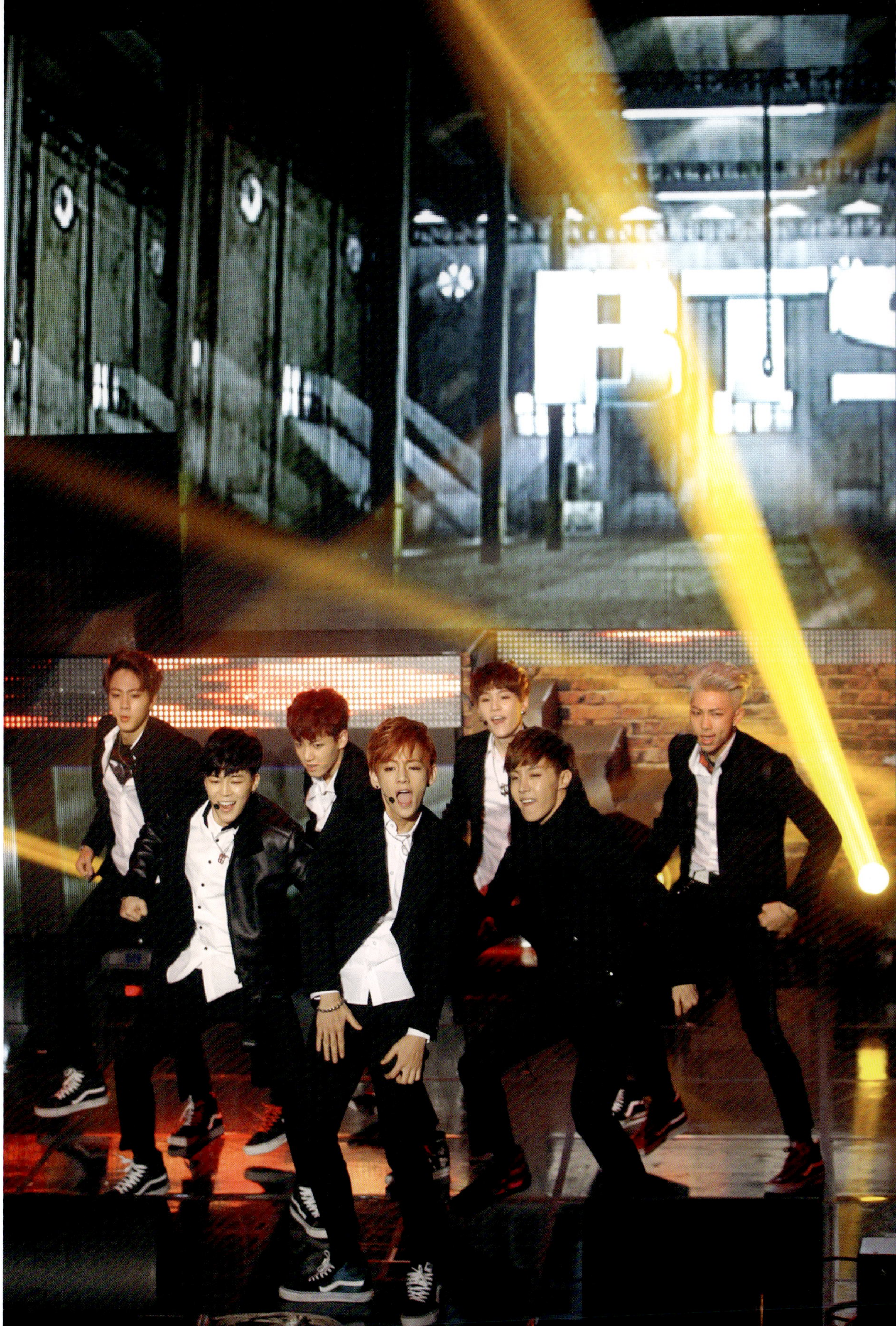

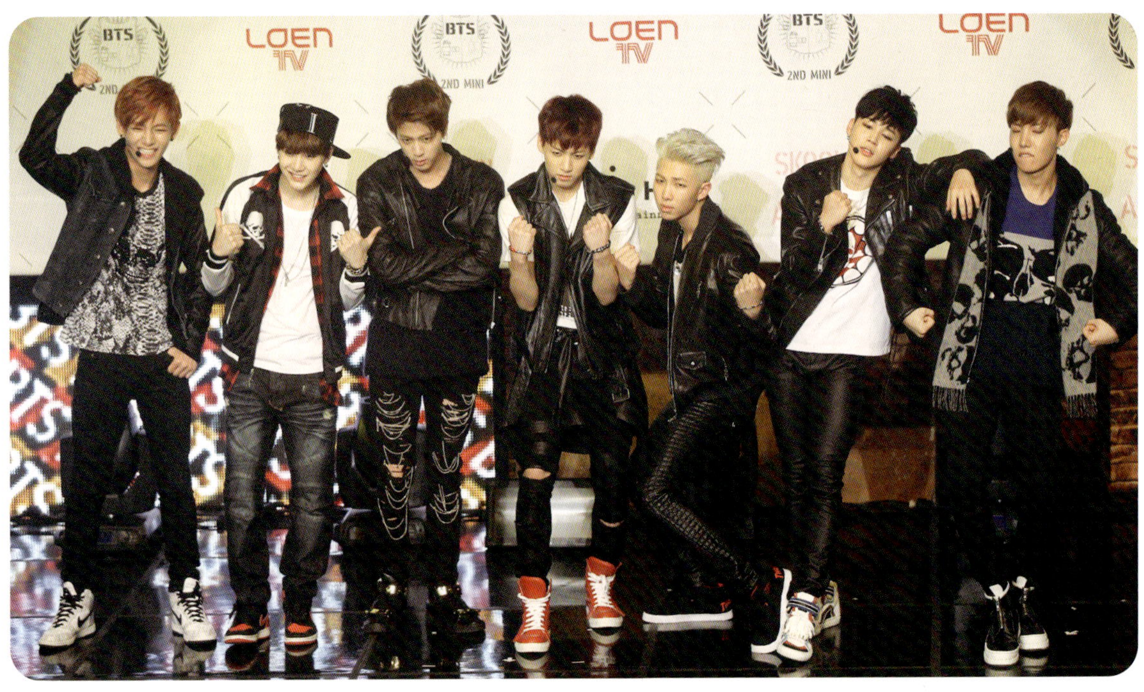

They were warming up for their first official BTS fan club muster that would take place just over a month later, when they wore the monochrome suits once more, thrilling the 3,000 supporters who had turned out for the song-and-games event. It was a special experience, where ARMYs got to know their idols just a little bit better. The boys not only performed favourite tracks like 'We Are Bulletproof Pt.2' and 'If I Ruled the World', but also games like Real Man – won by Jung Kook – and a classic dance battle, which was won by j-hope for shaking to ex-Wonder Girls, Sunmi's, '24 Hours'.

‘ Through our album,
we wanted to talk about
teenage peers and school.
We talk about dreams,
happiness, and love.
I think these three are the biggest
interests of teenagers. ’

RM, *etoday.co.kr***, 11 February 2014.**

Suits You, Sirs

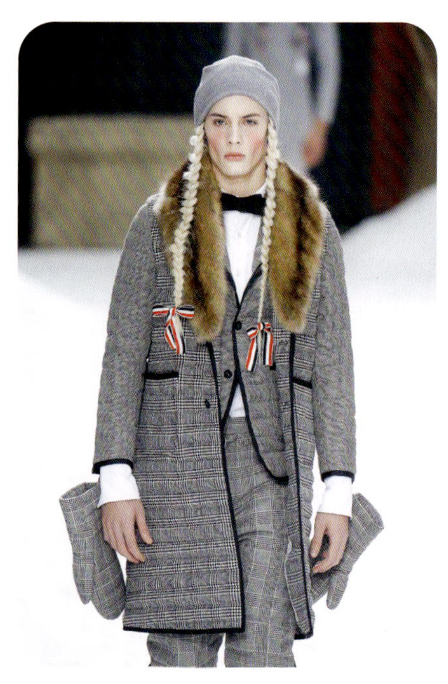

Way back in 2017, BTS were one of many K-Pop bands at the SBS K-Pop festival who worked the '#1' blockbuster theme, mixing up favourite hits from the early 2000s in tribute as well as playing their own winning songs from that year. BTS sang their now classics 'MIC Drop', 'DNA' and 'Not Today' – tracks that could almost be covered today as beloved retro sounds. The evening was all about remembering super-fun blasts from the past and BTS rose to the challenge by winning the award for the 'most wanted Christmas song'. During an interview with the singer IU, Jin, V and Jung Kook performed a few bars of 1980s British pop supremos Wham's iconic 'Last Christmas', much to the delight of the audience. It was an ultra-cute evening, and the band wore equally charming suits by the American designer Thom Browne. Bow ties and crisp shirting, blazers edged with red, white and blue trim, preppy striped polo shirts and mix-and-match college jackets were all on display, effortlessly

THIS PAGE: *Thom Browne Menswear A/W 2018-19 show, Paris Fashion Week, 20 January 2018.*
OPPOSITE: *Bow ties and blazers. K-Pop festival hosted by SBS in Seoul, 25 December 2017.*

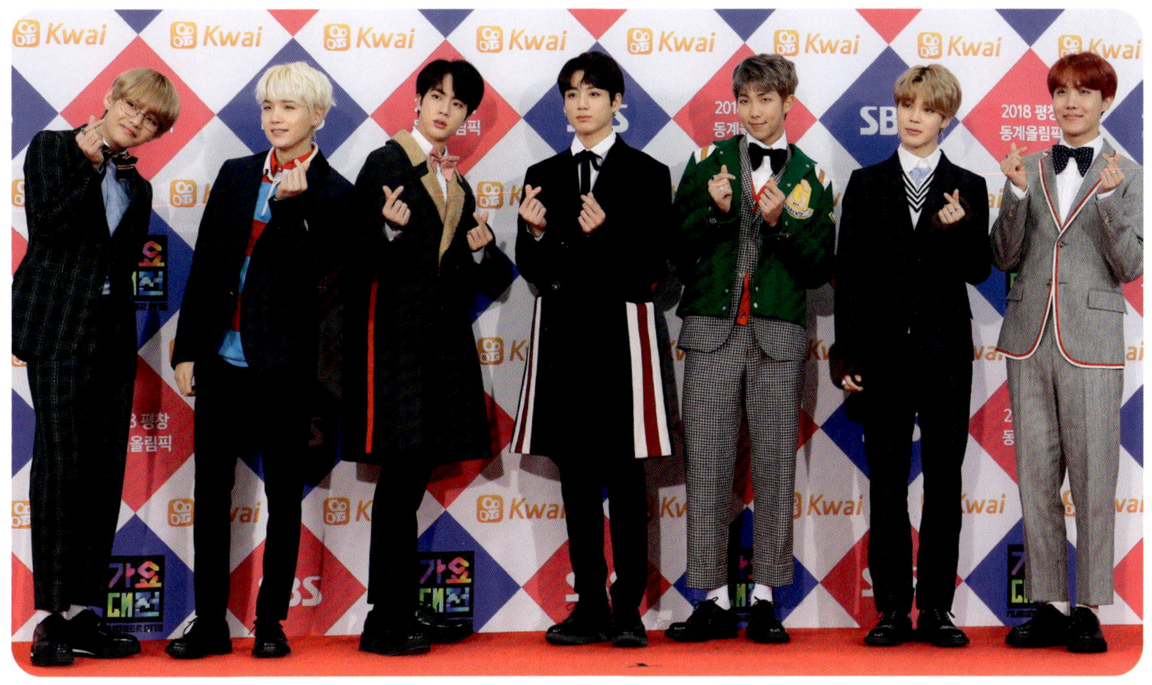

showcasing Browne's Ivy League Americana vibe. Browne is known for slick cartoonish collections and his signature shrunken suiting has become a fashion-forward silhouette that perfectly complements BTS and their hip personae. Over the years, Jin has especially gravitated towards the brand. In his noteworthy 2022 video for his debut solo music 'The Astronaut', co-written by Coldplay, he chose a Thom Browne windowpane-check two-piece.

Sweet St Laurent

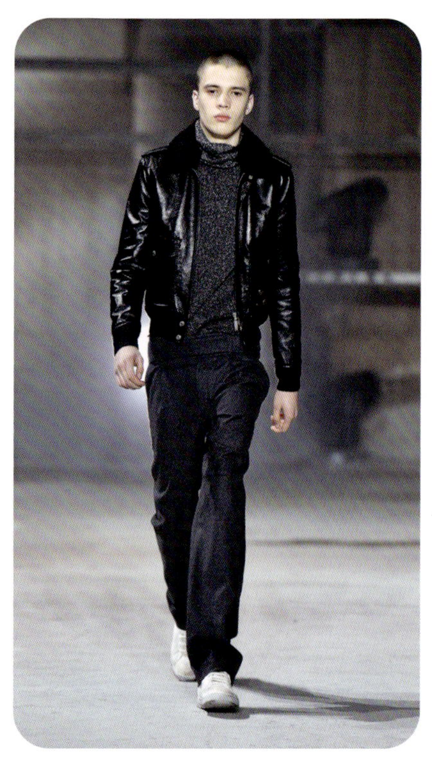

When Anthony Vaccarello joined Saint Laurent in 2016, BTS were already firm fans of the brand as previously helmed by Hedi Slimane, the French designer and photographer famed for his rock 'n' roll silhouettes. Under Vaccarello, the Parisian brand sustained Slimane's fluid approach to menswear and continued to cultivate an androgynous attitude that felt in tune with contemporary fashion's evolving zeitgeist.

In 2017, the band arrived wearing Vaccarello Saint Laurent to the AMAs (changing to Gucci for the performance) and since then they have consistently supported the house by sporting pieces at high-profile events. In December 2019, BTS accepted their Group of the Year Award at the Variety Hitmakers Brunch all dressed in Vaccarello's Summer 2020 Saint Laurent. The collection, which had been shown in Malibu, in many ways embodied the freedom of Yves's 1960s womenswear bohemian silhouettes; Vaccarello told WWD.com: 'When I design for a woman, I think about a

THIS PAGE: *Saint Laurent by Vaccarello A/W 2017–18, Paris Fashion Week, 28 February 2017.*
OPPOSITE: *Looking sweet at the American Music Awards, Microsoft Theater, LA, 19 November 2017.*

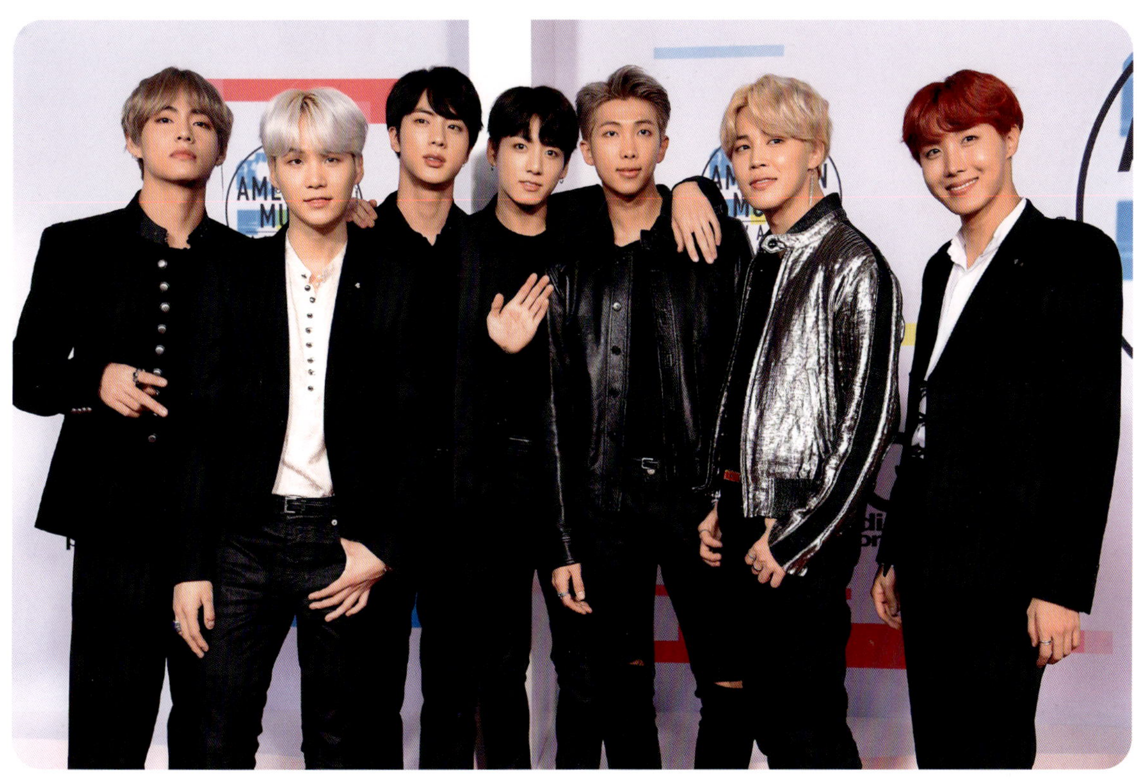

man and when I design for a man, I think about a woman's wardrobe.'

The line of BTS's outfits that night spoke of embellished luxe suiting and was more form-fitting than some of the more voluminous pieces shown on that season's Saint Laurent runway. However, it was the boys' impeccable make-up that really elevated their sartorial statement. Their brand of soft masculinity was new for some, as on entering West Hollywood's Soho House for the private brunch, a bystander was heard remarking on the boys' use of cosmetics. Jin made a joke about this on Twitter (now X) the next day, posting: 'I felt like putting on make-up was a waste, so I took a picture.'

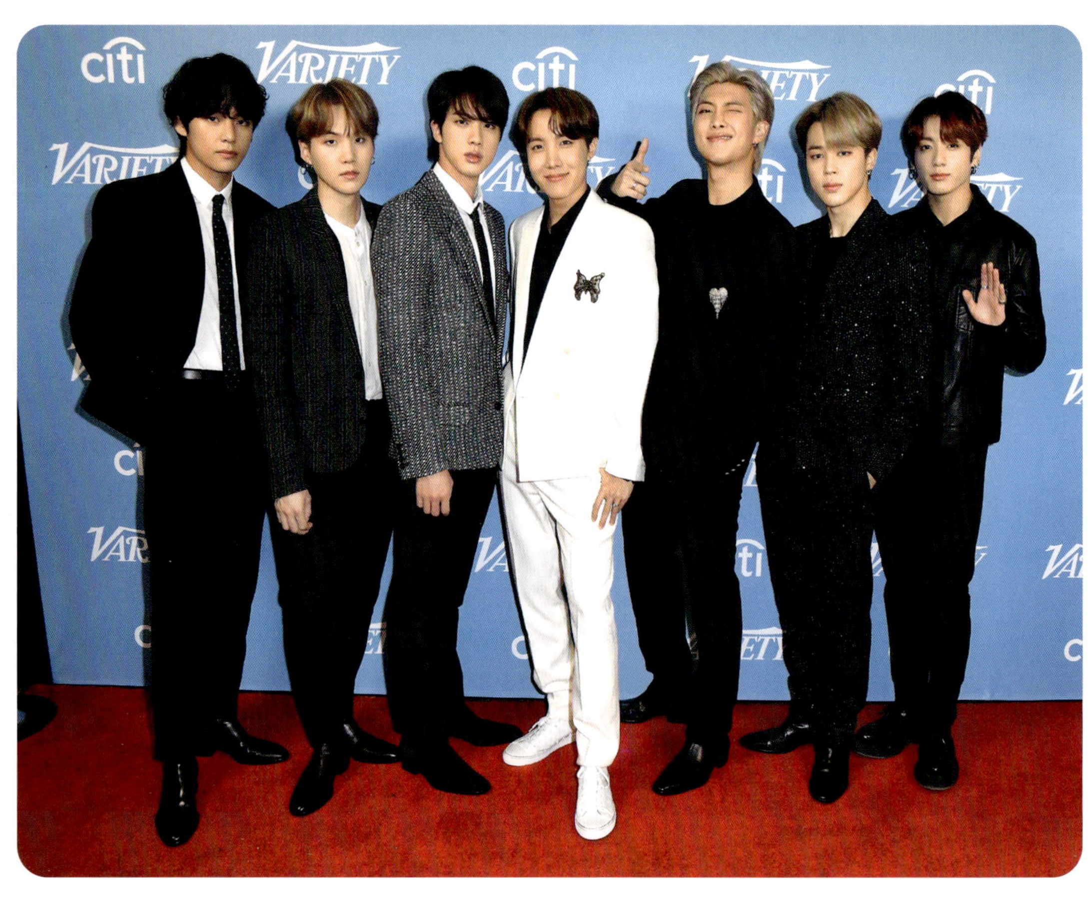

V, SUGA, Jin, j-hope, RM, Jimin, and Jung Kook at the Variety Hitmakers Brunch at Soho House, Hollywood, 7 December 2019.

'2019 was truly a very surprising and exciting year for us, and this event has made it even more so. And even though we are here to accept this award from very far away, none of this would have been possible without the efforts of Mr Bang, all the producers and staff from our label. And we have to say thank you to all the ARMYs around the world for their greatest love and support. '

**RM, accepting Group of the Year Award
at the Variety Hitmakers Brunch, December 2019.**

Kkonminam Man

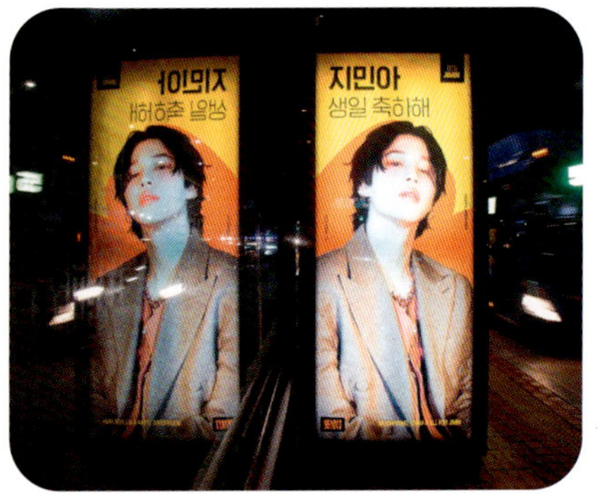

In many countries today it's seen as no big deal for men to wear foundation, lip gloss, or nail varnish, and the male beauty industry is booming. Statista reported in January 2024 that: 'by 2028, the global male grooming market is estimated to be worth about 115 billion U.S. dollars, up from nearly 80 billion U.S. dollars as of 2022'. Androgyny is also embedded in the fashion industry: designers including Rick Owens and Jean Paul Gaultier have pioneered men in skirts for decades and it's not unusual for high-profile celebrities such as Billy Porter, Brad Pitt and Harry Styles, to step out in non-binary outfits and openly enjoy a fluid approach to red-carpet dressing and self-care.

In South Korea, there has been an appreciation of *kkonminam* since the end of the 1990s, when actors and musicians moved away from the concept of the macho male ideal and, instead, adopted a more feminised identity. BTS's soft masculinity is part of this stylish trajectory and the band's

THIS PAGE: *A bus stop in Seoul decorated to celebrate Jimin's 28th birthday on Friday 13 October 2023.*
OPPOSITE: *RM, Jimin and j-hope at the Gaon Chart K-Pop Awards, Jamsil Arena, Seoul, 22 February 2017.*

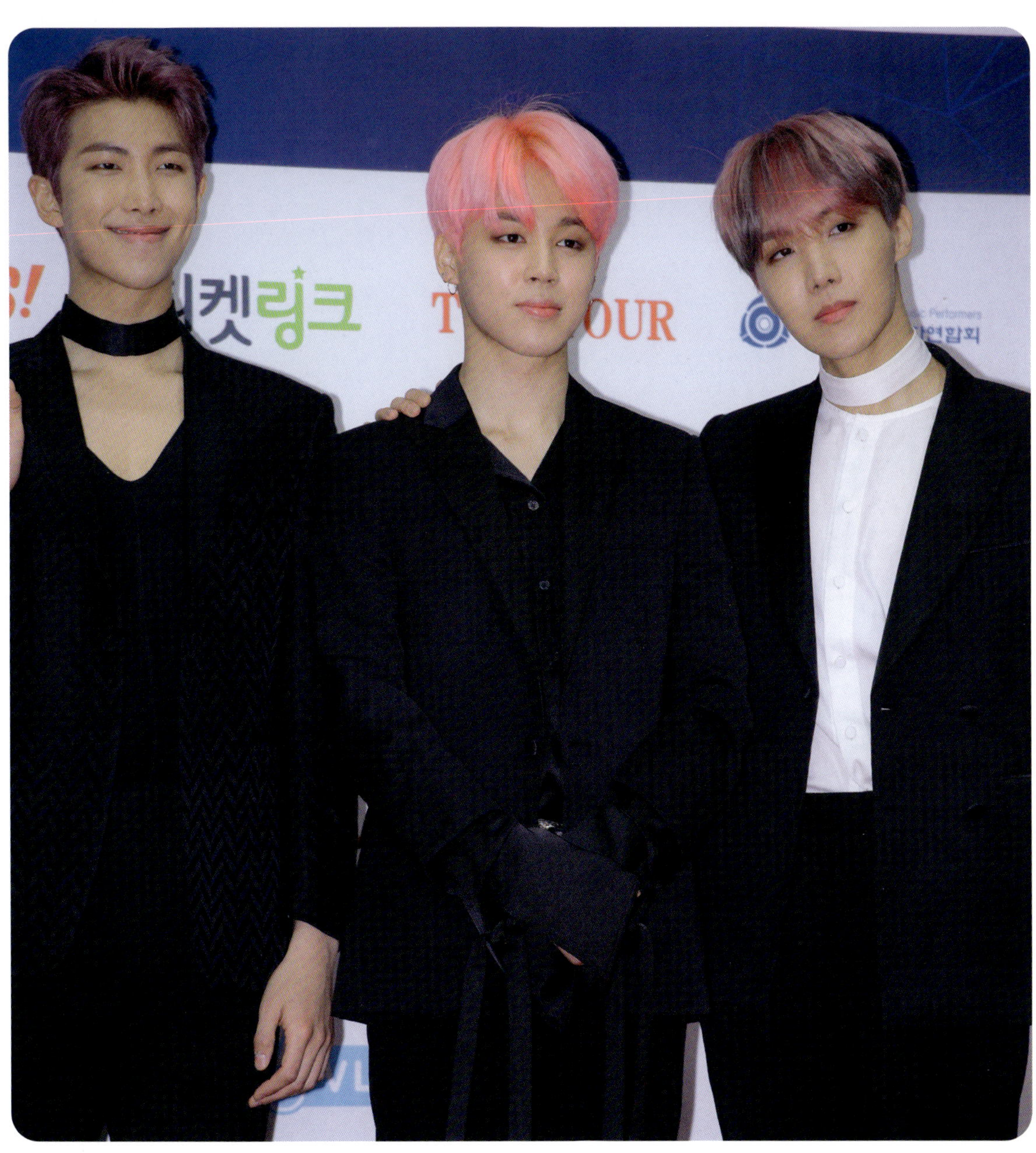

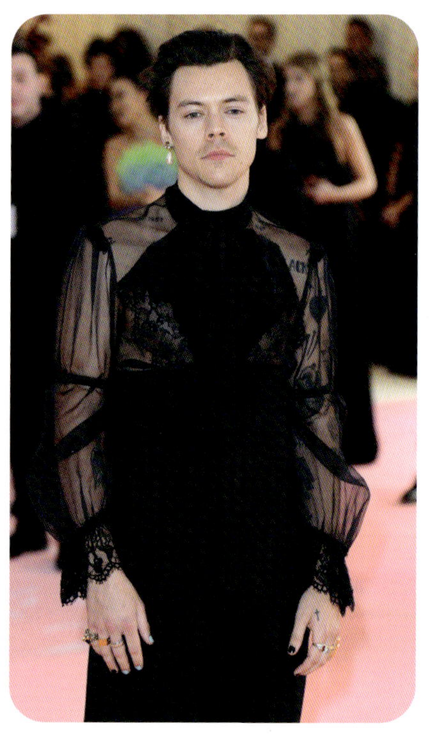

success has been built not just on their hard work to become skilled dancers and vocalists, but also on their dedication to perfecting a flawless idol aesthetic.

The South Korean beauty industry – 'kbeauty' – has not only been riding high on the *kkonminam* concept, but also surfing the so–called Korean Wave, or *Hallyu* (a surge of global interest in South Korean culture). In turn, this has helped familiarise Western audiences with BTS's professional approach to taking pride in their hair and to their make–up prowess.

BTS's confident identity and their grooming routines, however frivolous to some, have undoubtedly helped to break down toxic barriers. Fashions change and while men in make–up is nothing new – think rock 'n' roll heroes such as Little Richard and punk legends the New York Dolls, who took their cues from subcultural codes – BTS have helped normalise everyday male beauty for the mainstream. And not just in South Korea; their achievements have crossed cultures and helped establish powerful new ways of being a man.

THIS PAGE: *Frills thrills. Harry Styles arrives for the 2019 Met Gala*
OPPOSITE: *The picture of* kkonminam. *Jung Kook promotes the* Love Yourself *mini album, 18 September 2017.*

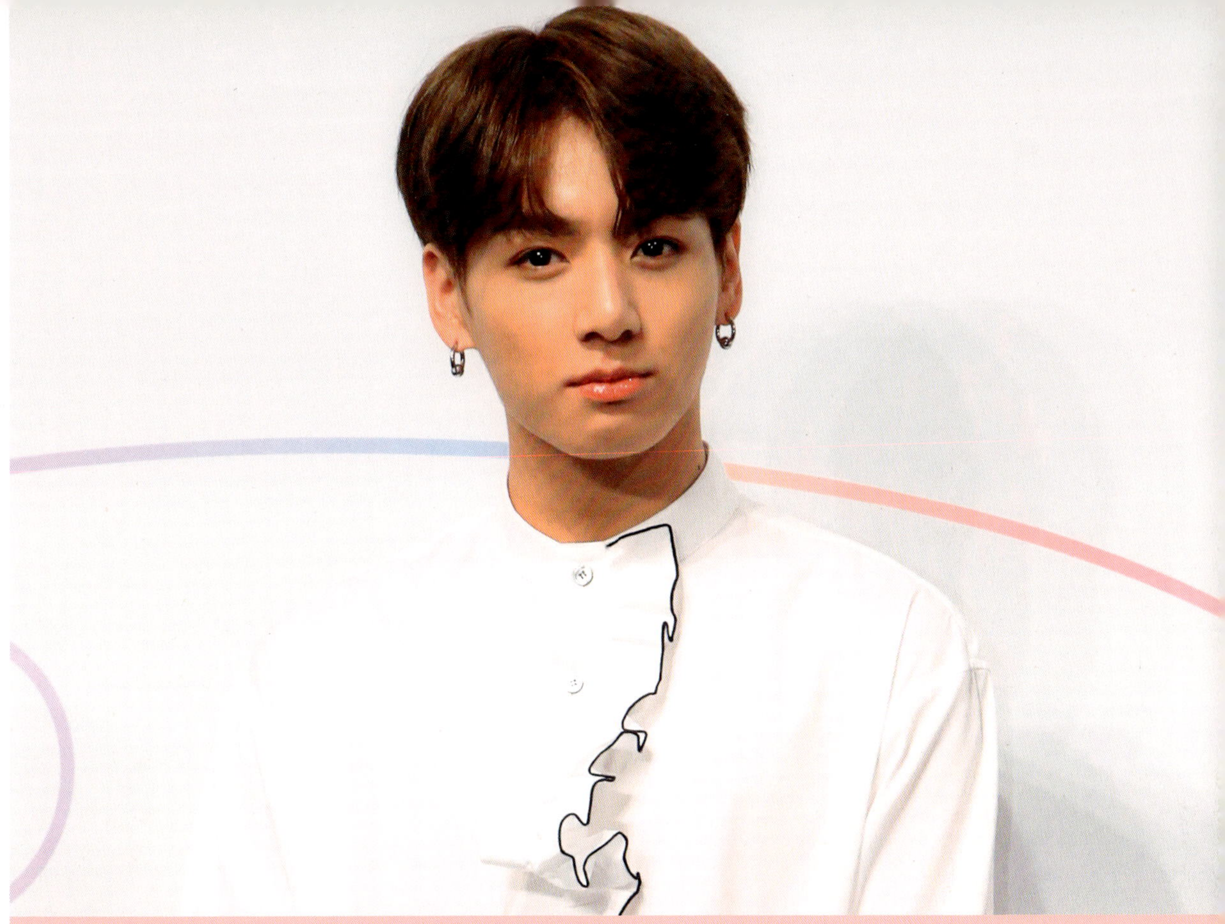

' Great style is...
wearing anything you like,
regardless of gender. '
— Jung Kook, Vanity Fair, September 2019.

Kutie Beauties

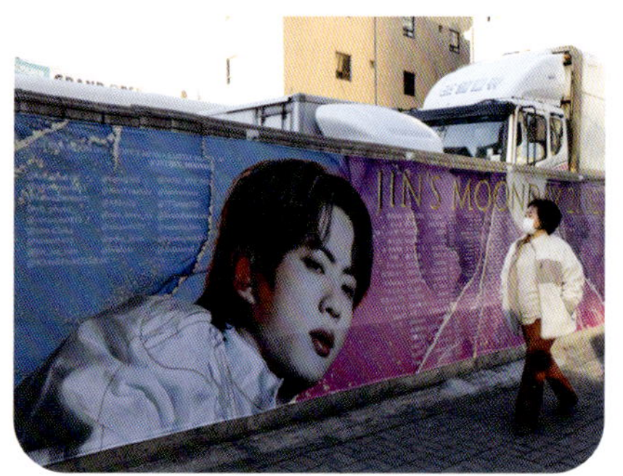

BTS are at the vanguard of the male beauty movement and throughout their careers have helped question established gender dictates through their unproblematic experimentation with make-up. They take their skincare as seriously as their clothes and music and after debuting a colour-correcting collagen pact in collaboration with Korean beauty brand VT in October 2017, they went on to create a fully fledged line under the BT21 merchandising umbrella the following year, selling lip gloss in syrup red and awesome pink alongside tinted CC creams and luminisers. Packaging is typically hyper-cute and decorated with the cartoon characters Tata, Mang, Chimmy, RJ, Koya, Cooky and Shooky, who the boys had created. Mang is a dancing purple chipmunk, who wears a horse mask; Shooky is a playful chocolate-chip cookie afraid of milk and mischievous: all the creatures are loveable and appear in an

THIS PAGE: *All made-up. Mural near the Hybe Co. headquarters in Seoul promoting Jin's Moonday project, 2023.*
OPPOSITE: *Picture perfect. Jimin at the 26th High1 Seoul Music Awards, Jamsil Arena, Seoul, 19 January 2017.*

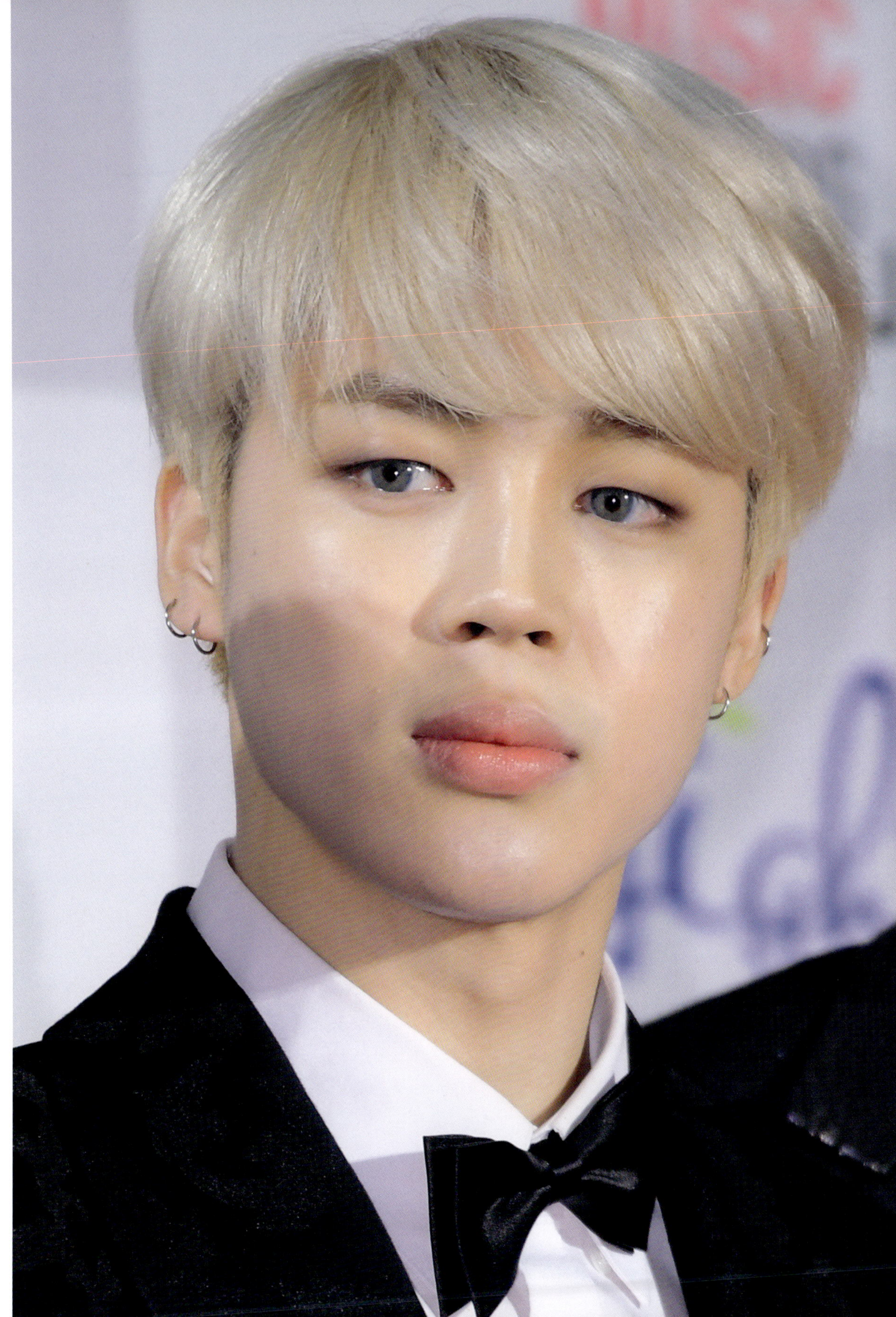

animated web-series called *BT21 Universe* as well as on a wide range of BTS merchandise. The gang wouldn't be the same without its vital eighth member, Van, a 'giant space robot' and BTS's guardian, designed to represent ARMY.

BT21 cosmetic products epitomised the world, not just of BTS, but also the K-Beauty industry which has disrupted skincare and beauty business worldwide with its USP of innovative formulations and accessibility. Subsequent BT21 beauty collaborations include with The Crème Shop (which introduced a whole shop front of new products, such as sheet masks, sanitising sprays, and gel-nail strips), the cruelty-free LA company ColourPop, South Korean natural brand Innisfree, and a hugely popular limited edition LANEIGE Amorepacific lip sleeping mask that came in a set of three named after the band's hit tracks, 'Butter', 'Permission to Dance' and 'Dynamite'.

Perfect foundation and lip gloss, even in the heat of the stage lights. Jung Kook performs for the Good Morning America *Summer Concert Series at the Rumsey Playfield/Summer Stage in Central Park, NYC, 14 July 2023.*

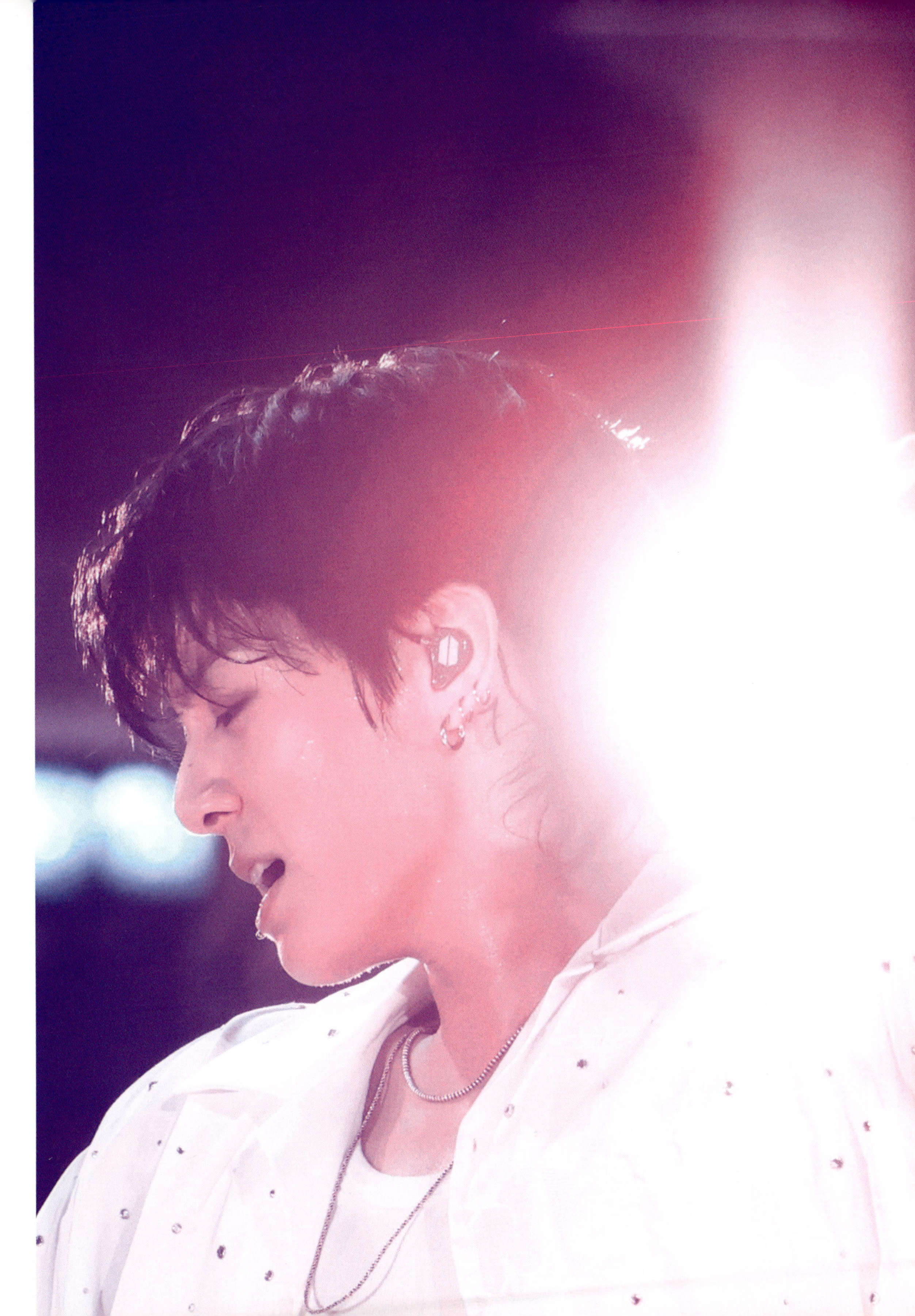

Hair Care

Every ARMY has a favourite BTS hair colour moment, whether it's Jimin looking prettier than ever in pink, memorably shown off on 19 June @bts.bighitofficial when he had his family portrait taken for the BTS 2019 FESTA opening ceremony, or in 2021 when j-hope chopped his hair into a pixie crop and turned it platinum white and Twitter (now X) went into a flurry of excitement and christened him Jack Frost. A pivotal moment in the chronology of BTS's hair evolution came in 2018 when remarkably the whole band simultaneously revealed black locks for the launch of their *Love Yourself: Tear* album, which came in co-ordinating dark packaging. The musical theme was similarly momentous, as RM explained the thought process behind the album title in a 2018 koreaboo.com interview, saying: 'Basically love is complex. There's sort of some sides that make us really feel bad or depressed. There could be tears, there could be sadness. So, this time we wanted to focus on some of the parts of love that we want to run away from. So, the name is Tear.'

In the pink. V with strawberry blonde locks at the SBS Gayo Daejeon Battle of the Bands, Gocheok Sky Dome, Seoul, 25 December 2018.

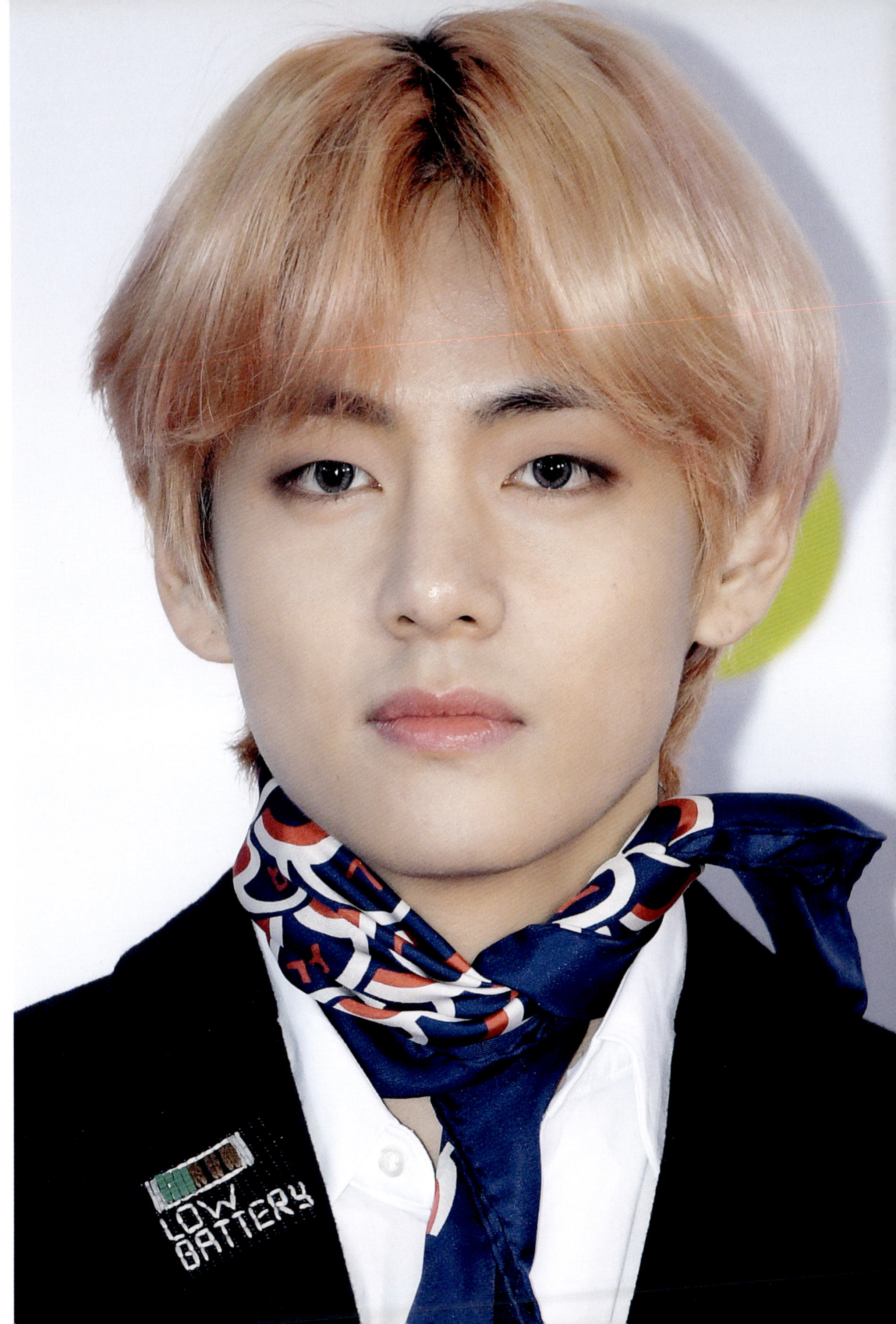

LOW
BATTERY

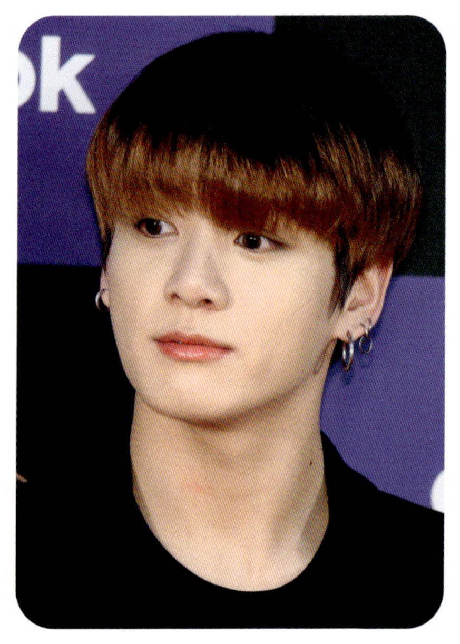

Similarly, in 2020, BTS released their concept album, *BE*, and their hair went dark again to coincide with the Covid pandemic and the mood of many who felt lost and dispirited. Hair is very much part of the language of BTS – a fresh shade tells their stories or can announce a comeback or launch.

Even on hiatus, catching sight of a freshly dyed BTS mane is cause to send ARMY into speculation. A month before the group's 10-year anniversary, in May 2023, V posted a picture of a new blonde hairstyle and 1.6 million fans saw it. That might have been reason enough for the dye-change, but there was more and later that year to much anticipation, V's debut studio album *Layover* dropped. In December 2023 Jin, Jimin, j-hope, Jung Kook, RM, and V showed off their military buzz-cuts while SUGA, who's serving in the public sector, displayed a shorter style. Looking to 2025, fans can only hope for more hair-flair excitement to welcome the group's biggest come-back. We will all be watching.

THIS PAGE: *Jung Kook, sporting an auburn Beatle mop arrives at the photocall for the 34th Golden Disc Awards in Seoul, 5 January 2020.*
OPPOSITE CLOCKWISE FROM TOP LEFT: *V, Jin, j-hope and SUGA keep ARMYs on tenterhooks with their ever-changing hairstyles.*

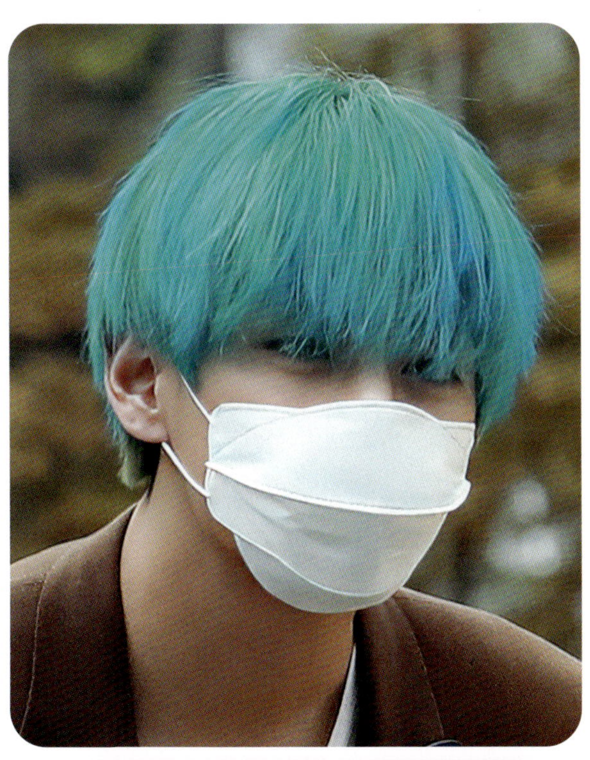
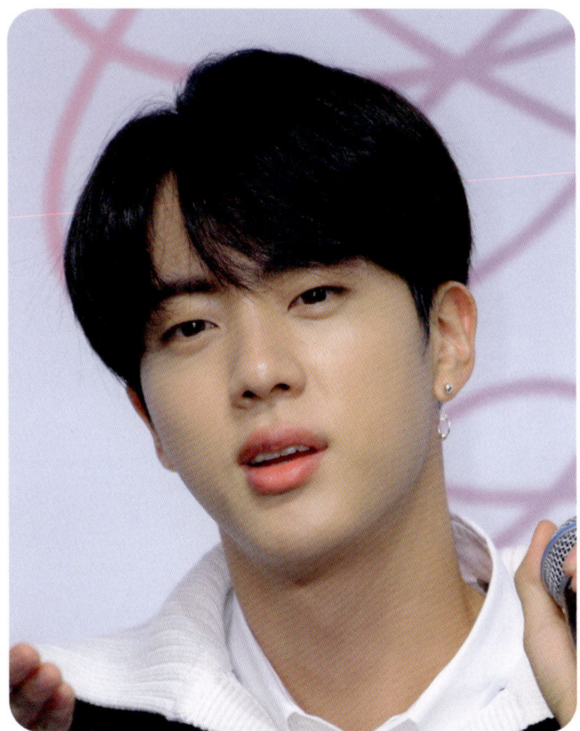
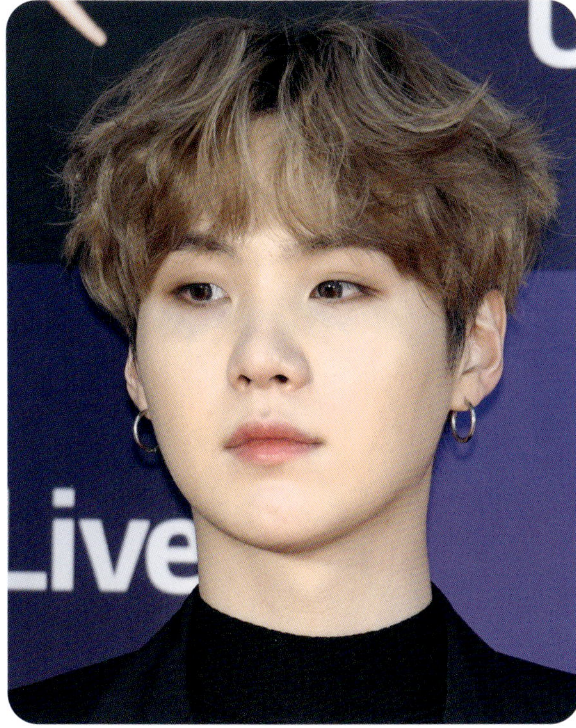
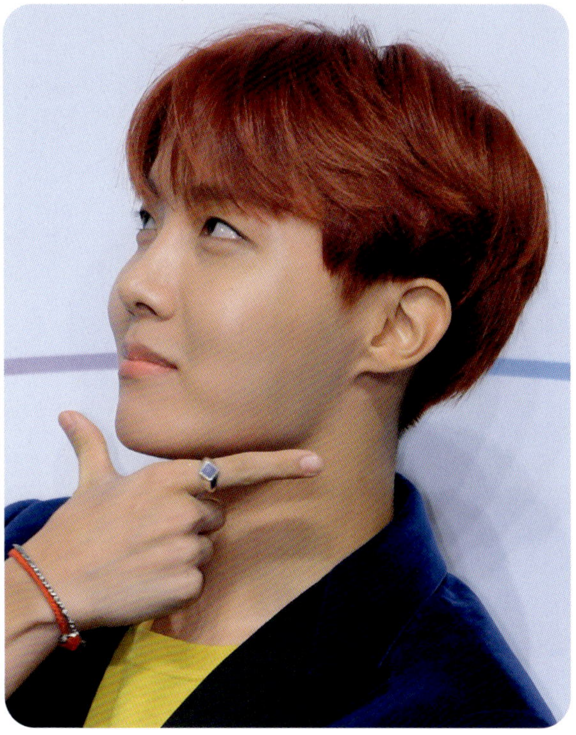

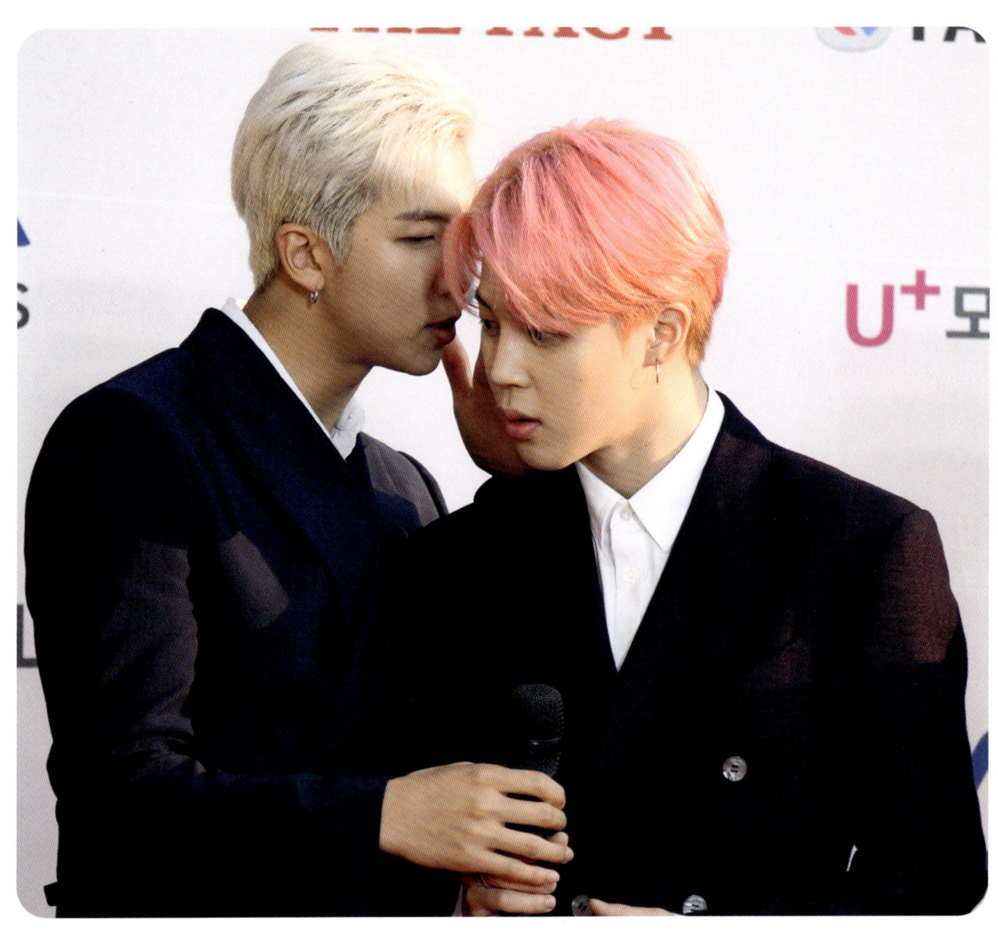

RM and Jimin, with striking platinum and pink hair, at the Fact Music
Awards held at Namdong Gymnasium, Incheon, 24 April 2019.

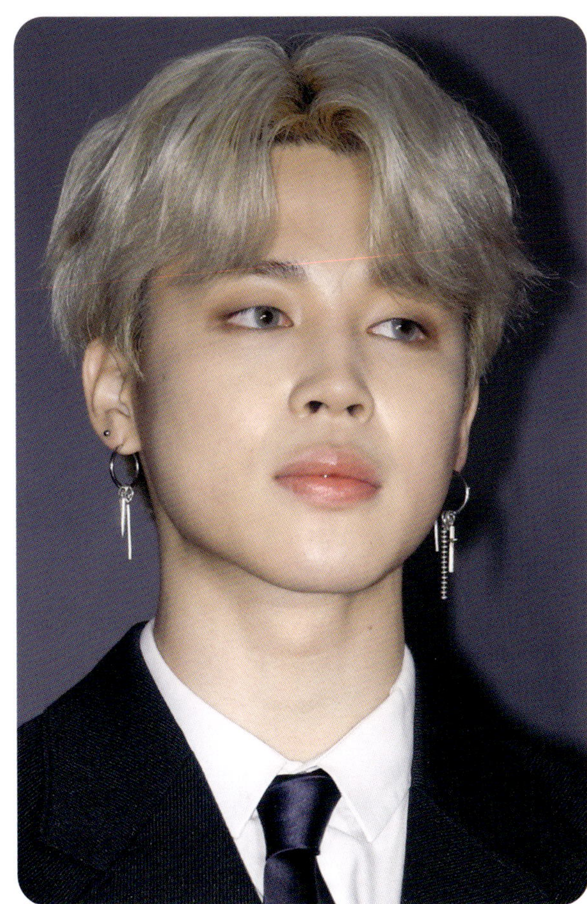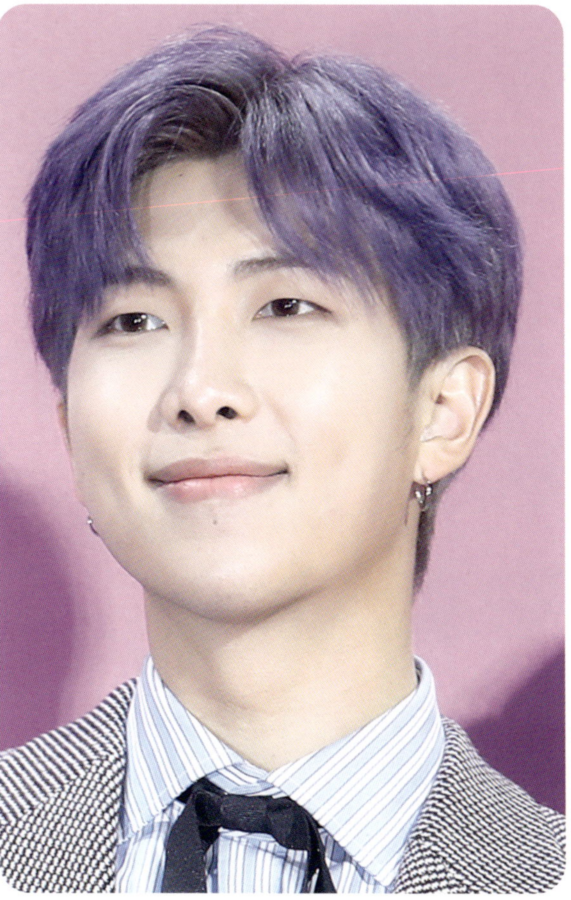

LEFT: *Jimin goes blonde for the MBC Plus X Genie Music Awards (MGA) at Namdong Gymnasium, Incheon, 6 November 2018.*
RIGHT: *i purple you. RM at the Melon Music Awards at Gocheok Sky Dome, Seoul, 1 December 2018.*

Showing Up

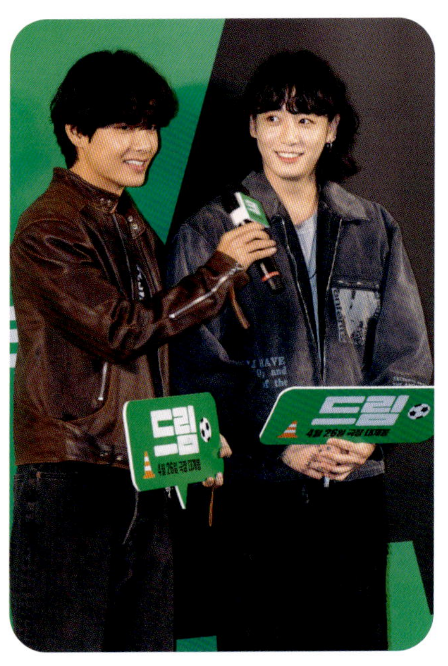

To the *Dream* movie premiere in April 2023, Jung Kook wore a super-rare jacket by the conceptual LA and Paris label, Enfants Riches Déprimés, which translates as 'depressed rich kids' – but he was anything but. He arrived at the Megabox COEX, in Gangnam, Seoul with his best friend V – aka Kim Tae-hyung – and the two not only attracted the most attention, but also clearly revelled in each other's company. V was there to support his WOOGA crew member, actor Park Seo-joon, starring alongside the singer IU in the sports comedy-drama based on a true story. It had started production in 2020 but had been put on ice due to Covid, so its eventual release was something to celebrate. And Jung Kook made sure to dress to impress, especially as it was also a chance for ARMY to see their beloved Taekook (the popular ship name that refers to the close friendship between V and Jung Kook) back in action.

THIS PAGE: *'Taekook' all smiles on the red carpet for the* Dream *VIP preview at the COEX Megabox cinema, Seoul, 24 April 2023.*
OPPOSITE: *Jung Kook, happily rocking the worn-in look.*

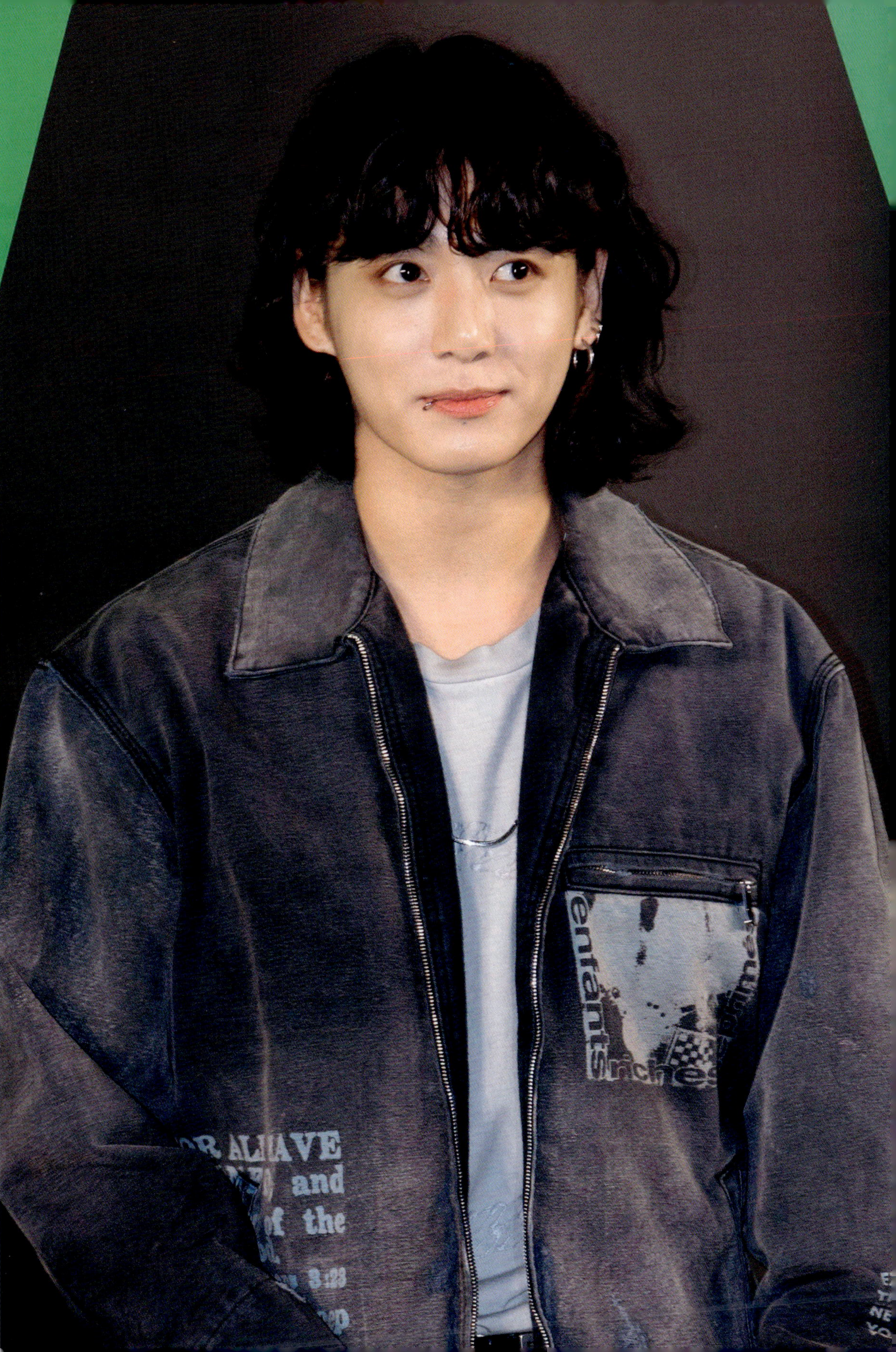
enfants
riches
FOR ALL HAVE
and
of the
3:23

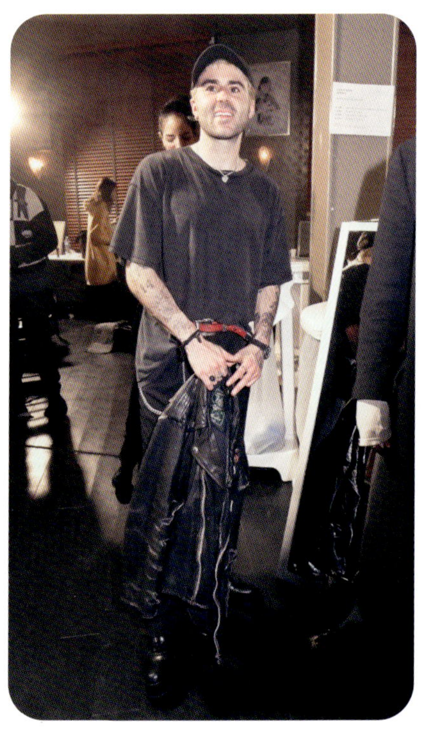

Enfants Riches Déprimés, or ERD, was founded in 2012 by American designer Henri Alexander Levy and is well known amongst the rock cognoscenti as an ultra-exclusive label: it's uber expensive and restricts production. Levy told hollywoodreporter.com in 2017: 'I won't keep releasing a product just because it's popular'. Which means when it's gone, it's gone. Jung Kook chose a vintage-feel work jacket in worn black denim for the high-profile movie launch and trend spotters immediately clocked it was a piece that had already sold out, despite its reported $2,750 (₩3.66 million) price tag. Jung Kook is a fan of the brand and later, in September that year, just before his 26th birthday, was spotted wearing an ERD T-shirt outside a restaurant; again, having fun, not the least bit miserable, and taking a few selfies with fans.

Henri Alexander Levy at the Enfants Riches Déprimés Womenswear A/W 2023-24 show, Paris Fashion Week, 3 March 2023.

'I was really shy during
my trainee days
and lacked sociability.
But it got better after V joined the
company. V and I have similar
personalities and it's
thanks to him that I
came out of my shell.
The more I became close to V
the more I liked him. '

Jung Kook, 'My Biography'
interview for *Volume 8, FC* magazine, Japan.

V Good

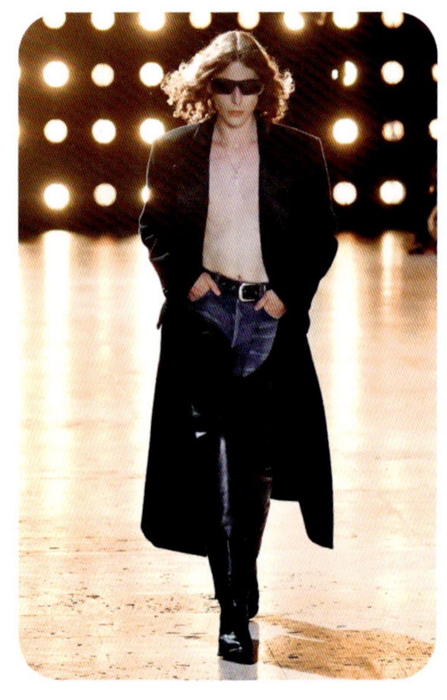

In March 2023, the House of Celine officially announced Kim Tae-hyung as brand ambassador. It was no surprise to ARMY who had watched V wear Hedi Slimane's creations at numerous high-profile events, including the Celine Men's S/S 2023 show in Paris. Timed to publish with the reveal, V featured on the cover of the April edition of Korean *Elle*. In an extended shoot by the celebrated style photographer, Hong Jang-hyun, inside the magazine, V wore key Celine Homme pieces, including a sequined hoodie, a fringed denim vest and studded leather blouson, a palm tree-patterned maxi skirt, sci-fi sunglasses and a pearl necklace with a logo charm.

It was the beginning of the formalisation of a beautiful fashion friendship. In November later that year, V posed for a series of portraits taken and styled by Slimane himself, showcasing key Celine silhouettes: a starburst embroidered cowboy shirt, a trucker jacket, rock 'n' roll shades and an over-the-shoulder

THIS PAGE: *Celine Ready to Wear S/S 2023, Paris Men's Fashion Week, June 2022.*
OPPOSITE: *V at the Celine pop-up store opening at The Hyundai, Seoul, 30 March 2023.*

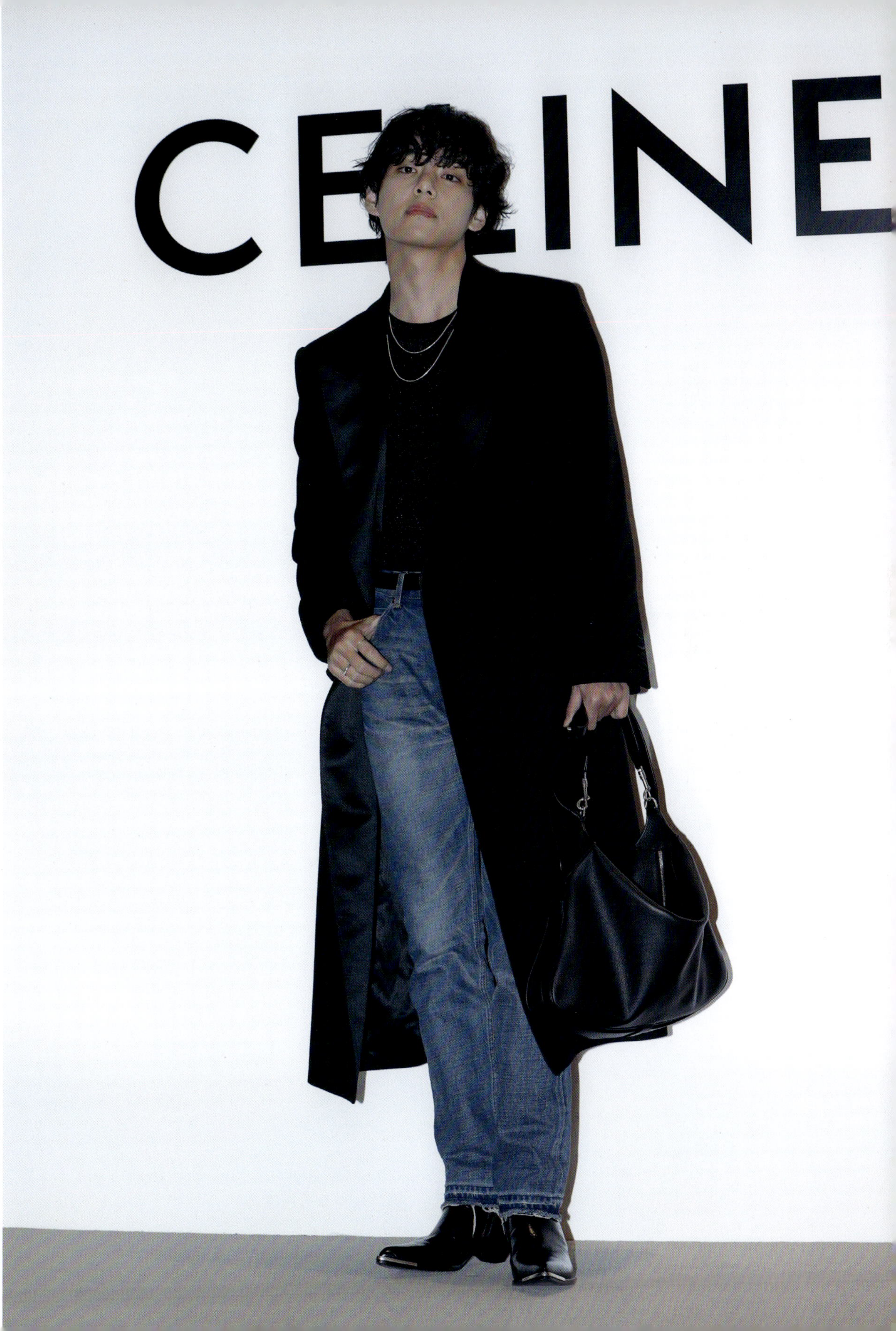

CELINE

Ava Triomphe bag. He looked like a smouldering young Asian Elvis Presley and the black-and-white campaign became an instant classic. In January 2024, allkpop.com reported that in the first ten months of the deal, V had 'generated $274 Million of Earned Media Value (EMV) for CELINE by posting only 31 stories and posts'.

The love was mutual. V had been a huge fan of Hedi's since 2017 when he showed off an homage to the creative director with a 'Vedi Slimane diary' – snapshot images of his own released on Twitter (now X), including one of Slimane's and BTS's constant references, the grunge band Nirvana's crooked smiley face T-shirt. Equally, V's muse-like influence on Slimane was detected in February 2024 when Celine dropped new camo-detailed pieces, including caps and a bi-material jacket that ARMY instantly speculated was informed by V's military service.

OPPOSITE: *V leaving Gimpo International Airport on his way to the Celine Men's Summer 2023 show, 24 June 2022.*

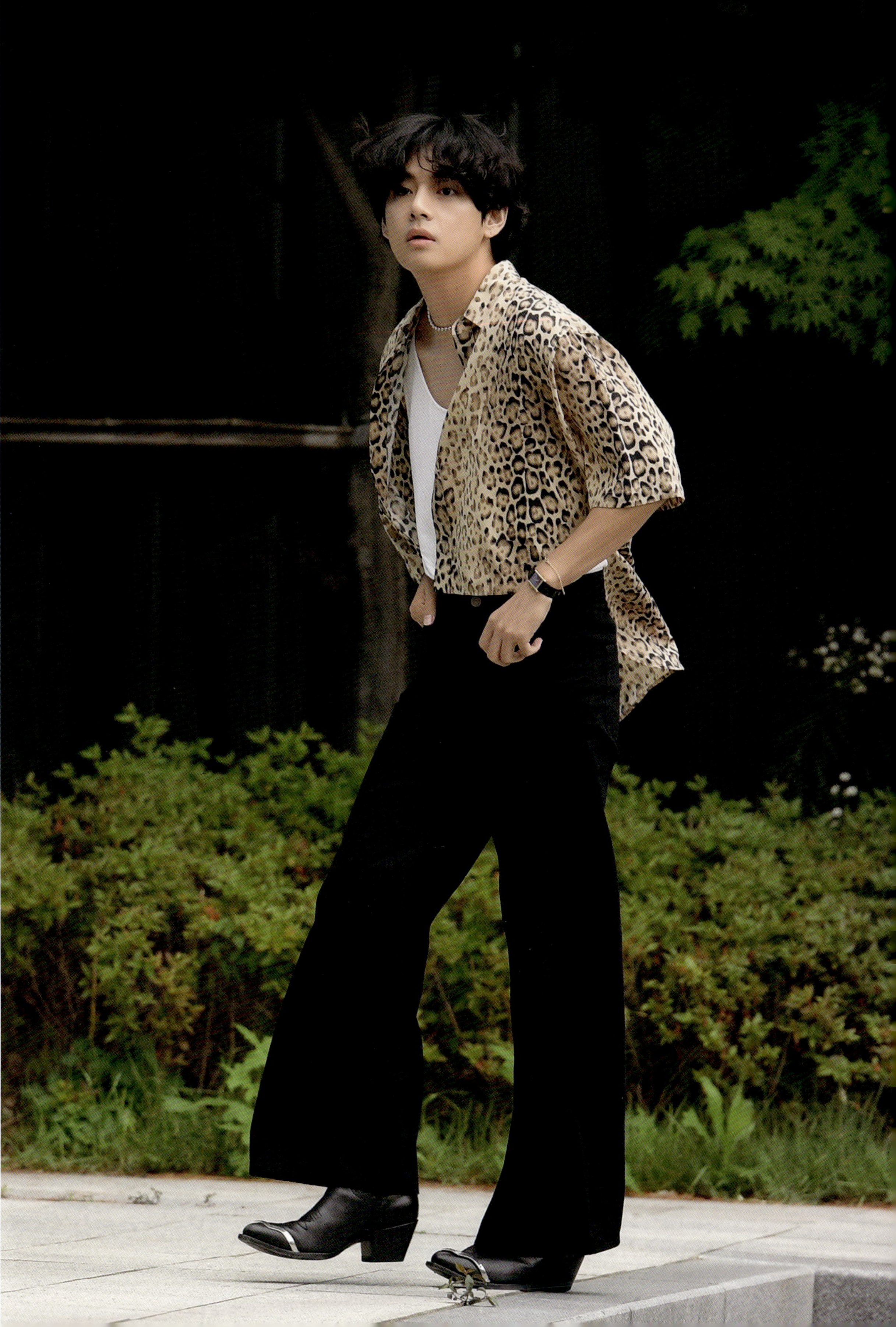

Fashion Taskforce

Before Jung Ho-seok enlisted for military service on 18 April 2023, he made sure that fans had plenty of stylish j-hope memories to remember him by. He arrived at the Louis Vuitton show in January wearing a full look to support the collection put together by the interim team with the help of KidSuper designer Colm Dillane and stylist Ibrahim Kamara.

On Valentine's Day, Pharrell Williams, the polymath music producer-turned-designer, was announced as creative director at the fashion house and shortly afterwards j-hope was made house ambassador and commissioned to star in the A/W campaign for the brand, with images shot by maestro photographer, Mario Sorrenti. The move placed j-hope right at the heart of the fashion industry, celebrated by creatives who are internationally revered.

OPPOSITE: *Dressing to be seen? j-hope at the Louis Vuitton Menswear A/W 2023–24 show, Paris Fashion Week, 19 January 2023.*

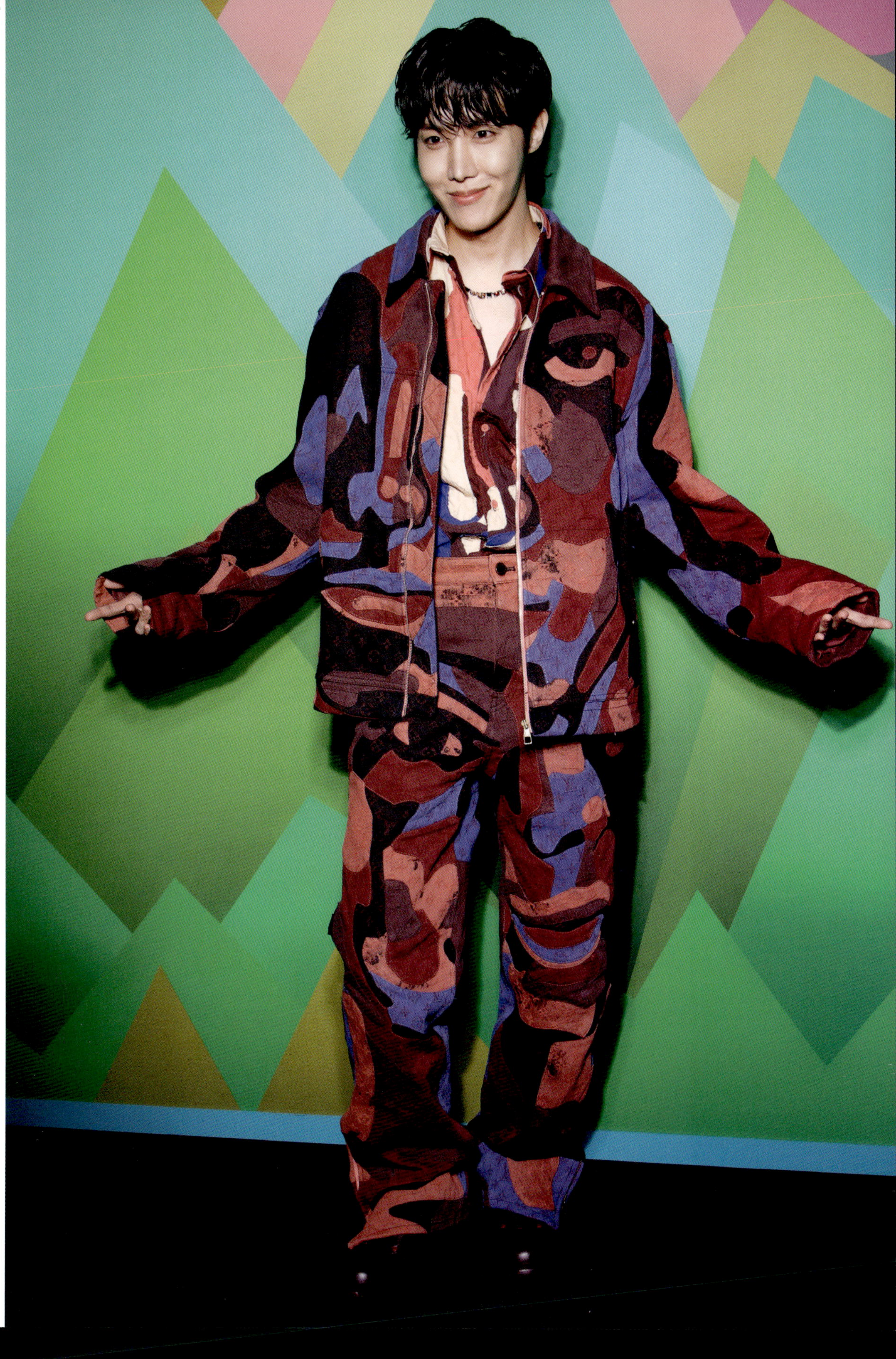

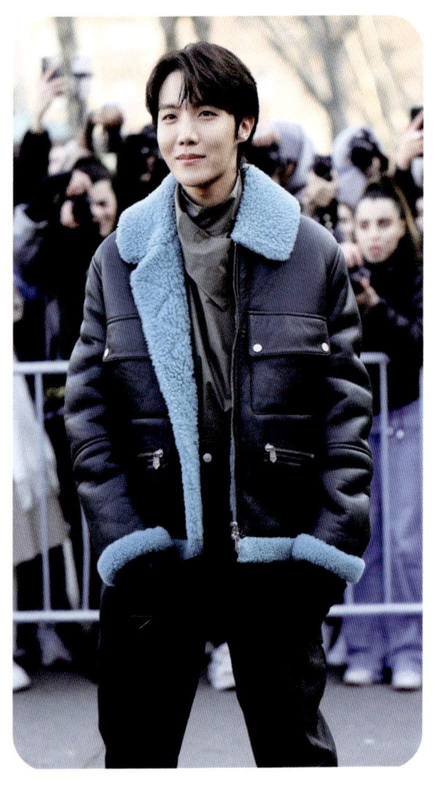

At the Paris shows he had been also feted by Hermès and invited to sit front row – wearing a turquoise shearling-lined leather jacket, Hobi arrived to possibly the biggest crowds that week. Hermès is notoriously discreet and rarely collaborates with influencers. Founded in 1837 it has few celebrity connections, instead relishing in its exclusive status and quiet, ultra-luxurious collections that speak for themselves. There couldn't have been a higher profile moment.

As well as slaying fashion, the BTS star went on to reveal a Weverse and Disney+ documentary, *j-hope IN THE BOX*, which would show the making of his debut solo album *Jack in the Box*, as well as his 2022 Lollapalooza performance where he headlined. Fans needn't have worried about missing him though, as during his time in the South Korean army, ARMY were happy to see him rising to the challenge of new responsibilities and treated to marching shots of him leading trainee soldiers on a hike, and regularly showing off stylish camo 'fits.

j-hope attends the Hermès Menswear A/W 2023–24 show as part of Paris Fashion Week, 21 January 2023.

' This year... I went to awards ceremonies alone, attended big (fashion) shows in Paris, made a collab song with someone I respected to give you a big gift before enlisting in the military and prepared content to let you feel a little bit of my warmth while I'm serving in the military. ,

j–hope, *Weverse,* **December 2023.**

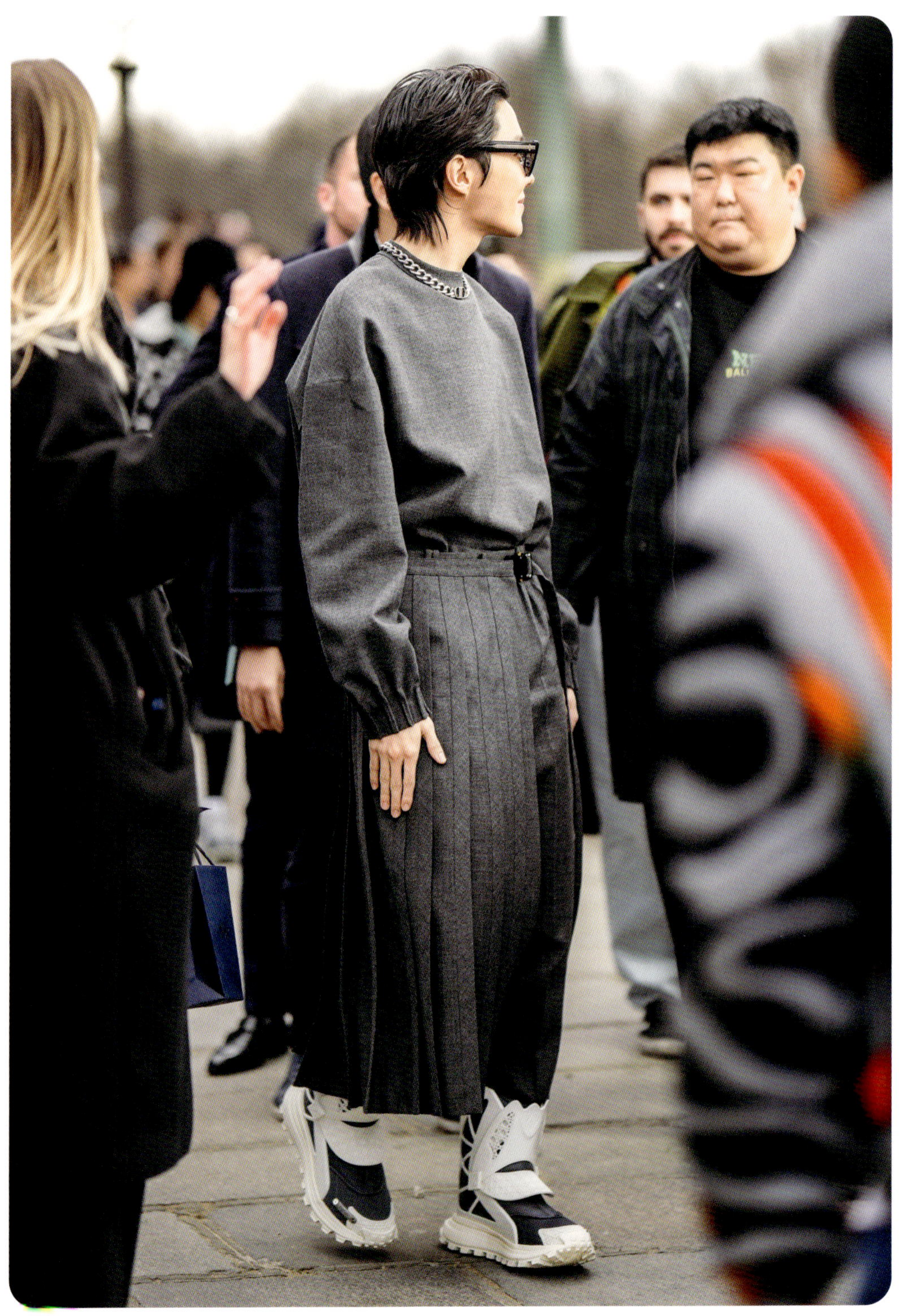

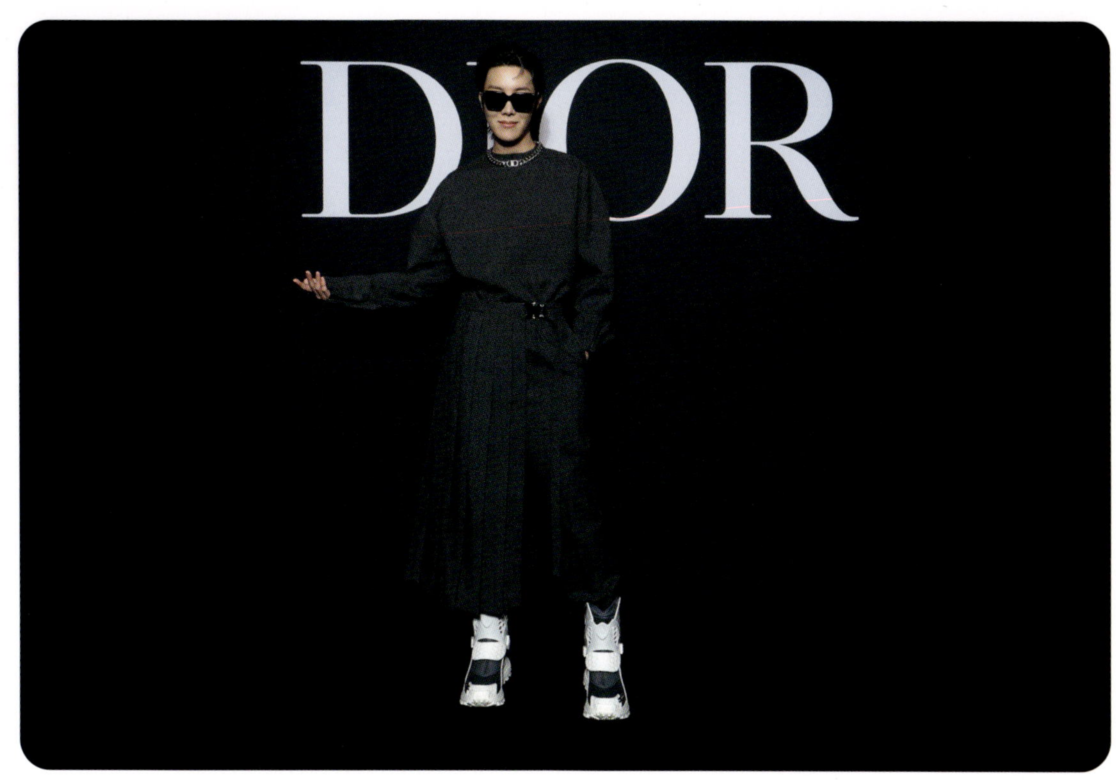

OPPOSITE: *j–hope top-to-toe in Dior during Paris Fashion Week, 2023.*
THIS PAGE: *j–hope at the Dior Homme Menswear A/W 2023–24 show, Paris Fasion Week, 20 January 2023.*

Part of the Bottega Family!

As part of the Kering luxury conglomerate, Milanese leather company Bottega Veneta is in good company – Kering also owns Gucci, Saint Laurent, and Balenciaga. They are at the very top of the fashion tree and have the power and contacts to pick and choose exactly who stars in their campaigns and sits in their front rows. The Kering labels work with the biggest celebrities as a matter of course, so unsurprisingly in March 2023, RM was chosen to become the first ever Bottega Veneta VIP ambassador. He'd been a fan for a while, dressing in the label for the 2020 Grammys.

In retrospect it was an easy choice. RM is celebrated as the first member of BTS and their spokesperson and leader. He also enjoys an IQ of 148 and while at high school was ranked in the prestigious top 1% of all university entrants. His talents manifested early: in the 7th grade he had already begun writing hip–hop songs. So, it feels right that Namjoon would

RM wearing a Bottega Veneta plaid shirt during Milan Women's Fashion Week, A/W 2023–24, February 2023.

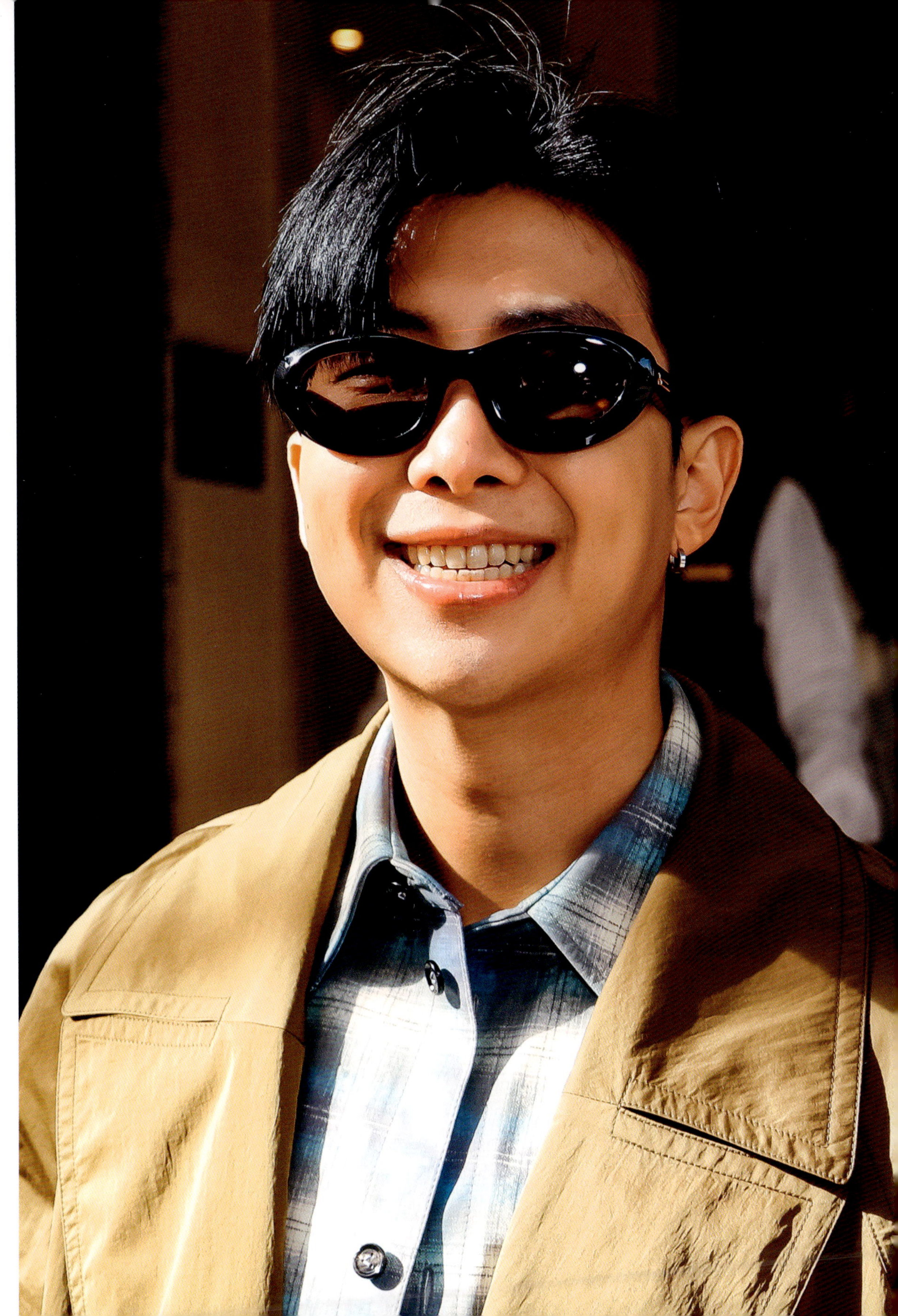

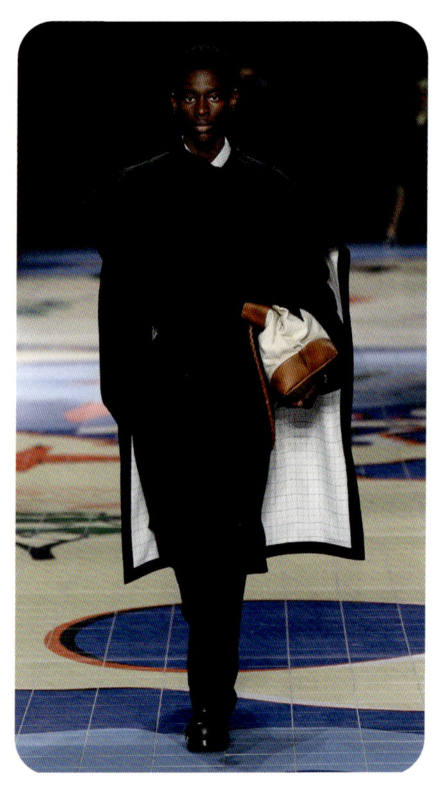

connect with one of the world's most intelligently cultured brands. Helmed since 2021 by Matthieu Blazy, formerly of Celine and Raf Simons, Bottega is less about trends and more about sophistication: perfect for the most grown up of the BTS team, who has evolved his own styling angle from the original Rap Monster to today, a slick, timelessly classic wardrobe. Explaining his new aesthetic, RM said in a March 2023 interview with the Spanish newspaper, *El País* as reported on koreaboo.com: 'Now I'm into timelessness. I'm over trends. I'm looking for vintage jeans, cotton T-shirts and natural things that don't scream "Hey, I'm here!" '

THIS PAGE: *Bottega Veneta Spring 2024 Ready to Wear show, Milan, 23 September 2023.*
OPPOSITE: *RM at the Bottega Veneta Autumn 2023 Ready to Wear runway show, Milan, 25 February 2023.*

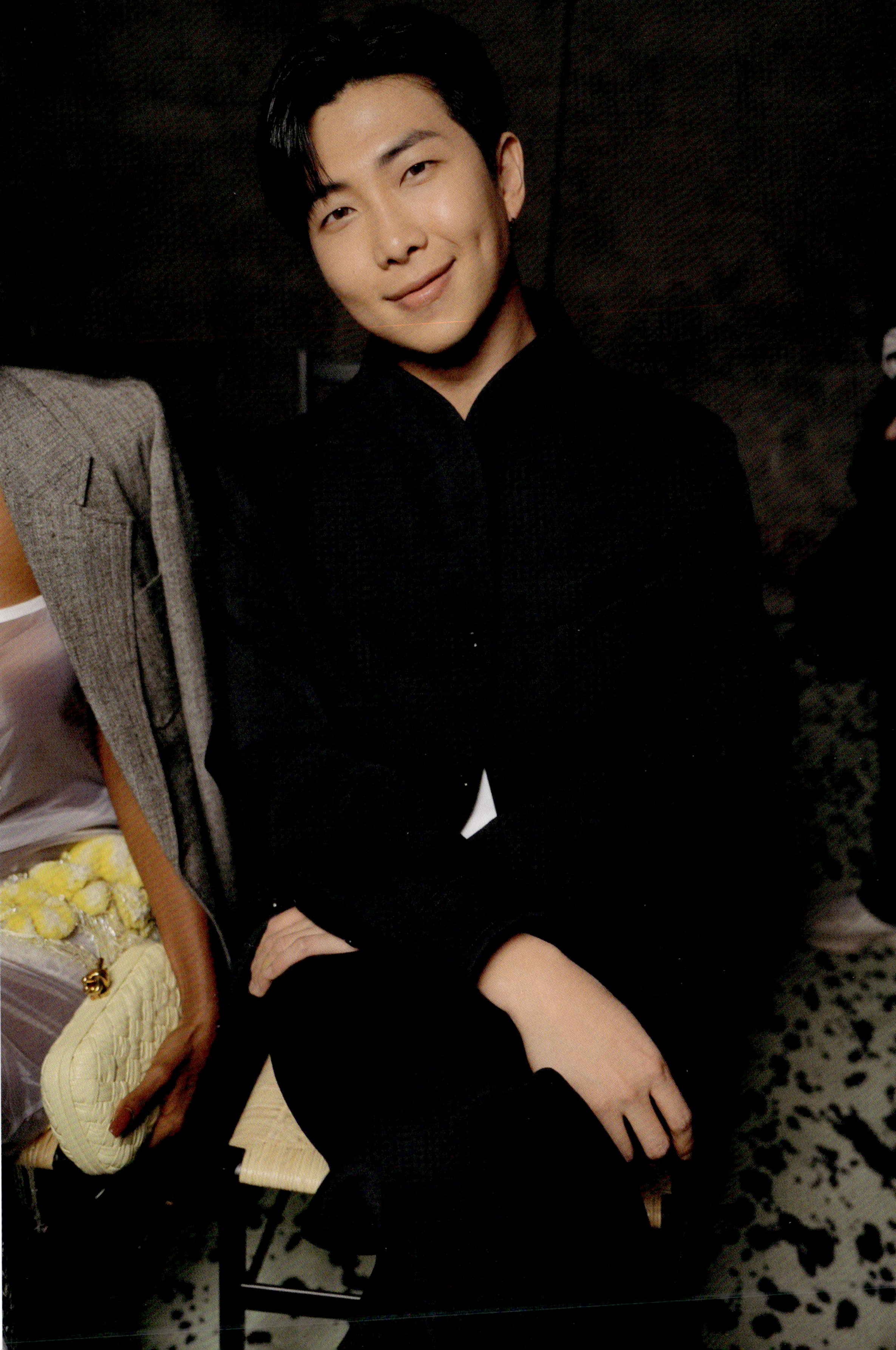

Good and Ready

Kim Nam-joon – aka RM – has always been the grown-up in BTS, but his maturity goes beyond just being the leader of the band. Whenever possible, he has made sure to be a role model by giving back to the community and good causes. In 2022, *Korea JoongAng Daily* reported the CHA and Overseas Korean Cultural Heritage Foundation had revealed that the singer had: 'donated 100 million won to our foundation, saying he wants the money to go toward preserving, restoring and utilizing artifacts outside of the country'. A similar gift the previous year helped preserve an important Joseon dynasty (1392–1910) *hwalot*, an exquisitely embroidered wedding robe; the 2022 donation went towards supporting Korean art. RM is well known for his sophisticated eye and his personal collection includes pieces by renowned artists, Kwon Jin-kyu and Jung Young-joo amongst others.

RM at Korea's 18th breast cancer awareness campaign 'Love Your W' event at Four Seasons Hotel, Seoul, 24 November 2023.

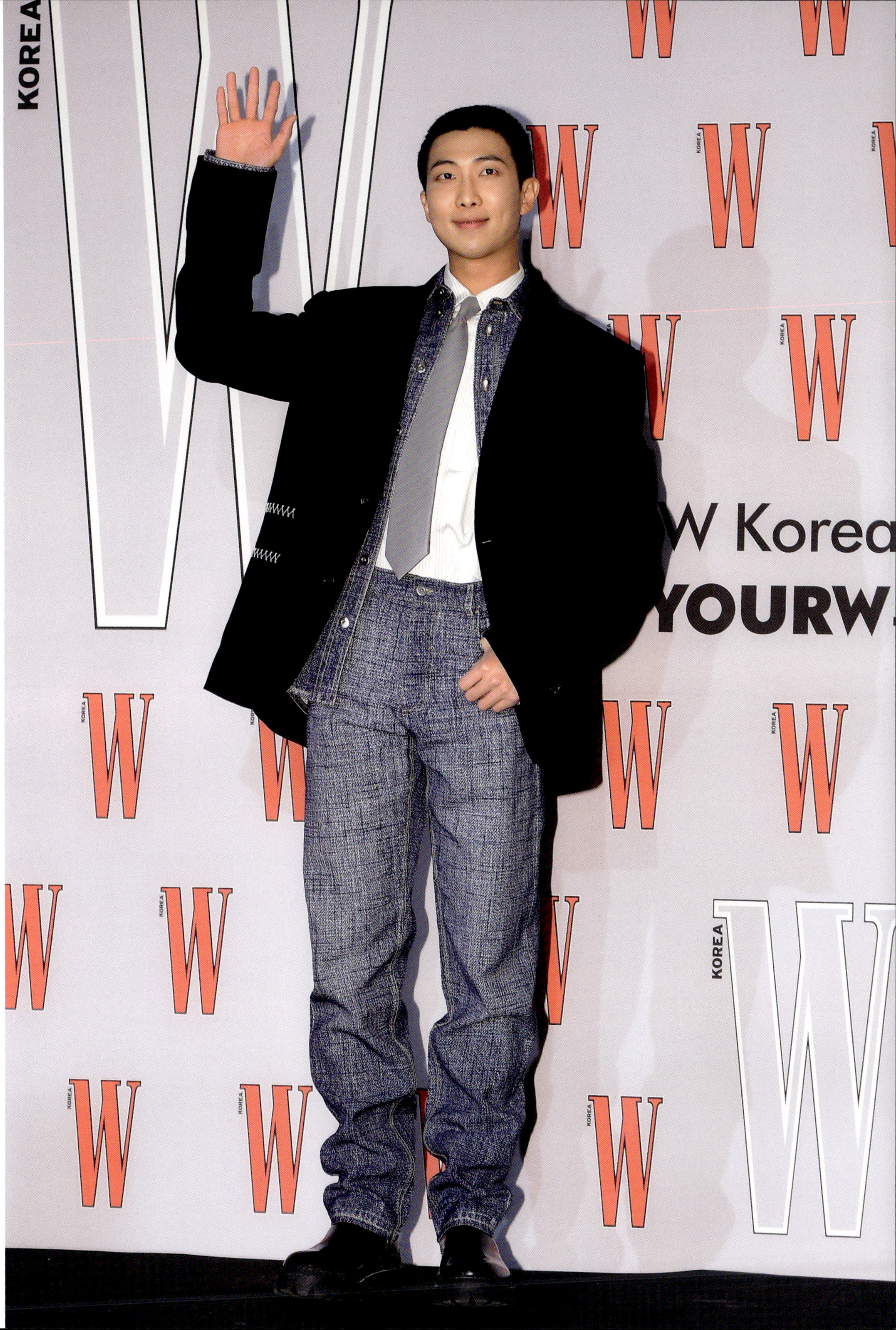

KOREA
W Korea
YOURW
W

More recently, the South Korean Ministry of Defence announced RM's role as public relations ambassador for MAKRI: a position previously held by Song Hae, the celebrated host of the National Singing Contest, and known throughout the country, before he died at the grand age of 95, as 'South Korea's beloved Nation's Emcee'. It is a serious role, which involves promoting activity to return the overseas remains of soldiers to their families.

One of the last public outings that RM attended before military service was the 18th breast cancer awareness campaign event, W Korea, held annually since 2006. A cause close to RM's heart, he had performed there with j-hope in 2022. Necessarily a high-profile occasion, in 2023 RM arrived with short hair, wearing a smart-casual double denim shacket and jeans combo, tailored suit jacket and grey leather tie from his favourite brand Bottega Veneta's pre-Spring 2024 BV collection. Not forgetting his allegiance to the Italian House, earlier in June he had appeared as cover star of *Vogue Korea* in cream BV knitwear and lattice leather trousers, shot by fashion photographer Dukhwa Jang.

' For a decade, I was the leader of BTS, and it was very stable and fun; things only got better. In 2023, a lot of things have changed, professionally and personally, although I can't tell. As I'm about to turn 30, I like myself more than I did when I was 20. Now I will spend a year and a half in military service, which is a big deal in every Korean man's life. And after that, I am sure I will be a different human being, hopefully a better and wiser one. ,

RM, *English.elpais.com*, **March 2023.**

The New Look

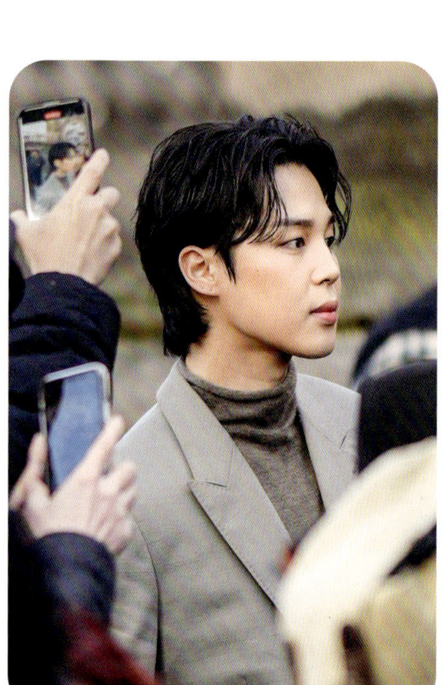

Jimin's friendship with the Parisian House of Dior goes back, along with the rest of BTS, to 2019 when its menswear Creative Director, Kim Jones, designed a wardrobe for the group's Love Yourself: Speak Yourself world tour. Since then, Jimin has often been photographed in Jones's collections, wearing his cult classic pieces, which magpie-like fuse clever fashion references and esoteric inspirations from the worlds of streetwear, literature, art, clubland and music. In January 2023, Jimin was aptly chosen as house ambassador, obligingly going on to set Paris ablaze arriving at the Dior A/W 2023–24 show in greige soft-suiting matched with a polo neck jumper and commando boots. The appointment heralded a dynamic chapter in Dior's relationship with Jimin and all things South Korean.

In September that year, Dior's womenswear division brand launched an exhibition at it store in the hip Seongsu-dong district of Seoul, showcasing a collaboration with 24 Korean artists, including Bahk Seon Ghi, Choi Jeong Hwa, Gigisue and Gimhongsok, who re-imagined its iconic Lady Dior

THIS PAGE: *Jimin in Dior during Paris Fashion Week, January 2023.*
OPPOSITE: *FROW greige. DIOR Menswear A/W 2023–24, Paris, 20 January 2023.*

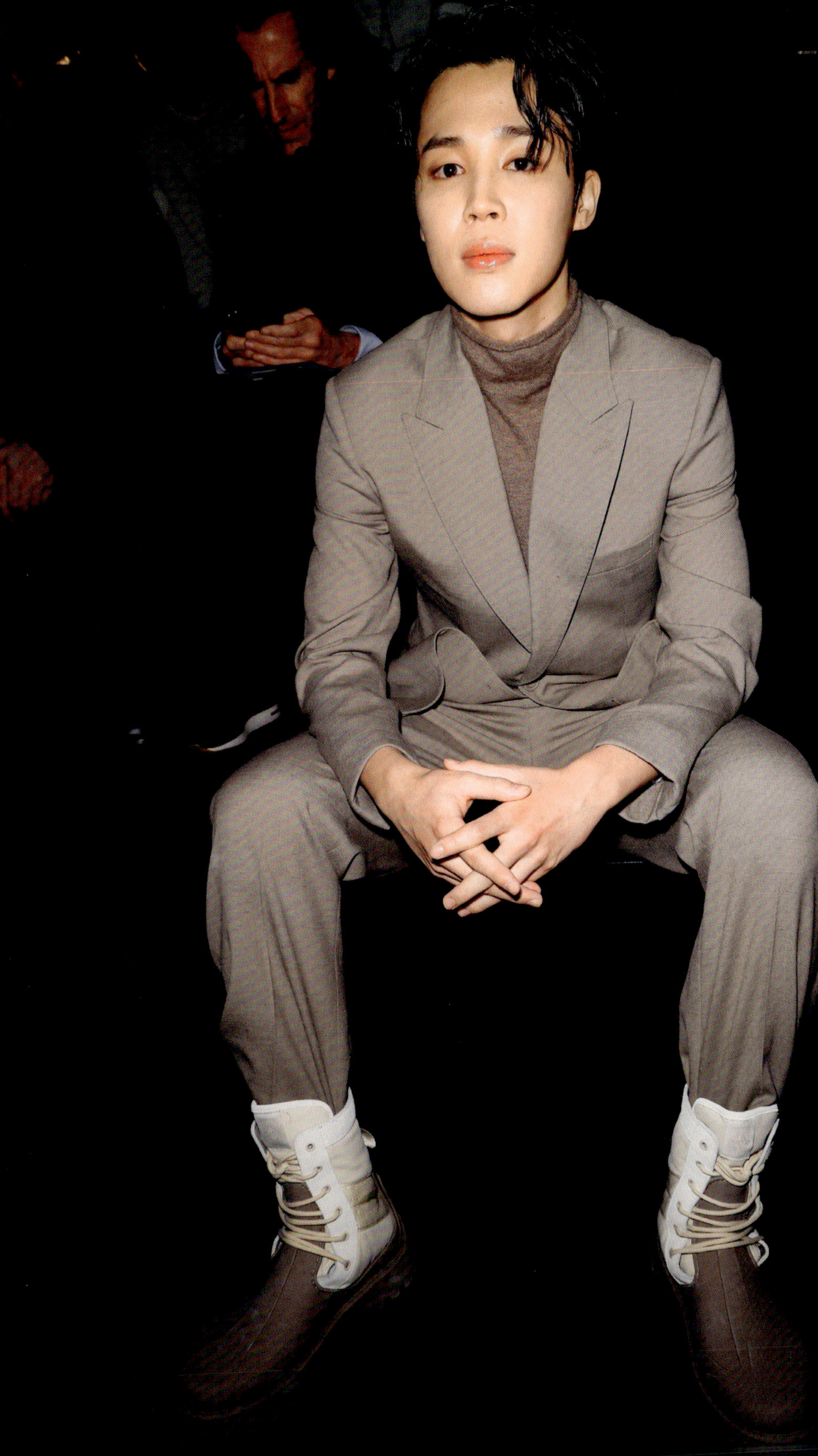

handbag. Jimin, wearing a taupe Dior cape–coat, was a guest of honour and ensured huge crowds turned up at the event, which prefaced Frieze Art week. A month later, he released images shot by Alasdair McLellan of the Dior S/S 2024 campaign via Instagram while at the same time, over on X, Dior proclaimed that Jimin 'incarnates' the new collection which was: 'redrawing the contours of the men's wardrobe in an artful mashup of genres, from streetwear to smart'. The campaign ran globally with ARMY supportively discussing online that the Dior adverts featuring Jimin had been spotted in over 50 locations around the world, including America, Australia, Europe, China, Korea and Thailand.

Like his fellow bandmates, Jimin's busy year, which also included the release of a debut album, *Face*, in March, as well as the Weverse documentary *Jimin's Production Diary*, preceded obligatory military service which began in December 2023. Before he took off, however, he had time to drop a final track, 'Closer Than This', which his record company revealed on billboard.com was a 'heartfelt fan song that encapsulates Jimin's genuine feelings for ARMY'.

Some heroes do wear capes. Jimin at the 'Lady Dior Celebration' event at DIOR Seongsu, Seoul, 1 September 2023.

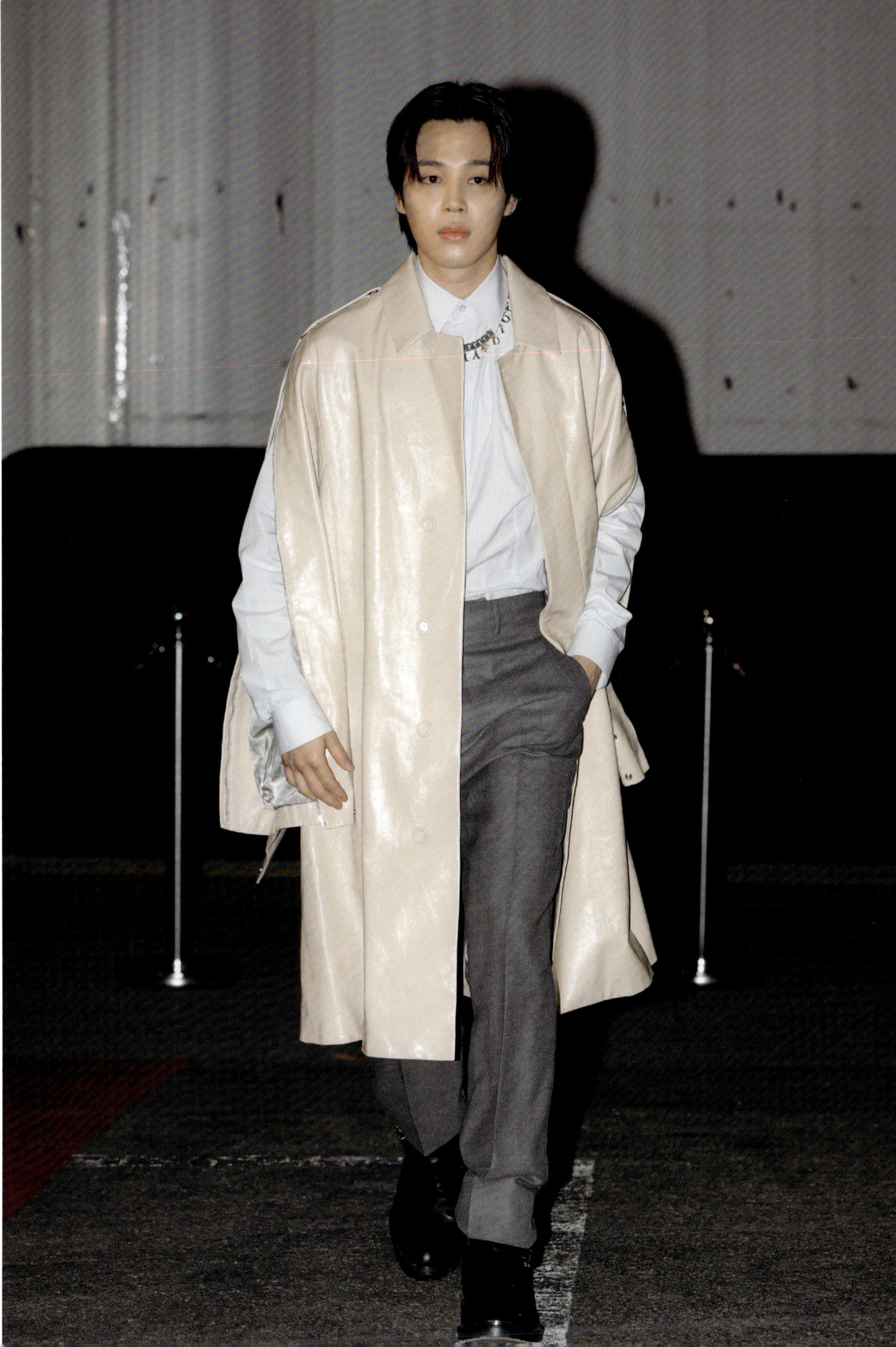

A Midas Touch

— Jimin, *Harper's Bazaar* Japan, 19 January 2024.

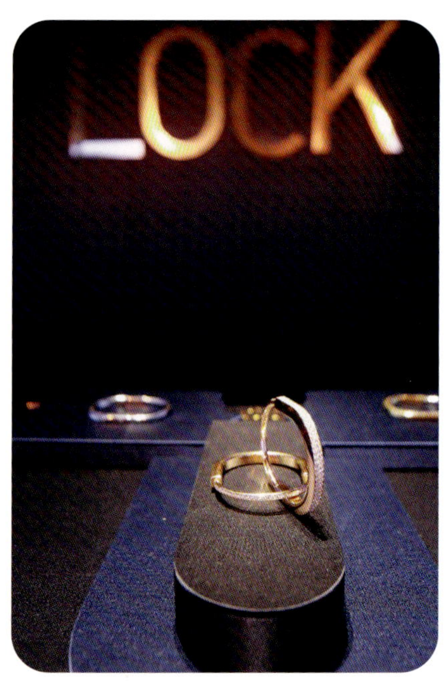

In March 2023 Jimin became an ambassador for the iconic jewellery company, Tiffany & Co. Founded in 1837, in New York, the company today is part of LVMH, the conglomerate that umbrellas luxury labels including Fendi, Loewe and Dior amongst many others. Jimin was a great appointment; his name has helped hyper-drive Tiffany's narrative across East Asia. WWD.com reported at the time that the brand announcement via X became 'Tiffany & Co.'s most-liked tweet of all time with 317,000 likes.' The first campaign saw Jimin wearing gender-fluid diamond-studded pieces selected from the Tiffany Lock Collection, which pays design tribute to a Tiffany & Co. padlock from 1883.

And, of course, he was guest of honour at the Fifth Avenue New York flagship store revamp party in April 2023, celebrating in its splendour alongside Pharrell Williams, and enjoying a set by Katy Perry and iconic dance troup, the Radio City Rockettes. Wearing a Tiffany flower brooch on the lapel of a pre-Fall 2019 Dior suit jacket, that night Jimin cleverly united two of his most high-profile collaborative alliances.

THIS PAGE: *Launch event for 'The Lock Collection' by Tiffany & Co., Mexico City, 8 November 2022.*
OPPOSITE: *Jimin sparkles at the reopening of The Landmark at Tiffany & Co., 5th Avenue, NYC, 27 April 2023.*

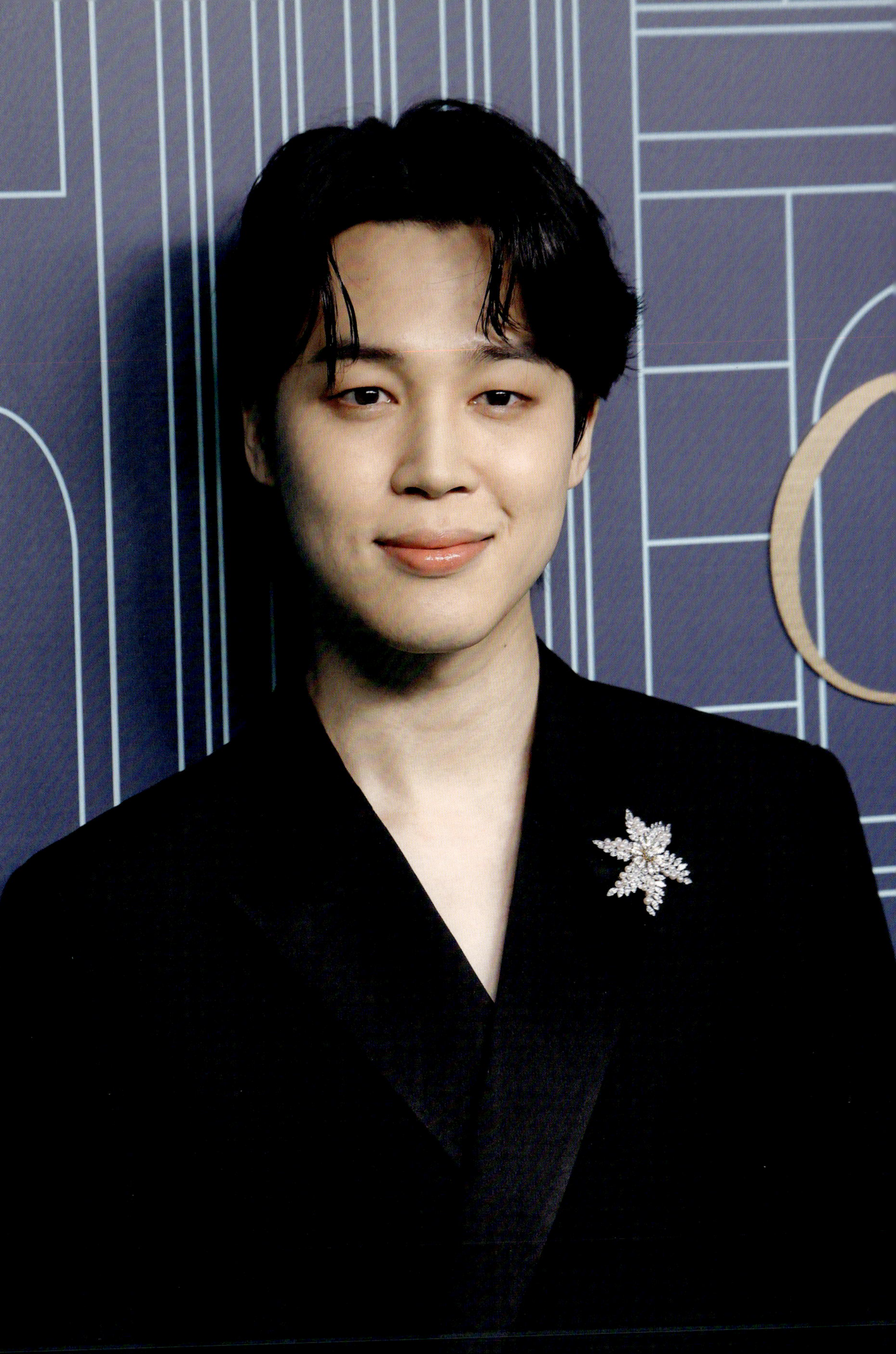

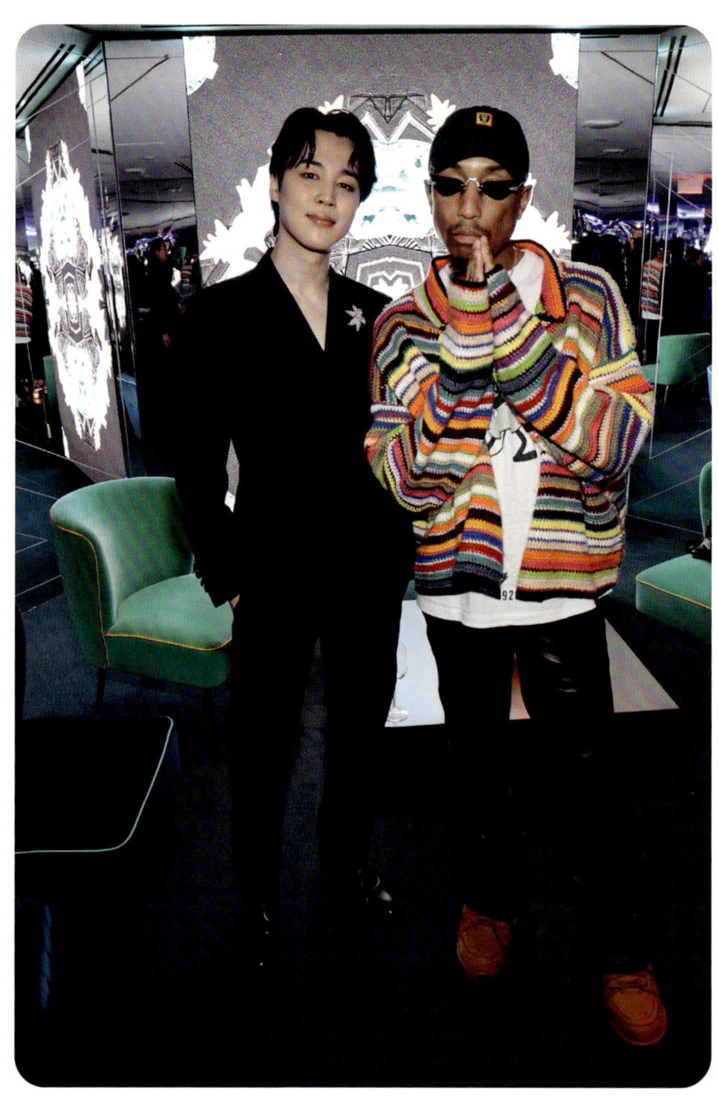

Jimin and Pharrell attend as Tiffany & Co. celebrates the reopening of its NYC flagship store, The Landmark, 27 April 2023.

'We are looking forward
to welcoming multifaceted artist and performer Jimin of BTS as our newest House ambassador. He embodies the energy, style and sense of modernity that epitomizes Tiffany and Co.'

Alexandre Arnault, Tiffany & Co. Executive VP, Product and Communications, March 2023.

Top Buzz

> **'** I always feel like every moment is the best moment.
> **How can anything be better than now? ,**
> — **Jin, *Weverse* interview, June 2022.**

In December 2022, Jin became the first member of BTS to join the South Korean military. As the eldest, it was natural he would lead the way, but in an extraordinary bow to the group's success, the Korean government changed the law in 2020 to allow him and the rest of BTS to defer their service to accommodate their ongoing world-wide accomplishments. This meant that when Jin was coming up to 28 years old, the age he would have had to sign up, he was given a reprieve because it was deemed that 'a pop culture artist who was recommended by the Minister of Culture, Sports and Tourism to have greatly enhanced the image of Korea both within the nation and throughout the world would be allowed to postpone their military service until age of 30'. This effectively gave Jin two more years before enlisting. It wasn't a question of refusing; the BTS star admitted way back in a 2019 CBS interview that he was sanguine about serving his country saying: 'As a Korean, it's natural. And someday when duty calls, we'll be ready to respond and do our best'.

Still with longer rock locks before the military chop. Jin at the 64th Annual GRAMMY Awards at the MGM Grand Garden Arena, Las Vegas, 3 April 2022.

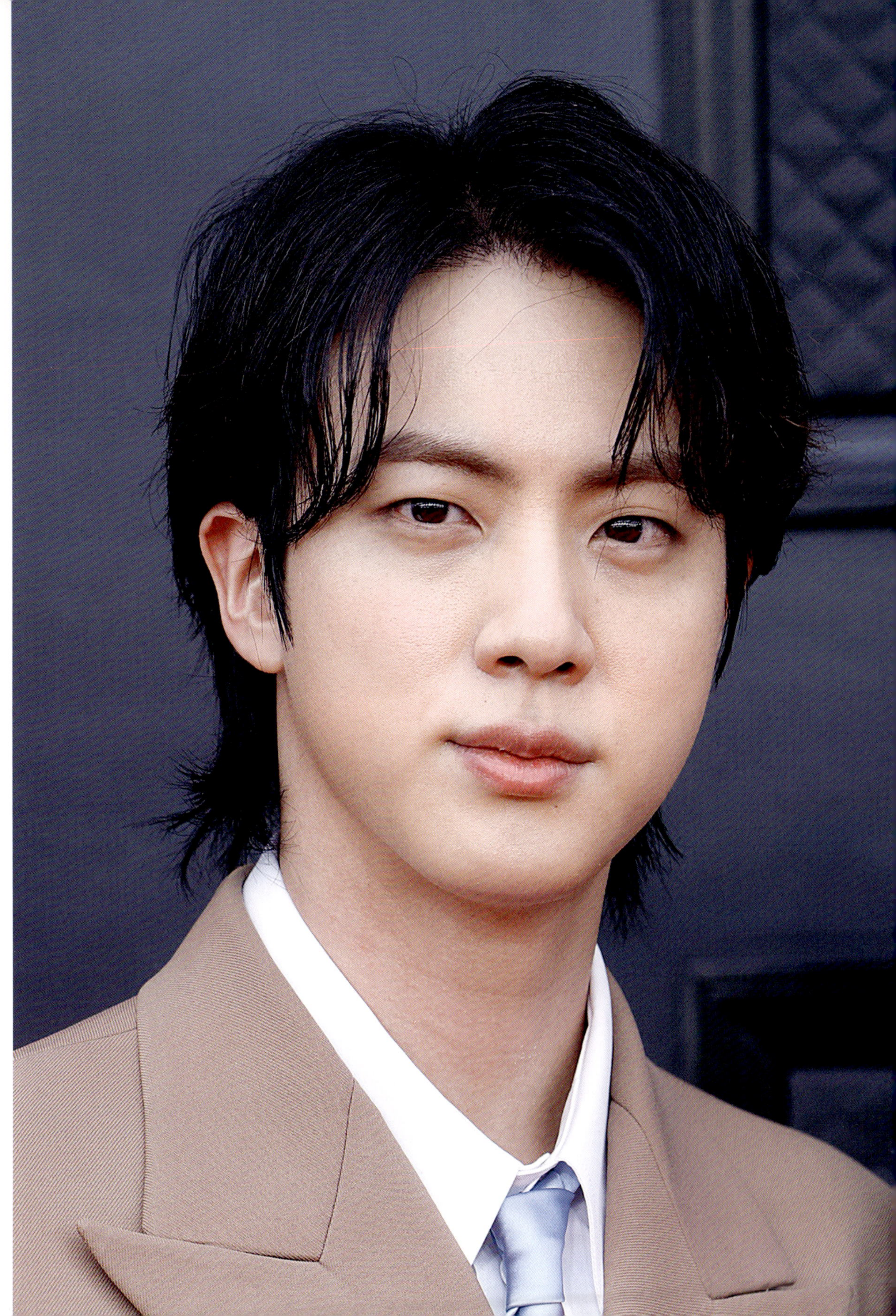

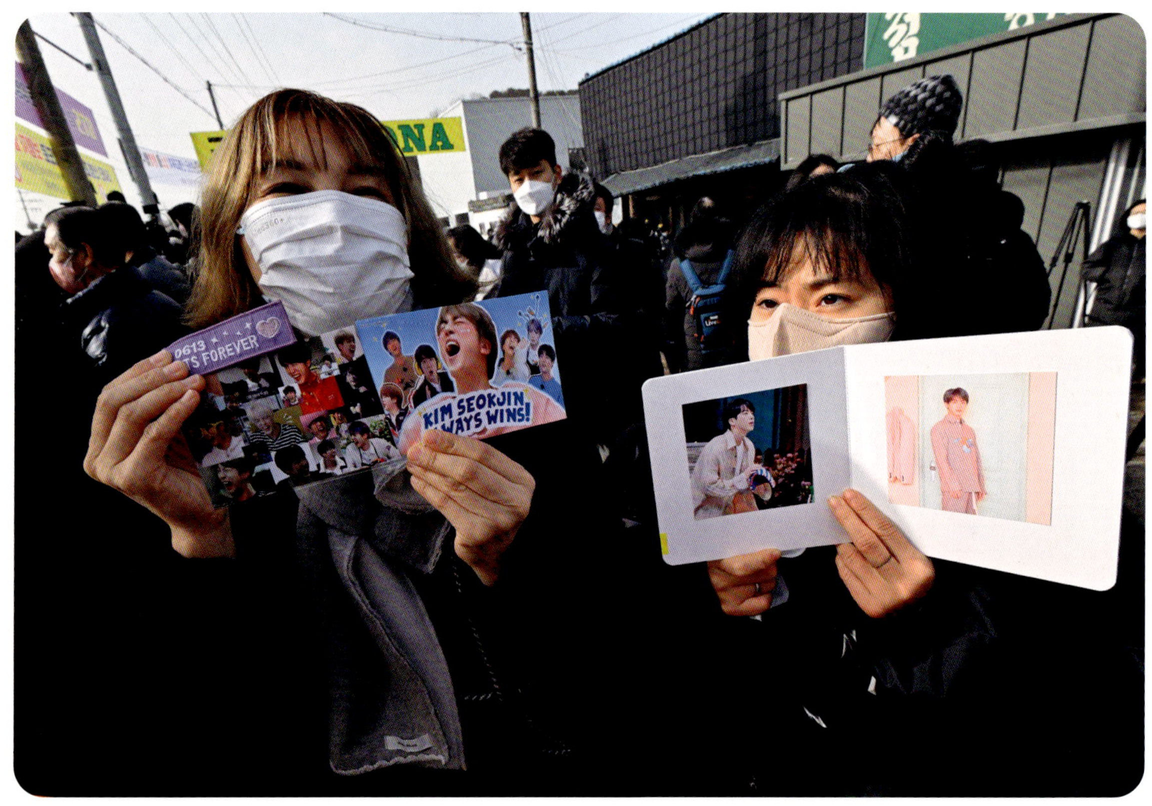

And true to form, when the time came, Jin took to his new role enthusiastically and with no regret, encouraged by ARMYs who waited at the camp gates to show their support. In January 2023, after five-week basic training at a camp in Yeoncheon, two hours north of Seoul, he emerged on Weverse and posted images of himself showing off a khaki camo uniform, beret and boots, standing in the snow and signalling the peace sign. His hair cut short in a buzz cut and face half hidden by a mask, ARMY were thrilled to see their IT-Boy looking spruce and ready to do his best.

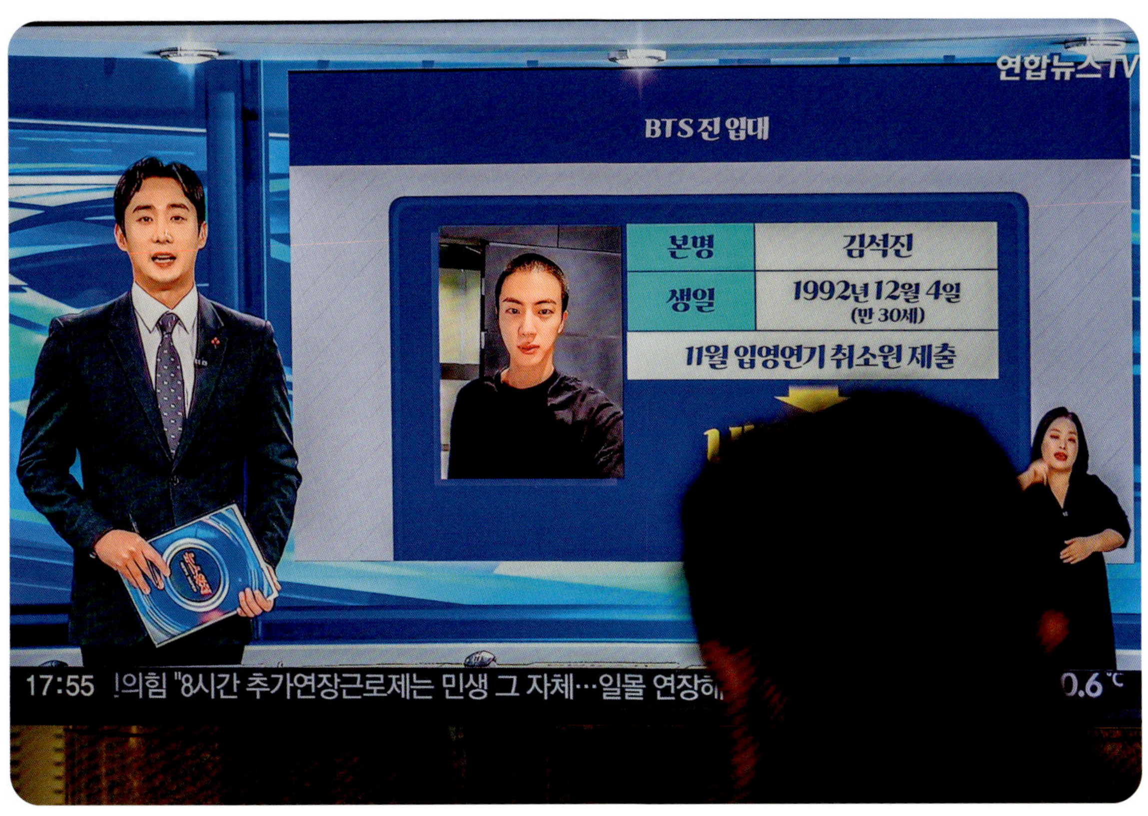

OPPOSITE: *Fans hold pictures of Jin in front of the military training unit in Yeoncheon waiting for him to arrive to begin his military service, 13 December 2022.*

THIS PAGE: *Jin's crewcut and enlistment in the South Korean army make the news. The first member of BTS to serve in the military, the 30-year-old entered a boot camp of a front-line Army 5 division in Yeoncheon, 60 kilometres north of Seoul, on 13 December to undergo a five-week basic training programme.*

Older and Wiser

Jin's birthday is a special day for all ARMY and holds special memories: it's often been celebrated while BTS have been on tour and always a highlight to look forward to. One of the biggest moments was on day four of BTS's Permission to Dance tour in 2021 at the enormous 298-acre SoFi Stadium in Inglewood, California, when the crowd performed a Mexican wave with their 'ARMY bomb' light-sticks while chanting for him. In a 2022 Weverse interview Kim Seok-jin reflected on that extraordinary night, saying: 'I was seriously moved in a way I have never been before. Honestly, where else could you experience something so touching? 50,000 people, all singing happy birthday, and the man of the hour is me. It was like being the protagonist in a novel. And to think, when we debuted, I thought it would be so nice just to have a concert in front of 3,000 people.'

In December 2023 then, when it came to his birthday while in the military, he sent a message to everyone via Weverse, saying: 'It's already been a year since I joined the military. There's still a lot of time left, but I'm already excited to be with you if I spend only a third of the total time. Oh, and our members are going to join the army...LOL. LOL. I'm going to cry. I hope that time passes quickly, and I can have a good time with the members and the Army.' While he was away, fans arranged LED advertisements to flag up his 31st

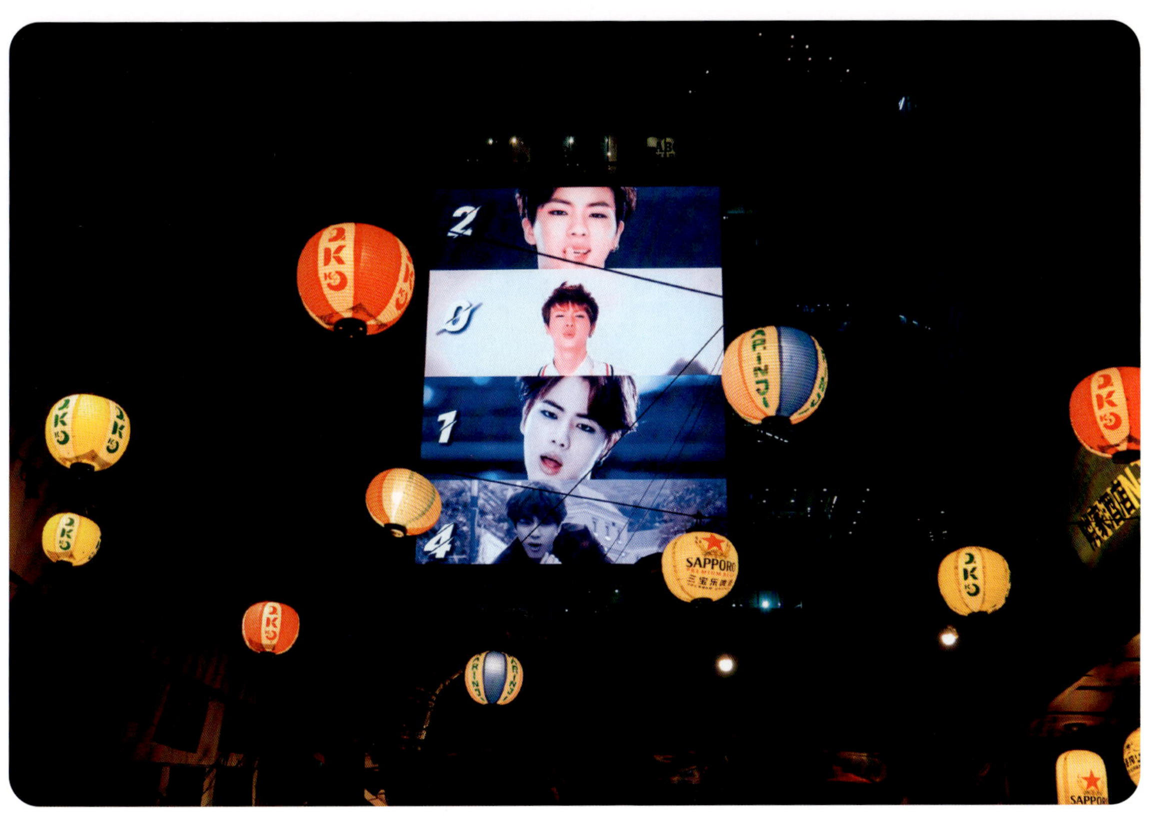

An ad arranged by Jin's fans to celebrate his birthday on an LED board of a department store building in central Seoul. Jin turned 31 on 4 December 2023. He began his military service in December 2022.

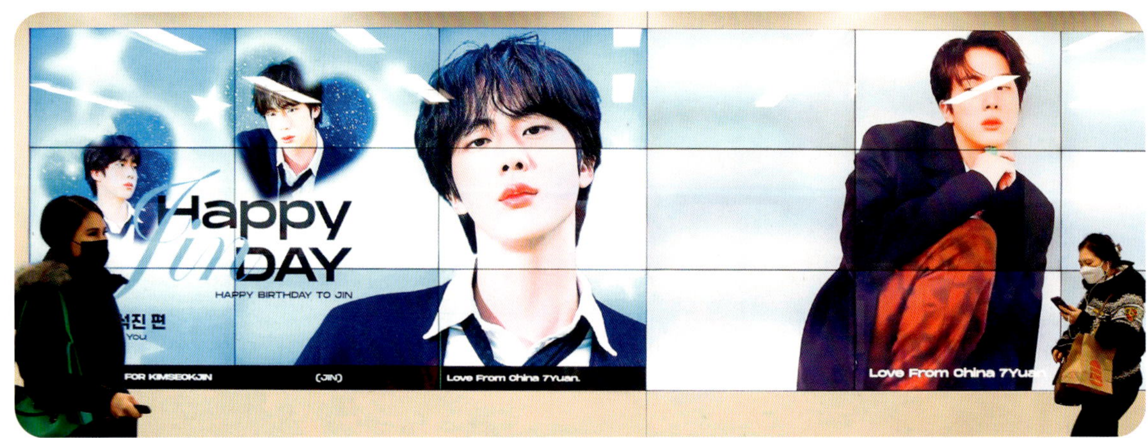

birthday and show he wasn't forgotten. Fans needn't have worried. In January 2024, koreanscoop.com announced he was that year's 'ultimate star to watch'.

It's hard to comprehend the impact of Jin, and although it might have been a less usual ambassadorship than the rest of his band-mates, when he was made the face of Ottogi Jin Ramen, it packed the usual BTS-worthy punch, with allkpop.com posting in 2023 that the brand's exports 'reached a recording number of $208 million sales in the 1st quarter of 2023'.

He is confident in his decisions and this equally translates to his fashion choices. Way back in 2020, during a *GQ* video, the magazine asked him who his style hero was, and he retorted: 'I am my own hero'. Something we can all celebrate.

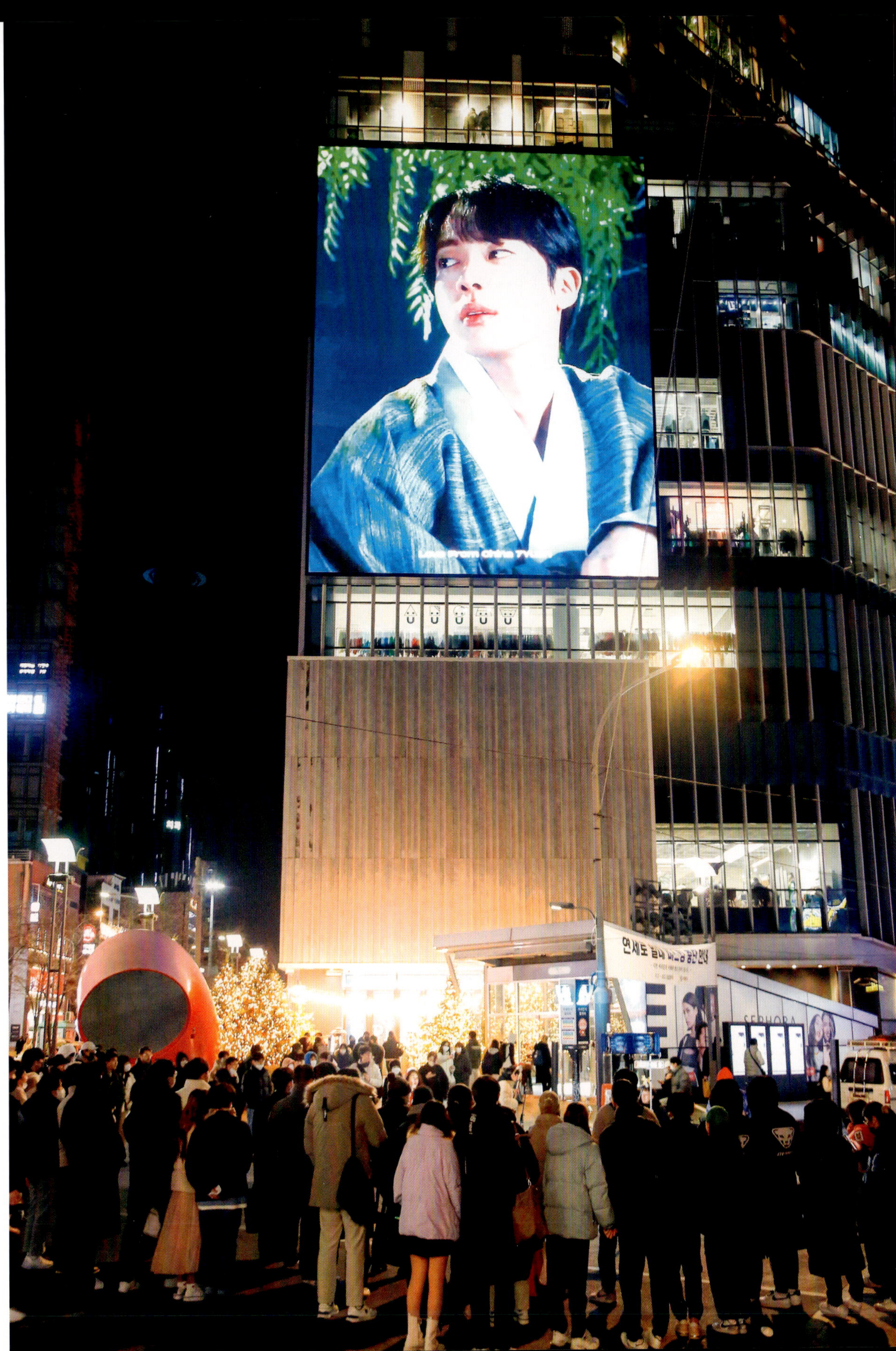

Slam-Dunk Success

SUGA's 2023 was busy. He released his studio album, *D-Day*, in April and went on tour, playing venues across the States, including New York, then on to Indonesia, Japan, and Thailand, concluding in South Korea. Min Yoon-gi's solo projects began back in 2016 with a youthful mixtape of rap tracks. In an nme.com interview in April 2023, he reflected poignantly: 'I released "Agust D" when I was still very young, so, even as I listen to it now, it kind of sounds immature'.

Nevertheless, for fans, it's part of the BTS star's journey and they were ecstatic when, during his penultimate gig at the Olympic Gymnastics Arena in Seoul, SUGA was joined by Jimin onstage to perform one of his classic tracks, 'Tony Montana'. Though he has developed through subsequent projects, including his second mixtape, *D-2* (2020), loneliness remains a central theme in his music away from BTS. In a July 2023 billboard.com feature, he mused: 'People might see me as someone who wouldn't have any concerns or worries or that I don't feel any agony, but I feel those emotions too. I'm trying to find a way to fight those and

SUGA watches the pre-season NBA basketball game between the Golden State Warriors and Washington Wizards at the Saitama Super Arena, north of Tokyo, 30 September 2022.

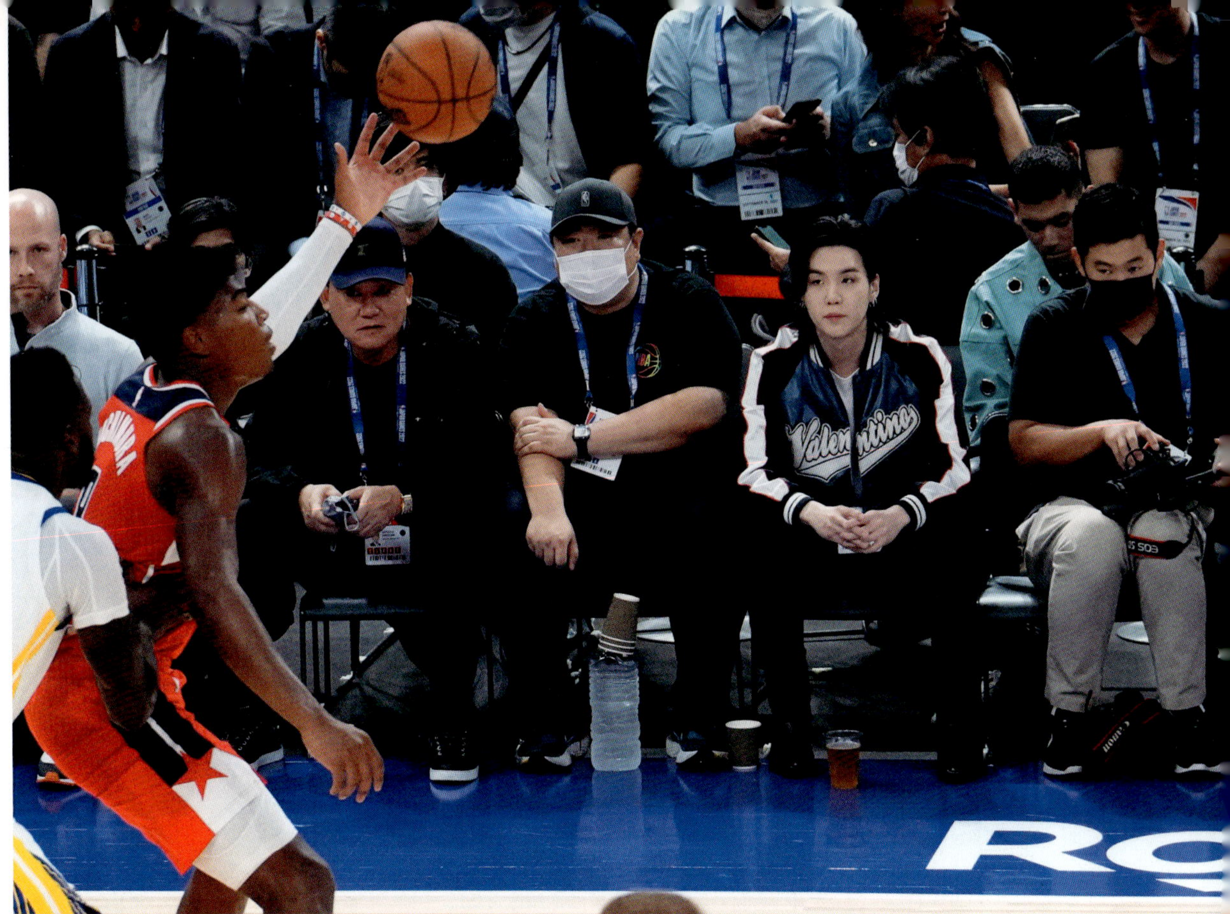

' Things change, situations change –
people have no choice but to change...
Everybody changes, but what's important
is the way that we change...
I think I changed very nicely. '

— SUGA, *nme.com*, April 2023.

overcome those too.' At his final concert, singing 'Snooze', a song about the pressures of fame, SUGA visibly began to cry, while the audience chanted: 'everything will be okay'. With such support there is no doubt this is true.

He's used to cheering on from the crowd himself too and has often been spotted at high-profile basketball games. It's a sport he has loved for many years – even his stage name SUGA is derived from the position he played as a student. So, it seemed a natural fit when he announced a collab with the NBA alongside the tour, who said at the time: 'We're thrilled to join forces with Suga – a superstar musician, fashion icon, and passionate NBA fan'. Later that year in a unique merch moment, a capsule range of sporty 'fits inspired by SUGA's solo tour dropped and included hoodies, T-shirts and caps created by Philadelphian heritage brand, Mitchell & Ness Nostalgia Co.

In 2024, a year ahead of his departure from the military, Yoon-gi's record company announced a concert film, *Agust D Tour 'D Day' The Movie*, would roll out in select cinemas, helping to keep everyone happy till his swish comeback when he will again, shoot, score, and make a difference.

Still from D–DAY The Movie.

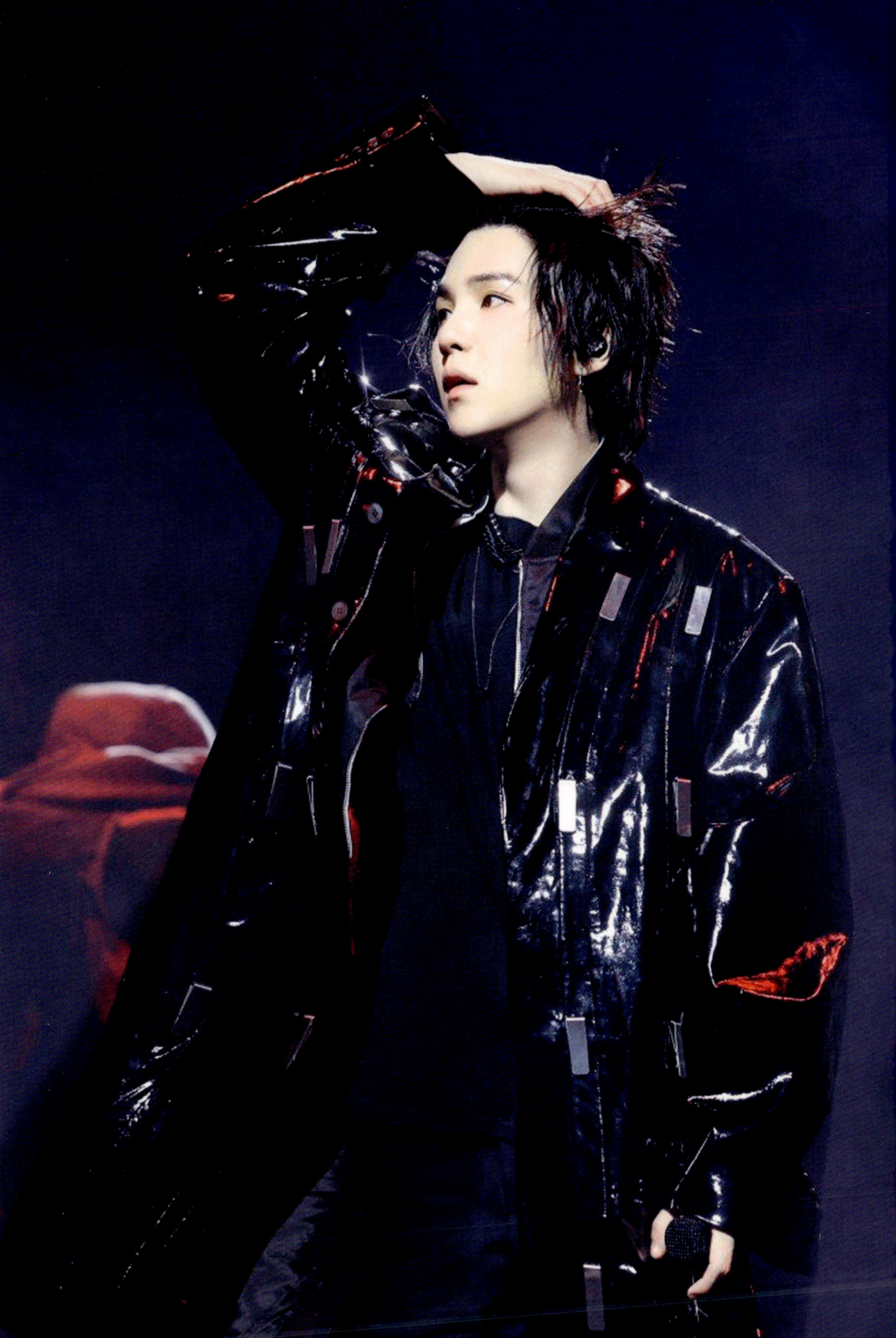

Boys on Film

A total of 290,000 fans watched SUGA perform his Agust D tour, showcasing *D-Day*, the debut album which forbes.com reported: 'According to the Hanteo chart–one of the two main music charts in South Korea–the album recored a remarkable 1,072,311 copies sold on its first day of release'. The gilded concert experience was captured for the big screen and while Min Yoon-gi was doing his military service, the film, *D-Day the Movie*, was released in March 2024 to rapturous applause in cinemas around the world. Alongside guest appearances by Jimin, Jung Kook and RM, viewers caught a rewind glimpse of SUGA's gig wardrobe, including, as @maisonvalentino posted on their Instagram, a mic-drop, finale outfit: 'For the last stop on his D-Day tour, the Brand Ambassador and #ValentinoDiVas opted for a "D-Day" double-breasted suit and #ValenTie, custom-made for him by Creative Director @pppiccioli.'

Luckily for his fans, it wasn't the last they saw of him though, as the singer stayed connected while he was away via his *Suchwita* web series, recorded prior to his enlistment.

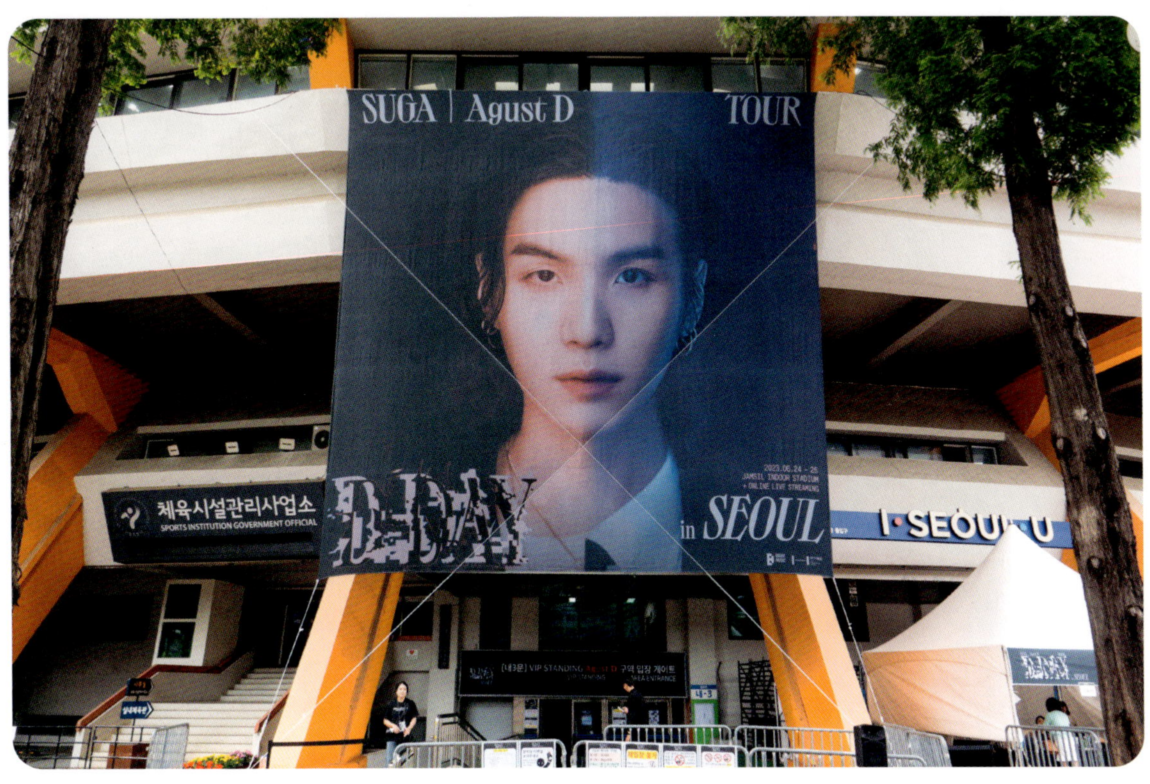

A placard promoting SUGA's solo concert 'D–DAY in SEOUL', at the
Jamsil Arena, Seoul, 24 and 25 June 2023.

On a Weverse live in September before he headed off, he urged everyone to keep watching, saying: 'I can't do Suchwita anymore. But I filmed a lot! Please look forward to it'. The programme is a fun watch for fans, who relish the camaraderie SUGA enjoys with his interview guests, but also the gossip and news that's revealed. An August 2023 episode saw Min Yoon-gi revealing he looks forward to aging with his fans and mused on their nickname: 'ARMY. It sounds really pretty. In French "ami" means friend. In English it's ARMY. So people think of it as...it sounds like they are gonna protect us from everything.'

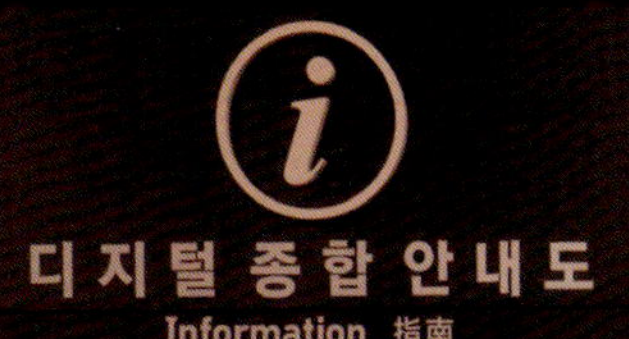

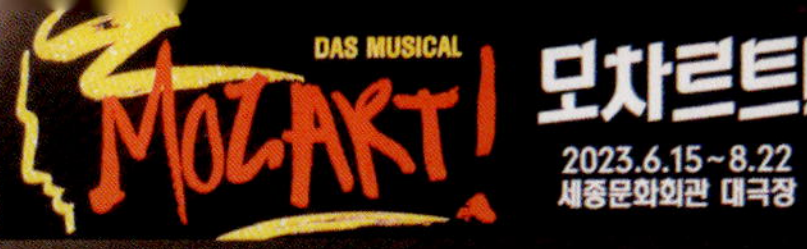

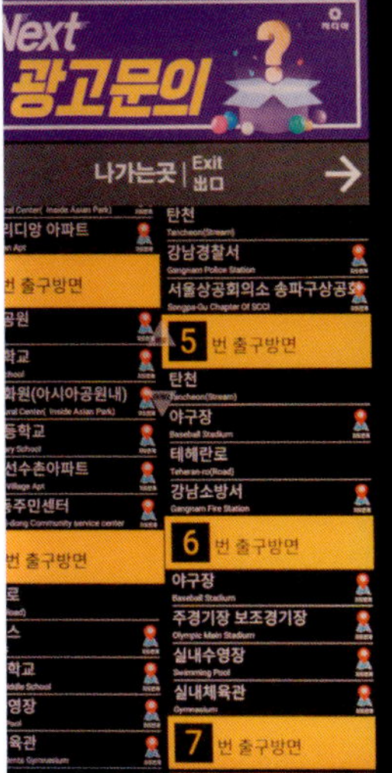

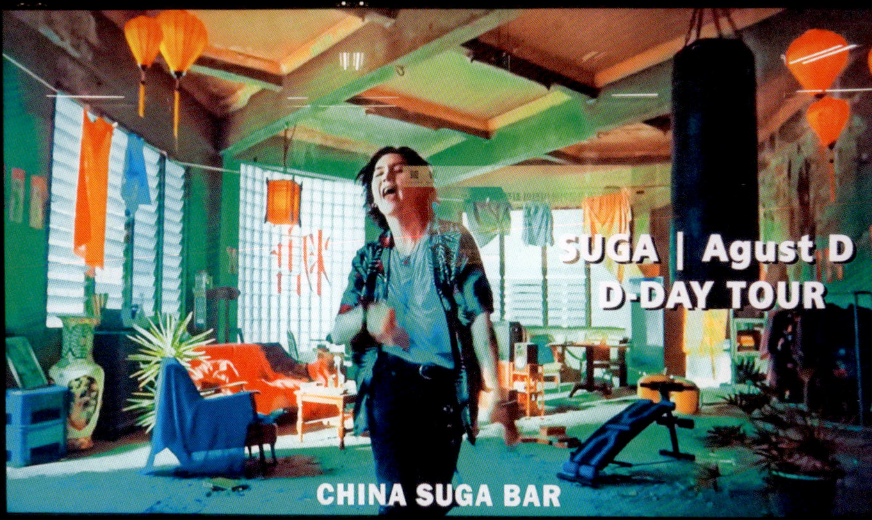

' Everything is possible
thanks to those fans who listen to your music. '
— SUGA, *Suchwita*, August 2023.

In the Long Run

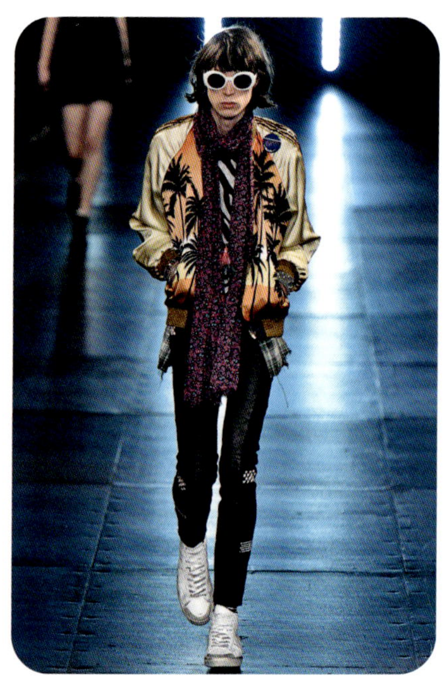

Part of the 2016 DMC Festival, the 'Korean Music Wave' concert took place on 8 October. BTS performed two songs. They burnt it up on stage, playing 'Fire' wearing now collectible pieces from Hedi Slimane's much-loved final S/S collection for Saint Laurent, sporting his teen-dream Hawaiian shirts, faux tour jackets and fringed camo cowboy shirts. The event has gone down in BTS history as a treasured moment in time when the band's reputation was rising. Memorably, they sang 'Run', released in November the year before and taken from their fourth EP, *The Most Beautiful Moment in Life, Pt 2*.

ARMY know by now that the boys love using the word run in their work and won't confuse it with the band's webseries, *Run BTS*, also known to fans as *Dallyeora Bangtan!*, which began in August 2015. The show was initially put together

THIS PAGE: *Hawaiian sunset jacket. Saint Laurent Ready to Wear Menswear S/S 2016 show, Paris Fashion Week, 28 June 2015.*
OPPOSITE: *BTS wearing Hedi Slimane St Laurent to the MBC Korean Music Wave DMC Festival in Seoul, 8 October 2016.*
OVERLEAF: *The Some Sevit, a man-made floating island on the south of the Han River in Seoul is lit up in purple to celebrate BTS's 10th Anniversary Festa, 12 June 2023.*

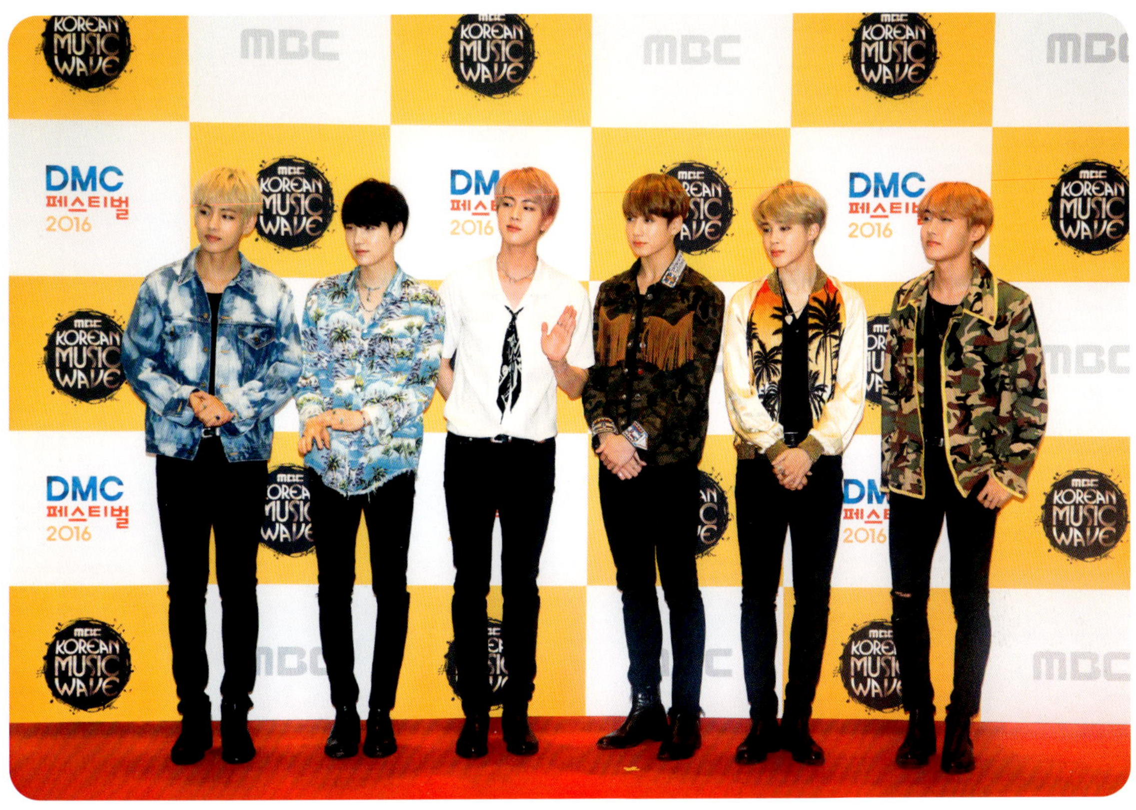

because, unbelievable as it sounds today, the group were rarely asked to appear on variety shows and so instead produced their own. It was a smart move as their fans got to know their personalities and this made their funny and cute programmes a huge hit. The symbolism behind the track and series name also tells of BTS's cohesive philosophy: when things set you back, get up and keep running! It's an attitude that has ensured their career triumphs.

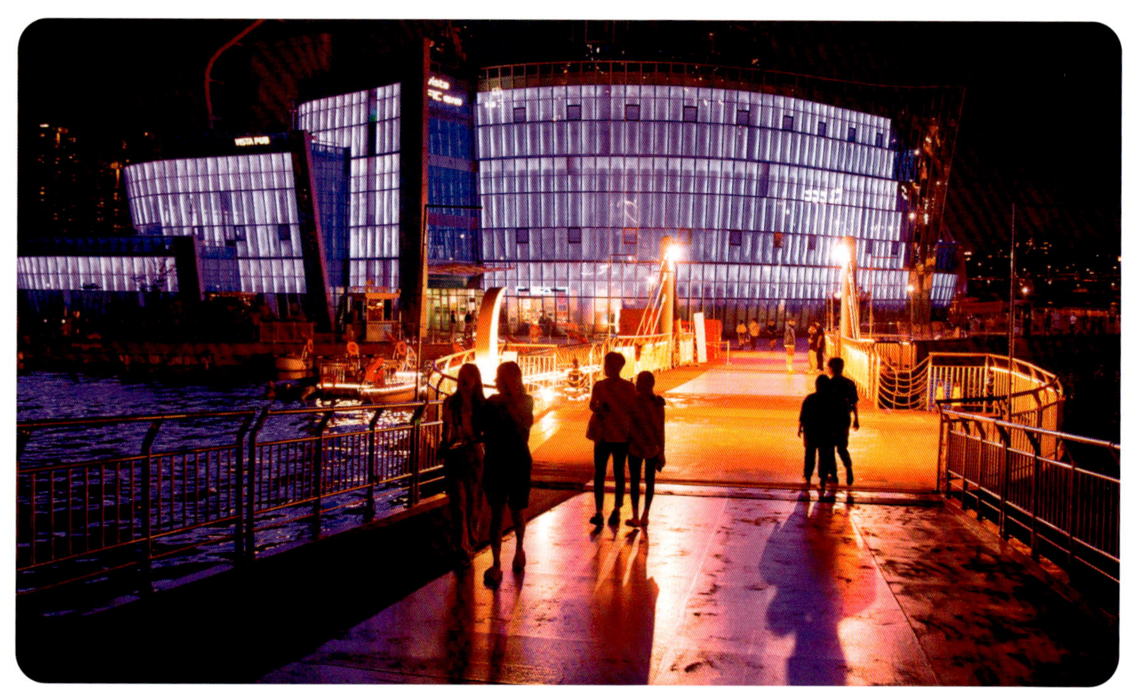

Going full circle, in 2022 the group released their first compendium album, *Proof*, featuring some of their best-loved music as well as a handful of new tracks including: 'Run BTS'. SUGA revealed to *Weverse* magazine: 'We kept saying we wanted to try doing a song in our older style, so we chose a title that both shares its name with our variety show and reflects who we are – always running. All the members have come a long way, and there's times when we're exhausted but there's also things we want to do moving forward, so I think we tried to include those desires as well.' The album, which takes the listener on a sightseeing tour of BTS's finest tunes, coincided with a fresh episode of *Run BTS* that aired in August 2022: a gift to fans before they took time away. Jung Kook explained at their BTS Festa: 'We're each going to take some time to have fun and experience lots of things. We promise we will return someday, even more mature than we are now.'

'We're each going
to take some time to
have fun and experience
lots of things.
We promise we will return someday,
even more mature
than we are now. '

Jung Kook, BTS Festa, August 2022.

Image Credits

COVER: Dave Bedrosian/Geisler-Fotopress/ Alamy Stock Photo
p.2: Steven Ferdman/Getty Images Entertainment
p.6: Jose Perez/Bauer-Griffin/Getty Images
p.7: ANTHONY WALLACE/AFP/Getty Images
p.10: Everett Collection/Alamy Stock Photo
p.11: Everett Collection/Alamy Stock Photo
p.15: JUNG YEON-JE/AFP/Getty Images
p.16: WENN/Alamy Stock Photo
p.17: Jason LaVeris/FilmMagic/Getty Images
p.18: Estrop/Wirelmage/Getty Images
p.19: ZUMA Press/Alamy Stock Photo
p.21: Kevin Winter/Getty Images Entertainment
p.22: Frazer Harrison/Getty Images Entertainment
p.23: Everett Collection/Alamy Stock Photo
p.24: Frazer Harrison/Getty Images Entertainment
p.25: Roy Rochlin/Getty Images Entertainment
p.26: ABACAPRESS/Alamy Stock Photo
p.27: Image Press Agency/Alamy Stock Photo
p.29: Sipa US/Alamy Stock Photo
p.30 TOP: Nippon News/Alamy Stock Photo
p.30 BOTTOM: Han Myung-Gu/Wirelmage/ Getty Images
p.31: Nippon News/Alamy Stock Photo
p.32: Vianney Le Caer/Alamy Stock Photo
p.32 BOTTOM: Swan Gallet/WWD/Getty Images
p.35: Paul Froggatt/Alamy Stock Photo
p.36 TOP: Nippon News/Alamy Stock Photo
p.36 BOTTOM: Pictorial Press/Alamy Stock Photo
p.37: Daniel Zuchnik/Billboard/Getty Images
p.38: Swan Gallet/WWD/Penske Media/Getty Images
p.39: Frazer Harrison/Getty Images Entertainment
p.40: Nippon News/Alamy Stock Photo
p.41: The Chosunilbo JNS/ImaZinS/Getty Images
p.45: Jim Ruymen/Alamy Stock Photo
pp.46/47: Everett Collection/Alamy Stock Photo
p.49: White House Photo/Alamy Stock Photo
p.50: White House Photo/Alamy Stock Photo
p.52 TOP: dpa/Alamy Stock Photo
p.52 BOTTOM: Peter White/Getty Images Entertainment
p.53: dpa/Alamy Stock Photo
p.54: Han Myung-Gu/GC Images/Getty Images
p.55: Kevin Mazur/Getty Images Entertainment
p.57: Jeff Kravitz/Getty Images Entertainment
p.59: Media Punch/Alamy Stock Photo
pp.60/61: BJ Warnick/Alamy Stock Photo
p.62 TOP: Frédéric VIELCANET/Alamy Stock Photo
p.62 BOTTOM: ARCHIVIO GBB/Alamy Stock Photo
p.63: The Chosunilbo JNS/ImaZinS/Getty Images
p.64: Estrop/Getty Images Entertainment
p.65: The Chosunilbo JNS/ImaZinS/Getty Images
p.67: The Chosunilbo JNS/ImaZinS/Getty Images
p.68: ED JONES/AFP/ Getty Images
p.69: Imaginechina/Alamy Stock Photo
p.71: BJ Warnick/Alamy Stock Photo

p.72 TOP: BJ Warnick/Alamy Stock Photo
p.72 BOTTOM: Bryan Steffy/Getty Images Entertainment
p.73: BJ Warnick/Alamy Stock Photo
p.74: BJ Warnick/Alamy Stock Photo
p.76: Pietro D'Aprano/Getty Images Entertainment
p.77: The Chosunilbo JNS/ImaZinS/Getty Images
p.78: The Chosunilbo JNS/ImaZinS/Getty Images
p.79 LEFT: The Chosunilbo JNS/ImaZinS/Getty Images
p.79 RIGHT: The Chosunilbo JNS/ImaZinS/ Getty Images
p.80: Everett Collection/Alamy Stock Photo
p.81: Han Myung-Gu/Wirelmage/Getty Images
p.82: Francois Durand/Getty Images Entertainment/Getty Images
p.83: ilgan Sports/ImaZinS/Getty Images
p.84: ilgan Sports/ImaZinS/Getty Images
p.86: Richard Bord/Wirelmage/Getty Images
p.87: BJ Warnick/Alamy Stock Photo
p.88: Pascal Le Segretain/Getty Images Entertainment
p.89: OConnor/AFF-USA/Alamy Stock Photo
p.90: Steve Granitz/Wirelmage/Getty Images
p.92: Nippon News/Alamy Stock Photo
p.93: The Chosunilbo JNS/ImaZinS/Getty Images
p.94: Karwai Tang/Getty Images Entertainment
p.95: BJ Warnick/Alamy Stock Photo
p.96: SeongJoon Cho/Bloomberg/Getty Images
p.97: The Chosunilbo JNS/ImaZinS/Getty Images
p.99: UPI/Alamy Stock Photo
p.101: THE FACT/ImaZinS/Getty Images
p.102: The Chosunilbo JNS/ImaZinS/Getty Images
p.103 TOP LEFT: JTBC PLUS/ImaZinS/Getty Images
p.103 TOP RIGHT: The Chosunilbo JNS/ ImaZinS/Getty Images
p.103 BOTTOM LEFT: The Chosunilbo JNS/ ImaZinS/Getty Images
p.103 BOTTOM RIGHT: The Chosunilbo JNS/ ImaZinS/Getty Images
p.104: The Chosunilbo JNS/ImaZinS/Getty Images
p.105 LEFT: The Chosunilbo JNS/ImaZinS/ Getty Images
p.105 RIGHT: JTBC PLUS/ImaZinS/Getty Images
p.106: Sipa US/Alamy Stock Photo
p.107: Sipa US/Alamy Stock Photo
p.108: Foc Kan/Wirelmage/Getty Images
p.110: Victor VIRGILE/Gamma-Rapho/Getty Images
p.111: Han Myung-Gu/Wirelmage/Getty Images
p.113: The Chosunilbo JNS/ImaZinS/Getty Images
p.115: Julien Hekimian/Getty Images Entertainment
p.116: Jacopo Raule/GC Images/Getty Images
p.118: Edward Berthelot/Getty Images Entertainment
p.119: Pascal Le Segretain/Getty Images Entertainment

p.121: NurPhoto/Alamy Stock Photo
p.122: Giovanni Giannoni/WWD/Getty Images
p.123: Swan Gallet/WWD/Getty Images
p.125: The Chosunilbo JNS/ImaZinS/Getty Images
p.128: Edward Berthelot/Getty Images Entertainment
p.129: dpa/Alamy Stock Photo
p.131: The Chosunilbo JNS/ImaZinS/Getty Images
p.132: Manuel Velasquez/Getty Images Entertainment
p.133: Taylor Hill/Getty Images Entertainment
p.134: Jamie McCarthy/Getty Images Entertainment
p.137: Frazer Harrison/Getty Images Entertainment
p.138: JUNG YEON-JE/AFP/Getty Images
p.139: SOPA Images/Alamy Stock Photo
p.141: Nippon News/Alamy Stock Photo
p.142: Nippon News/Alamy Stock Photo
p.143: Nippon News/Alamy Stock Photo
p.145: Eugene Hoshiko/Alamy Stock Photo
p.147: TCD/Prod.DB/Alamy Stock Photo
p.149: Nippon News/Alamy Stock Photo
p.151: Nippon News/Alamy Stock Photo
p.152: Victor VIRGILE/Gamma-Rapho/Getty Images
p.153: Nippon News/Alamy Stock Photo
p.154: Nippon News/Alamy Stock Photo

References

https://www.koreaboo.com/stories/bts-jin-exo-kai-cardigan-different-vibes/
https://sbsstar.net/article/N1007356575/kim-nam-gil-tells-what-it-is-like-to-be-in-the-same-room-with-his-good-friend-bts-jin
https://www.sportskeeda.com/pop-culture/news-bts-jin-korean-male-celebrity-mentioned-on-list-top-20-instagram-influencers-usa
https://magazine.weverse.io/article/view?lang=en&num=211
https://elle.in/bts-kim-seok-jin-style-evolution/
https://sbsstar.net/article/N1007356575/kim-nam-gil-tells-what-it-is-like-to-be-in-the-same-room-with-his-good-friend-bts-jin
https://hypebeast.com/2022/5/erl-x-dior-new-california-couture-capsule-collection-spring-2023
https://www.koreaboo.com/news/bts-jhope-new-years-eve-dick-clark-rockin-fashion-outfit/
https://www.kpopstarz.com/articles/302525/20211106/bts-jimin-sells-out-celine-tshirt-globe-release-2022-seasons-greetings-preview.htm
https://magazine.weverse.io/article/view?colca=1&artist=&searchword=&num=437&lang=en
https://www.sportskeeda.com/pop-culture/all-brands-bts-wore-grammys
https://kpopherald.koreaherald.com/view.php?ud=201903241528324693672_2
https://kpopherald.koreaherald.com/view.php?ud=201903081420161738407_2
https://www.youtube.com/watch?v=OovjtA1qSPw&list=PLwFs58D1XAMaobsvgXJm3TgkXYnayY-mQ
https://inkistyle.com/bts-incheon-airport-november-17-2021/
https://www.rollingstone.com/music/music-news/jung-kook-misses-bts-1234874254/
https://www.voguehk.com/en/article/fashion/style-file-bts-jungkook/
https://kpoplife.com/jungkook-calvin-klein-style/
https://kpopherald.koreaherald.com/view.php?ud=201902120943009634578_2
https://www.koreaboo.com/news/bts-rm-shares-luxury-fashion-brands-except-one/
https://www.vogue.co.uk/miss-vogue/article/bts-2019-mnet-asian-music-awards-celine
https://www.alethea-magazine.com/Maison-Valentinos-latest-catch--Suga-becomes-brand-ambassador--whats-next-after-singing-break-Jan23#:~:text=24%20January%202023%3A%20Maison%20Valentino,appointed%20so%20far%2C%20(DI.
Maison Valentino Instagram, 17 January 2023/quote for DI.VA for Ever.
https://www.marieclairekorea.com/celebrity/2023/04/suga-valentino/
https://www.j-14.com/posts/bts-v-best-fashion-and-red-carpet-moments-photos-outfits/
https://kpop.fandom.com/wiki/No_More_Dream#cite_note-14
https://time.com/5681494/bts-bang-si-hyuk-interview/
https://www.kpopbehind.com/2014/02/kpop-behind-scenes-bts-showcase-for.html
https://k-popped.com/2014/04/event-coverage-bts-muster-own-army-at-their-1st-fan-meeting/
https://magazine.weverse.io/article/view?lang=en&num=435
https://www.refinery29.com/en-us/2018/05/199674/bts-bbmas-billboard-music-awards-2018-tweets
https://www.forbes.com/sites/bryanrolli/2018/05/19/bts-fake-love-video-k-pop-youtube-record/?sh=2f536fe47502
https://www.koreaboo.com/news/bts-billboard-boycott-backlash-fans-boycott-apology/
https://variety.com/2019/music/news/bts-2019-tour-map-of-the-soul-persona-1203423364/
https://kpopherald.koreaherald.com/view.php?ud=201801031308372445454_2
https://www.koreaboo.com/news/bts-jhope-blonde-black-hair-short-debut-no-era/
https://www.koreaboo.com/news/bts-explains-meaning-behind-love-tear-next-goal/
V blonde hair on X: https://twitter.com/miiniyoongs/status/1663743681713651713?ref_

Acknowledgements

Many thanks to Carrie Kania at Iconic Images; to James Smith and his team at ACC Art Books, in particular Craig Holden, Susannah Hecht and Sue Bennett; and special credit to Holly Hill for her editorial input. Also, to Andrew, Freddie and William Newman, Mick Rooney, Gina Gibbons, Pippa Healy, Michael Costiff, Francine Bosco and Jo Unwin for their love and encouragement.

Biography

Terry Newman is a fashion historian who lectures at Regent's University London. She has worked in the industry for over 15 years as a journalist and stylist and now writes about fashion, art and culture. Recent books include *Legendary Authors and the Clothes they Wore, Legendary Artists and the Clothes they Wore, Harry Styles and the Clothes He Wears, Taylor Swift and the Clothes She Wears* and *Beyoncé and the Clothes She Wears*. During the 1990s, she was employed as Shopping Editor at *i-D* magazine, Associate Editor at *Self Service* magazine, and Consumer Editor at *Attitude* magazine, and as a TV presenter for Channel 4 fashion programmes. Her journalism has been published in the *Guardian, The Times* and *The Sunday Times, Viewpoint* and the *Big Issue*, amongst others and she has contributed to *i-D*'s *Fashion Now, Fashion Now 2* and *Soul i-D* books. Newman lives in London with her husband and two sons.

'Hearing our fans saying that we **changed their lives** changes our lives in turn. We got to know about the weight that our words and music carry, and we're truly thankful for that. We've realized that despite our love for music, the most important thing about this job is to have people who listen to you. We thank our fans for listening to our messages and music. '

SUGA, *rollingstoneindia.com*, November 2020.

ISBN: 978 1 78884 269 3

A CIP catalogue record for this book is available from the British Library

The author and publisher gratefully acknowledge the permission granted to reproduce the copyright material in this book. Every effort has been made to trace copyright holders and to obtain their permission for the use of copyright material. The publisher apologises for any errors or omissions in the text and would be grateful if notified of any corrections that should be incorporated in future reprints or editions of this book.

Editor: Susannah Hecht

Designer: Craig Holden

Cover: *BTS keeping it cool at the American Music Awards, Microsoft Theater, LA, 19 November 2017.*

Frontispiece: *Conquering The States. BTS visit the Empire State Building, NYC, 21 May 2019.*

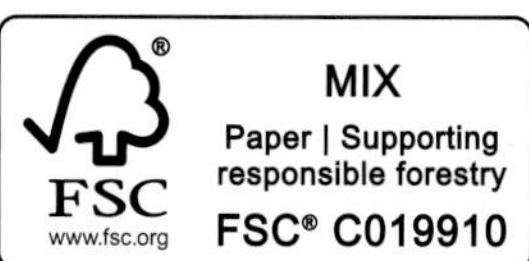

Printed in China

for ACC Art Books Ltd., Woodbridge, Suffolk, UK

www.accartbooks.com

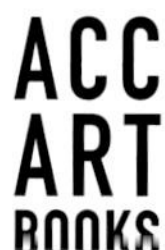